American Literature by Negro Authors

Herman Dreer, PROFESSOR
OF ENGLISH, STOWE TEACHERS
COLLEGE, ST. LOUIS, MISSOURI

THE MACMILLAN COMPANY
New York: 1950

To My Daughter, Vivian Emma,
A Student and Teacher of English,
I Dedicate This Book

Preface

THIS VOLUME is intended primarily for use as a textbook. Accordingly much realistic material, though regarded by some as showing artistic skill, has been omitted as unsuitable for classroom use. The aim has not been to cover the entire field, but to present representative authors and some of their works, in order to show how Negro writers have treated each type of American literature.

The range of writings is from the age of Phillis Wheatley to current times. The book is divided into nine sections: folklore, poetry, letters, biography and autobiography, essays, addresses, short stories, novels, and plays.

This text can be made to serve several purposes. It can introduce students to most of the classic and better-known Negro authors and to many rising authors who are talented but who at present may not be nationally known. It offers some idea as to how the Negro has thought in the past and how he thinks today. The selections will show also how American Negroes have adapted themselves to the American way of life in their effort to solve their problems. The text demonstrates how Negroes have interpreted life. The selections reveal also the aspiration and the idealism of the Negro. Finally, the book will show to what extent the Negro is a literary artist.

As to how the book is to be used, each teacher's own plan is best for his class. No method can be stated which would suit every class, since the personality of each class is different from that of any other. However, some suggestions may be offered here for the teacher to incorporate into his plans.

First, the biographical approach can be effective. A knowledge of the life of an author often is sufficient to inspire the student to read that author's works.

Next, the historical approach sometimes is necessary, because the pupil can not appreciate a literary work when he does not know the background out of which it was created. If the teacher discovers that his class does not have the background for the appreciation of a work, he would do well to see to it that the student acquires the background before the work is presented for study or appreciation.

The comparative method is also effective in the study of literature. For example, if a student reads several poems by one author which employ dialect, he can understand and appreciate the use of dialect in a poem better than he could if he studied only one. The same is true if he reads dialect poems of several authors; he would thus be helped by the comparisons he would make. For example, one might consider Lowell's "The Courtin'." In it Lowell uses dialect to portray the character of a Yankee suitor in an old New England setting. The student might then turn to Robert Burns' "The Cotter's Saturday Night" and see how he portrays in dialect the character of the humble Scotch farmer. Or the student might make a comparison with Paul Laurence Dunbar's portrayal of a Negro tenant farmer in "Little Brown Baby." The comparisons here are apt, since each poet is using dialect to portray an aspect of rural life.

Burns and Dunbar could be extensively compared as to their lives, their aspirations, their writings, their friends, their romances, and their rise to fame. They could even be compared with reference to the subjects upon which they wrote and their treatment of them.

Teachers might take such a theme as death and immortality and show by comparison the different ideas of the poets on these subjects and their different ways of treating the same general idea. If Paul Laurence Dunbar should be the focal poet, the teacher might present the following poems of Dunbar on these themes: "A Death Song," "Ships That Pass in the Night," and "When All Is Done." For comparative purposes he might use Ralph Waldo Emerson's "Goodbye" and "Terminus" and Alfred (Lord) Tennyson's "Crossing the Bar." These suggestions reveal the opportunity to develop appreciation for literature and to stimulate wide reading. The comparative method is a valid one for arousing the curiosity of the student and deepening his love for literature. However, these are merely suggestions; for any best method of teaching literature must be determined by the teacher and the personality of each particular class.

For the privilege of reprinting the works presented in this collection we are indebted to the generosity of those who felt that a work of this sort would be generally helpful to all. These literary works may bring pupils to see that the Negro's culture is an American culture; that the Negro's aspirations are the aspirations of an American citizen.

Where the authors no longer dwell among us, their relatives put their works at our disposal and welcomed our use of them. The publishers, too, were generous in allowing us to have the selections we desired. To all these we are especially indebted. Our gratitude extends also to Mr. Ulysses S. Donaldson, a teacher of English at Sumner High School, and to Miss Helen Flowers, Chairman of the English Department of Stowe Teachers College, who assisted in the reading of the manuscript. To these and all others who in any way contributed to the preparation of this book, the author expresses his thanks.

HERMAN DREER

St. Louis, Missouri
April 15, 1950

General Introduction

IN ORDER to appreciate better the work of the Negro author, one would do well to consider how he arose. This can best be understood by considering the source from which he came. The American Negro is a composite or mixture of African Negro, European Caucasian, and American Indian.[1]

His basic stock, however, is African; that is, his physique. The home of the "true Negro," as described by A. C. Haddon in his *Races of Mankind,* is West Africa. Although some Negroes were brought to the United States from East and South Africa, most of them came from West Africa, since that region was nearest to America. Hundreds of different dialects were spoken by those who came.

The many dialects contributed to the delay of more than a hundred years in the appearance of a representative Negro author. Since the Negroes of Africa were warlike, as indicated by such leaders as Chaka, Soni Ali, Mohammed Askia,[2] and Cetawayo,[3] it became the policy of slave traders to place on a single plantation a group of Negroes speaking not one dialect but many dialects. This difficulty of intercommunication reduced insurrections and made easier the subjugation of the Negro. By the time all had learned to speak a common language, English, they had become somewhat docile and more inclined to accept their enforced condition. Literature is a social product requiring an audience or group of readers who can see in the literary artist one who understands their problems, sympathizes with them, and inter-

[1] Melville Hertskovits' *The American Negro,* a summary of his *Anthropometry of the American Negro,* a study based upon the measurements of parts of the bodies of thousands of living American Negroes, African Negroes, Caucasians, and American Indians.
[2] Chaka, a Zulu, a race fanatic like Adolph Hitler, a great general of the eighteenth century, who lived in South Africa and sought to destroy all peoples but his own; Soni Ali, a despotic king of North Africa, who ruled a territory almost as large as Europe; Mohammed Askia, a Negro king of North Africa, who ruled a territory larger than Europe for twenty-four years. Cf. Gollock, *Sons of Africa.* Cf. C. G. Woodson, *African Heroes and Heroines.*
[3] A South African king, who held the English at bay until 1895. H. R. Haggard, *Cetawayo and His White Neighbors.*

prets their experiences suitably for them and for others. Thus the
literary artist is supposed to be a specialist, a person of leisure, to
muse, to meditate, to dream, and to interpret the soul of humanity.

Slavery, however, does not inspire literary production; in fact, slavery discourages it. The laws of the various slave states forbade teaching
a Negro to read or write under severest penalties; yet many slaves did
learn to read and write. The wife of the master of Frederick Douglass
taught him to read while instructing her own son. When she informed
her husband of the rapid progress of the Negro slave, he forbade
further instruction, saying these immortal words, "Education is in-
compatible with slavery. If you educate a person, you make him love
freedom; if you are to enslave, you must not educate." The mother
of Paul Laurence Dunbar learned to read and write during slavery by
stopping the master's children on their way to school, when she talked
with them about their spelling, their exercises, and their copy books.
Many a slave was taught by a Quaker or by some minister or priest,
not in the open but clandestinely. For instance, Reverend John Berry
Meachum, the first pastor of First Baptist Church of Saint Louis, Missouri, conducted a clandestine school in the basement of his church.[1]
Mrs. Wheatley taught her slave, Phillis, not only to read and write
English, but to read Latin as well. Generally speaking, however, the
facts that several dialects were spoken on a plantation and that it was
forbidden to teach Negroes to read and write were partly responsible
for the long delay in the rise of a prominent Negro author.

Despite this, the Negro author did arise. In his ascent he was helped
and inspired by his natural gifts and by his literary heritage. His bodily
rhythms, the beating of his pulse and his heart, the swinging of his
arms as he walked or ran, and the regular motion of his legs as he
moved from place to place gave him the basis for appreciating and
creating the rhythms of poetry. Curiosity led him into adventure. These
experiences, tempered with emotions of love, joy, sympathy, hate, or
revenge, stirred his imagination and led to the expression of his feeling
in proverbs, poetry, and folk tales.

Lord Rattray of England collected and published hundreds of proverbs of the people of Ashanti.[2] Illustrative of these proverbs are the
following: "When you are courting, always keep both eyes open; but
after you get married, always keep one eye shut," and "Death has the

[1] George E. Stevens, *History of the Central Baptist Church.*
[2] A small country in West Africa.

key that opens the miser's chest." Blaise Cendrars [1] collected and published a group of folk tales, prose and poetical charms, and proverbs that he called *The African Saga*. Barker and Sinclair [2] published an interesting collection of African folk tales that they called *The Anansi Stories*. Elephantine and Dayrell [3] published a collection which they called *Folk Tales of West Africa*. This folk literature is an important heritage, a part of which the Negro brought to America. This can be recognized by comparing some of the stories published as collections of folklore of Negro Americans by Joel Chandler Harris [4] in his *Nights with Uncle Remus* with some of the tales in *The Anansi Stories*.

The literature produced before 1865 came almost entirely from free Negroes, many of whom had been taught by indentured white servants and religious leaders, white and black. This was rarely literature motivated by the spirit of art for art's sake; it was chiefly literature with a purpose, and that purpose was the full rights of citizenship for free Negroes and immediate emancipation of all slaves. The same aspiration underlay all the types of literature that arose before 1865, whether it was poetry, autobiography or biography, the sermon, the address, the news article or editorial, the letter, the essay, or history.

A few writers may be listed as representative of the period before the War Between the States. The first poet was Jupiter Hammon, a slave, who in 1760 published "An Evening Thought." This was just one hundred and forty-one years after 1619, when the first Negro slaves were brought to Jamestown, Virginia. Then other important writers followed: Phillis Wheatley in 1773 published *Poems on Various Subjects;* Gustavus Vasa, his *The Interesting Narrative of the Life of Olaudah Equiana, or Gustavus Vasa, the African,* in 1789. In 1827, Samuel Cornish, a minister, and John B. Russworm, the first Negro to graduate from an American college—his school was Bowdoin College—published the first Negro newspaper in America. Here was the formal beginning of the editorial writing of the Negro. In 1794 Richard Allen, founder of the African Methodist Episcopal Church, and his colleague, Absalom Jones, published a pamphlet entitled "A Narrative of the Proceedings of the Black People during the Late Awful Calamity in Philadelphia, and a Refutation of Some Censures Thrown upon Them in Some Publications." One of the earliest published ad-

---

1 A French writer.   3 English scholars.
2 English scholars.   4 An eminent author from the South.

dresses was William Whipper's "Eulogy on William Wilberforce," in 1833. Many of the addresses of Charles Lenox Remond, the most prominent Negro orator before Frederick Douglass, were published in the *Liberator,* which was edited by William Lloyd Garrison. William Wells Brown, who escaped from slavery, was one of the most prolific writers of this period. Among his important writings before 1865 were *The Black Man,* a collection of biographies of distinguished Negroes in various parts of the world, and his novel, *Clotelle,* both of which were published in 1863.

Such was the beginning of the Negro author. With the coming of freedom for all and public education, the Negro began to produce bountifully and to make a substantial contribution to American literature. This book presents a few types of these contributions and supplies a bibliography for those interested in going beyond the scope of this work in the study of the Negro American author.

The spirit of the Negro author is reflected in the theme-poem of the book of poems published by The Scribes, a literary club of college people interested in encouraging the writing of poetry. The writer keeps the title of the poem, which is the same as that of the book, *Sing, Laugh, Weep;* but he changes the order of the stanzas, to reflect the attitude that is most characteristic of the Negro and the Negro author.

Weeping is the beginning, the recognition of a difficulty the Negro faces; as the Negro weeps, he thinks, he plans a way out of his trouble. As he works, he laughs. Many a joke he has created as he worked. He uses his laughter to lighten the burden of his labor. When he has overcome his difficulty, he bursts out in song. All three of these moods are characteristic of the Negro; but the most important of these is expressed by his song, because his songs express his hope, his faith, his optimism. With song he moves from sorrow to joy, from defeat to victory. Thus he weeps, laughs, and sings.

Contents

CONTENTS

CONTENTS

CONTENTS

Part III—Letters

CONTENTS

Part VIII—The Novel ²

Part IX—The Drama

PART I

Folk Literature

Introduction   Every racial group, if it goes back far enough, will find that its ancestors produced folk material: folk music and folk literature. Folk material is that material whose composer or author is unknown. Whether it is literature or music, it is composed spontaneously and is handed down by word of mouth from generation to generation. As it goes from person to person, it may lose or gain something in substance or content; it may be varied as it goes from locality to locality. If the folk material happens to be a story of some deed of prowess performed by a warrior of the group, several versions of the incident may arise simultaneously in neighboring families or clans. This variation or the development of different versions of an incident is due to the lack of a written record of the original story. Once the folk material is recorded, it will be preserved without change.

An example of folk material in the Bible is the Book of Proverbs. Such proverbs are familiar the world over—for instance, "A soft answer turneth away wrath." "A good name is rather to be chosen than great riches."

Another example of folk material would be such Negro proverbs as "Who marries a beautiful woman marries beautiful trouble"; "The only secret a tattler can keep is the secret he does not know"; "Hold a true friend with both hands"; "Death is always new"; and "There is no cure for old age."

1

There are other examples. Richard Wagner used the folk material of his country and developed from it his great operas, such as "Lohengrin," "The Valkyrie," and "Tannhäuser." Franz Liszt took folk songs of Hungary and developed them into immortal rhapsodies. Likewise Giuseppe Verdi used many folk tunes of Italy as the basic material of some of his best operas. Similarly, R. Nathaniel Dett, the eminent Negro composer, has produced beautiful anthems from the folk material of the American Negro. Examples of such artistic compositions are his "Somebody's Knocking at Your Door"; "Let Us Cheer the Weary Traveler"; "Listen to the Lambs"; and the oratorio, "The Ordering of Moses."

The crude material is the spiritual. Parallel material to this would be some of the psalms in the Book of Psalms of the Christian Bible. The structure of the Negro spiritual, like all raw folk material, is simple. The setting is a camp meeting, a revival in the open on a plantation. In the earliest days there were no seats. The people sat on the ground. A tune would come to an individual; he would create the tune and the words. Generally he would start with the chorus or the refrain and sing it several times until all would know the melody and the words of the refrain. Then he would make up stanzas, which he would sing alone. At the end of each stanza, in order to strengthen the appeal to the emotions, the group would join in and at times vary the tune in spots.

As the leader would sing, he would wave his hands, and by his body movements he would dramatize the thought of his song, moving among the congregation. In the beginning, this leader was the minister on the slave plantation; later any deeply spiritual person, man or woman, minister, deacon, or layman, became the leader.

The leader might begin thus:

Refrain
Camp meeting, camp meeting, camp meeting, camp meeting!
Come on, let's go to the camp meeting!
Come on, let's go to the camp meeting!

No more I'll roam.
Camp meeting!

No more I'll roam.
Camp meeting!
I'm going home!
Camp meeting!
I'm going home!
Camp meeting.

Refrain
Camp meeting, camp meeting, camp meeting, camp meeting!
Come on, let's go to the camp meeting!
Come on, let's go to the camp meeting!

Here are presented a series of spirituals, which show how the slave thought on the plantation. They show his hope and aspiration. Note the absence of any desire for revenge. From the spirituals, one can get a conception of the Negro's idea of God; he can discern the Negro's faith in his religion. As manifested by "In Dat Great Gittin' Up Mornin'" and "Walk Together, Children," it is a triumphant faith.

The untutored Negro was not only a musician: he was also a poet. Thomas W. Talley, for many years professor of chemistry at Fisk University, in his leisure hours and during vacation times went among the lowly Negroes of the South, on the farms and in the cabins, collected folk rhymes, and published them in a volume called *Negro Folk-Rhymes*. The selection here made is sufficient to show that even the untutored mind can have the poetic gift.

In considering some of the poetry of our major poets—Paul Laurence Dunbar, Sterling Brown, Langston Hughes, Countee Cullen, and some of the more recent poets who are included in this volume —it would be well to read again these folk-rhymes and see to what extent the known poets are more artistic than the unknown ones who produced this folk material.

Zora Neale Hurston, a student of the anthropologist, Franz Boas, has specialized in collecting folk tales of the American Negro. Her method of collecting this material will readily be discerned by reading *Mules and Men,* from which one of the tales has been chosen for this work. The reader will find that Miss Hurston becomes one of the group, showing no sophistication; she dresses and behaves as one of the group from which she obtains her stories. In writing these tales she preserves the spontaneity and the natural freshness of the narrative that comes from simple, untutored people.

From her *Jonah's Gourd Vine,* which might be called a folk novel, the writer has chosen an excerpt from the folk sermon. A folk sermon may be regarded as one that has in it ideas and images that could be heard from many an untutored preacher. With slight variation that sermon could be heard today in many backwoods Southern communities. It could even be heard in some of the primitive congregations of metropolitan cities like St. Louis, Chicago, New York, and Philadelphia.

In studying this folk sermon, it would be well to compare it with the folk sermons and other folk material in James Weldon Johnson's *God's Trombones,* and with the excerpt of the polished sermon of Dr. Vernon S. Johns, "Civilized Interiors," or Dr. Charles H. Wesley's Baccalaureate Address on "The Pursuit of Things." In measuring achievement, one needs to consider the background of him who attains. As Frederick Douglass said, "Don't judge me by the height I have reached, but by the depth from which I have come."

IN DAT GREAT GITTIN' UP MORNIN'

I'm-a goin' to tell you 'bout de comin' of de Savior,
      Fare you well! Fare you well!
I'm-a goin' to tell you 'bout de comin' of de Savior,
      Fare you well! Fare you well!
Dere's a better day a'comin', Fare you well! Fare you well!
Oh, preacher, fol' yo' Bible, Fare you well! Fare you well!

Refrain
In dat great gittin' up mornin', Fare you well, Fare you well!
In dat great gittin' up mornin', Fare you well, Fare you well!

WALK TOGETHER, CHILDREN

Walk together, children,
Don't you get weary;

Walk together, children,
Don't you get weary;
Walk together, children,
Don't you get weary;
There's a great camp meeting in the Promised Land.

Refrain
Gwineter mourn and never tire;
Mourn and never tire;
Mourn and never tire;
There's a great camp meeting in the Promised Land.

Sing together, children,
Don't you get weary;
Sing together, children,
Don't you get weary;
Sing together, children,
Don't you get weary;
There's a great camp meeting in the Promised Land.

Refrain: Gwineter mourn etc.
Talk together, children, etc.
Refrain: Gwineter mourn etc.
Shout together, children, etc.
Refrain: Gwineter mourn etc.

STEAL AWAY

Refrain
Steal away, steal away, steal away to Jesus!
Steal away, steal away home;
I ain't got long to stay here.

My Lord, He calls me,
He calls me by the thunder.
The trumpet sounds within-a my soul;
I ain't got long to stay here.
Refrain: Steal away, etc.

My Lord, He calls me,
He calls me by the lightning.
The trumpet sounds within-a my soul;
I ain't got long to stay here.
Refrain: Steal away, etc.

EVERYBODY TALKIN' 'BOUT HEAVEN

I got a shoe, you got a shoe;
All-a God's children got shoes;
When I get to heaven, I'm goin' to put on my shoes;
I'm goin' to walk all over God's heaven.

Refrain
Heaven, heaven—everybody talkin' 'bout heaven ain't goin' there.
Heaven, heaven—I'm goin' to walk all over God's heaven.

I got a robe, you got a robe,
All-a God's children got robes;
When I get to heaven, I'm goin' to put on my robe;
I'm goin' to shout all over God's heaven.
Refrain: Heaven, heaven, etc.

I got a wing, you got a wing,
All-a God's children got wings;
When I get to heaven, I'm goin' to put on my wings;
I'm goin' to fly all over God's heaven.
Refrain: Heaven, heaven, etc.

MOUNT ZION

Refrain
Mount Zion, Mount Zion, Mount Zion, Mount Zion!
I wouldn't take nothing, Mount Zion, for my journey now, Mount
Zion!

I went down into the valley, Mount Zion;
I didn't mean to stay, Mount Zion.
My soul got happy, Mount Zion,
And I stayed all day, Mount Zion.
Refrain: Mount Zion, Mount Zion, etc.

You may talk about me, Mount Zion,
Just as much as you please, Mount Zion.
I'll talk about you, Mount Zion,
When I get on my knees, Mount Zion!
Refrain: Mount Zion, Mount Zion, etc.

JAYBIRD [1]

De Jaybird jump from lim' to lim';
An' he tell Br'er Rabbit to do lak him.
Br'er Rabbit say to de cunnin' elf:
"You jes want me to fall an' kill myself."

Dat Jaybird a-settin' on a swingin' lim'.
He wink at me an' I wink at him.
He laugh at me w'en my gun "crack."
It kick me down on de flat o' my back.

Nex' day de Jaybird dance dat lim'.
I grabs my gun fer to shoot at him.
W'en I "crack" down, it split my chin.
"Ole Aggie Cunjer" fly lak sin.

Way down yon'er at de risin' sun,
Jaybird a-talkin' wid a forked tongue.
He's been down dar whar de bad mens dwell.
"Old Friday Devil," fare—you—well!

[1] From *Negro Folk Rhymes*, by T. W. Talley. Copyright, 1922, by The Macmillan Company, New York. Reprinted with the permission of Dr. Thomas W. Talley.

THE LITTLE ROOSTER [1]

I had a liddle rooster,
He crowed befo' day.
'Long come a big owl,
An' toted him away.

But de rooster fight hard,
An' de owl let him go.
Now all de pretty hens
Wants dat rooster fer deir beau.

THE OLD HEN CACKLED [1]

De ole hen she cackled,
An' stayed down in de bo'n.
She git fat an' sassy,
A-eatin' up de co'n.

De ole hen she cackled,
Got long yaller laigs.
She swaller down de oats,
But I don't git no aigs.

De ole hen she cackled,
She cackled in de lot,
De nex' time she cackled,
She cackled in de pot.

I LOVE SOMEBODY [1]

I loves somebody, yes, I do;
An' I wants somebody to love me too.
Wid my chyart an' oxes stan'in' 'roun',
Her pretty liddle foot needn' tetch de groun'.

[1] From *Negro Folk Rhymes*, by T. W. Talley. Copyright, 1922, by The Macmillan Company, New York. Reprinted with the permission of Dr. Thomas W. Talley.

I loves somebody, yes, I do,
Dat randsome, handsome, Stickamastew.
Wid her reddingoat an' waterfall,
She's de pretty liddle gal dat beats 'em all.

BEDBUG [1]

De June-bug's got de golden wing,
De Lightning-bug de flame;
De Bedbug's got no wing at all,
But he gits dar jes de same.

De Punkin-bug's got a punkin smell,
De Squash-bug smells de wust;
But de puffume of dat old Bedbug,
It's enough to make you bust.

W'en dat Bedbug come down to my house,
I wants my walkin' cane.
Go git a pot an' scald 'im hot!
Good-by, Miss Lize Jane!

SHE HUGGED ME AND KISSED ME [1]

I see'd her in de Springtime,
I see'd her in de Fall,
I see'd her in de Cotton patch,
A-coming from de Ball.

She hug me, an' she kiss me,
And wrung my han' an' cried.
She said I wus de sweetes' thing
Dat ever lived or died.

1 From *Negro Folk Rhymes*, by T. W. Talley. Copyright, 1922, by The Macmillan Company, New York. Reprinted with the permission of Dr. Thomas W. Talley.

She hug me an' she kiss me.
Oh Heaben! De touch o' her han'!
She said I wus de puttiest thing
In de shape o' mortal man.

I told her dat I love her,
Dat my love wus bed-cord strong;
Den I axed her w'en she'd have me,
An' she jes say, "Go long!"

Zora Neale Hurston

"A girl! A girl? Lord, have mercy!" exclaimed the disappointed John Hurston, who handled bales of cotton like sacks of potatoes—this carpenter, farmer, and preacher—the father of Zora Neale. He had enough girls. He wanted boys, because "girls didn't bring in anything." However, since Zora resembled him more than any of the other children, he made her welcome and soon learned to love her.

She was born at Eatonville, Florida, the first Negro town in the United States to be incorporated. Her father wrote the first laws of this community and for three terms served as its mayor.

After getting the rudiments of an education in her home town, she did her preparatory work at Morgan College in Baltimore, Maryland. From there she went to Howard University, Washington, D. C., and completed her formal training at Columbia University, where under the inspiration of Franz Boas [1] she became especially interested in anthropology. Her specialty in this field is American Negro folk lore.

As to her writings, her short story, "Spunk," won first prize in the *Opportunity* contest of 1925. Her *Jonah's Gourd Vine,* a novel, was published by J. B. Lippincott Company of Philadelphia in 1934. The same company in 1935 published her *Mules and Men,* which is chiefly a collection of folk tales. Though she presents this folk material as a skilled literary artist, she has preserved the humor, the realism, and the naturalism of the people concerning whom she writes.

[1] Franz Boas, author of *The Mind of Primitive Man* and many other significant works, was Chairman of the Department of Anthropology at Columbia University.

THE MAN WHO WENT TO HEAVEN FROM JOHNSTOWN [1]

You know, when it lightnings, de angels is peepin' in de lookin' glass; when it thunders, they's rollin' out de rain barrels; and when it rains, somebody done dropped a barrel or two or bust it.

One time, you know, there was going to be a big doin's in Glory and all de angels had brand new clothes to wear and so they was all peepin' in the lookin' glasses, and therefore it got to lightning all over de sky. God told some of de angels to roll in all de full rain barrels and they was in such a hurry that it was thunderin' from the east to the west and the zig-zag lightning went to join the mutterin' thunder and, next thing you know, some of them angels got careless and dropped a whole heap of them rain barrels, and didn't it rain!

In one place they call Johnstown they had a great flood. And so many folks got drownded that it looked jus' like Judgment Day.

So some of de folks that got drownded in that flood went one place and some went another. And so one of de brothers in black went up to Heben from de flood.

When he got to the gate, Old Peter let 'im in and made 'im welcome. De colored man was named John, so John ast Peter, says, "Is it dry in dere?"

Old Peter tole 'im, "Why, yes it's dry in here. How comes you ast that?"

"Well, you know Ah jus' come out of one flood, and Ah don't want to run into no mo! Ooh, man! You ain't seen no water. You just oughter seen dat flood we had at Johnstown."

Peter says, "Yeah, we know all about it. Jus' go wid Gabriel and let him give you some new clothes."

So John went off wid Gabriel and come back all dressed up in brand new clothes and all de time he was changin' his clothes he was tellin' Old Gabriel all about dat flood, jus' like he didn't know already.

So when he come back from changin' his clothes, they give him a brand new gold harp and handed him too a gold bench and made him welcome. They was so tired of hearing about dat flood, they was glad

1 From *Mules and Men*. Copyright, 1935, by Zora Neale Hurston. Published by J. B. Lippincott Company, Philadelphia.

to see him wid his harp 'cause they figgered he'd get to playin' and forget all about it. So Peter tole him, "Now you jus' make yo'self at home and play all de music you please."

John went and took a seat on de bench and commenced to tune up his harp. By dat time, two angels come walkin' by where John was settin' so he throwed down his harp and tackled 'em.

"Say," he hollered, "Y'all want to hear 'bout de big flood Ah was in down on earth? Lawd, Lawd! It sho rained, and talkin' 'bout water!"

Dem two angels hurried on off from 'im jus' as quick as they could. He started to tellin' another one and he took to flyin'. Gab'ull went over to 'im and tried to get 'im to take it easy, but John kept right on stoppin' every angel dat he could find to tell 'im about dat flood of water.

Way after while he went over to Ole Peter and said: "Thought you said everybody would be nice and polite?"

Peter said, "Yeah, Ah said it. Ain't everybody treatin' you right?"

John said, "Naw. Ah jus' walked up to a man as nice and friendly as Ah could be and started to tell 'im 'bout all dat water Ah left back there in Johnstown and instead of him turnin' me a friendly answer he said, 'Shucks! You ain't seen no water!' and walked off and left me standin' by myself."

"Was he a *ole* man wid a crooked walkin' stick?" Peter ast John. "Yeah."

"Did he have whiskers down to here?" Peter measured down to his waist.

"He sho did," John tol' 'im.

"Aw shucks," Peter tol' 'im. "Dat was Old Nora. You can't tell *him* nothin' 'bout no flood."

THE FOLK SERMON [1]

Nobody pushed him uphill, but everybody was willing to lend a hand to the downward shove. Oh for the wings, for the wings of a dove! That he might see no more what men's faces held!

[1] From *Jonah's Gourd Vine*, by Zora Neale Hurston. Copyright, 1934, by J. B. Lippincott Company, Philadelphia.

Sunday afternoon, the sunlight filtered through the colored glass on the packed and hushed church. Women all in white. Three huge bouquets of red hibiscus below him and behind the covered Communion table. As he stood looking down into the open Bible and upon the snow-white table, his feelings ran riot over his body. "He that soppeth in the dish with me." He knew he could not preach that Last Supper. Not today. Not for many days to come. He turned the pages while he swallowed the lump in his throat and raised:

> "Beloved, Beloved, now are we the sons of God
> And it doth not yet appear what we shall be;
> But we know, but we know
> When He shall appear, when He shall appear
> We shall be like Him;
> We shall see Him as he is."

The audience sang with him. They always sang with him well, because group singers follow the leader.

Then he began in a clear, calm voice.

"Brothers and Sisters: De song we jus' sung, and seein' so many uh y'all out here tuh day, it reaches me in uh most particular manner. It wakes up uh whole family uh thoughts, and Ahm gointer speak tuh yuh outa de fullness uh mah heart. Ah want yuh tuh pray wid me whilst Ah break de bread uh life fuh de nourishment uh yo' souls.

"Our theme this morning is the wounds of Jesus. When the Father shall ast, 'What are these wounds in thine hand?' He shall answer, 'Those are they with which I was wounded in the house of my friends.' Zech. 13:6.

"We read in the Fifty-third Chapter of Isaiah where He was wounded for our transgressions and bruised for our iniquities, and the apostle Peter affirms that His blood was spilt from before the foundation of the world.

"I have seen gamblers wounded. I have seen desperadoes wounded; thieves and robbers and every other kind of characters, law-breakers, and each one had a reason for his wounds. Some of them was unthoughtful, and some for being overbearing, and some by the doctor's knife, but all wounds disfigures a person.

"Jesus was not unthoughtful. He was not overbearing. He was never

a bully. He was never sick. He was never a criminal before the law
and yet He was wounded. Now, a man usually gets wounded, says the
text, in the house of His friends. It is not your enemies that harm
you all the time. Watch that close friend. Every believer in Christ is
considered His friend, and every sin we commit is a wound to Jesus.
The blues we play in our homes is a club to beat up Jesus, and these
social card parties.

"Jesus have always loved us from the foundation of the world.

> When God stood out on the apex of His power
> Before the hammers of creation
> Fell upon the anvils of Time and hammered out the ribs of
> the earth
> Before He made any ropes
> By the breath of fire
> And set the boundaries of the ocean by the gravity of His
> power,
> When God said, ha!
> Let us make man
> And the elders upon the altar cried, ha!
> If you make man, ha!
> He will sin.
> God my master, ha! [1]
> Father!! Ha——aa!
> I am the teeth of time
> That comprehended de dust of de earth
> And weighed de hills in scales
> That painted de rainbow dat marks de end of de parting
> storm,
> Measured de seas in de holler of my hand
> That held de elements in a unbroken chain of controllment.
> Make man, ha!
> If he sin I will redeem him.
> I'll break de chasm of hell
> Where de fire's never quenched,
> I'll go into de grave
> Where de worm never dies, Ah!
> So God A'mighty, Ha!

[1] The exclamations, "Ha," and "Aa-ah," represent the preacher gasping for breath,
suggesting the coming of the Holy Spirit.

Got His stuff together
He dipped some water out of de mighty deep,
He got Him a handful of dirt
From de foundation sills of de earth,
He seized a thimble full of breath
From de drums of de wind, ha!
God, my master!
Now I'm ready to make man——
Aa-aah!
Who shall I make him after? Ha!
Worlds within worlds begin to wheel and roll,
De Sun, Ah!
Gethered up de fiery skirts of her garments
And wheeled around de throne, Ah!
Saying, Ah, make man after me, ha!
God gazed upon de sun
And sent her back to her blood-red socket
And shook His head, ha!
De Moon, ha!
Grabbed up de reins of de tides,
And dragged a thousand seas behind her
As she walked around de throne;
Ah-h, please make man after me.
But God said 'No!'
De stars bust out from their diamond sockets
And circled de glitterin' throne crying
A-aah! Make man after me,
God said, 'NO!'
I'll make man in my own image, ha!
I'll put him in de garden
And Jesus said, Ha!
And if he sin,
I'll go his bond before yo' mighty throne.
Ah, He was yo' friend.
He made us all, ha!
Delegates to de judgment convention.
Ah!   .   .   .   .
We notice at de supper table
As he gazed upon His friends, ha!

His eyes flowin' wid tears, ha! He said,
'My soul is exceedingly sorrowful unto death, ha!
For this night, ha!
One of you shall betray me, ha!
It were not a Roman officer, ha!
It were not a centurion,
But one of you
Who I have chosen my bosom friend,
That sops in the dish with me shall betray me.'
I want to draw a parable.
I see Jesus
Leaving heben with all of His grandeur,
Dis-robin' Hisself of His matchless honor,
Yielding up de scepter of revolvin' worlds,
Clothing Hisself in de garment of humanity,
Coming into de world to rescue His friends.
Two thousand years have went by on their rusty ankles;
But with the eye of faith, I can see Him
Look down from His high towers of elevation!
I can hear Him when He walks about the golden streets,
I can hear 'em ring under His footsteps;
I can see Him step out upon de rim bones of nothing,
Crying, 'I am de way
De truth and de light.'

. . . . .

He died for our sins.
Wounded in the house of His friends.

. . . .

When Jesus shall place one foot on de neck of de sea, ha!
One foot on dry land, ah,
When His chariot wheel shall be running hub-deep in fire,
He shall take His friends through the open bosom of an
                                  unclouded sky
And place in their hands de 'hosanna' fan
And they shall stand 'round and 'round his beatific throne
And praise His name forever,

                                  Amen."

PART II

Poetry

Introduction   Poetry is a rhythmic kind of expression. Whether the writer uses the classic style of Homer,[1] Milton,[2] Goethe,[3] or Shakespeare or the informal style of Amy Lowell,[4] Walt Whitman, or Langston Hughes, rhythm is a dominant characteristic of poetic writing. If the style is classic, the rhythm is prevailingly regular with some variation; if the style is informal, the rhythm is rather irregular with no, or with only occasional, regularity. Among the Negro poets, Paul Laurence Dunbar and Claude McKay adhered to the classic style; likewise, Countee Cullen. Langston Hughes blends the two, leaning preferably, it seems, toward the informal style, which is the use of free verse. In using the classic style, the writer pays great attention to form, deciding upon a pattern of verse or stanza and closely following it, as did Shelley, Keats, and Tennyson.[5] In free verse, form is subordinated to thought, and though a set rhythmic pattern may be in the mind of the poet he may not follow it. If rhyme is used, the classic writer will observe regularity of rhyme; the writer of free verse does not strive for rhyme. His poetry may contain rhyme, but with him rhyme is incidental and spontaneous, if there is rhyme at all.

1 Homer, Greek author of "The Iliad" and "The Odyssey," epic or heroic poems, about 9th century B. C.
2 John Milton, English poet, author of the epic, "Paradise Lost," 1608-1674.
3 Johann Wolfgang von Goethe, German author of the dramatic poem, "Faust," 1749-1832.
4 Amy Lowell, an American poet, advocate of free verse, 1874-1925.
5 Percy Bysshe Shelley, 1792-1822, John Keats, 1795-1821, Alfred (Lord) Tennyson, 1809-1892, English poets.

Naomi Long Witherspoon, a rising poet of great promise, used effectively both styles. Her "Quest" and "The Poet Deserts His Ivory Tower" are both examples of the classic style. "Not I Alone," on the other hand, is written in free verse.

Rhythm is an essential characteristic of poetry. It is the regularity of the rhythm that distinguishes poetry from prose. The more regular the rhythm, the more readily is the literary product recognized as poetry. Poetry is the discourse for the feelings of joy and gladness, of sorrow and love. The more skillfully the poet uses his rhythm, the easier is his appeal to the emotions.

Prose ordinarily has irregular rhythm; the more irregular its rhythm, the more readily is it recognized as prose. If the writer of prose should aim to stir the emotions, as does the orator or public speaker, he may use rhythmic prose, as did Daniel Webster [1] in his "Reply to Hayne" and Frederick Douglass [2] in his "Fourth of July or Independence Day Oration."

The other essential of poetry aside from rhythm is figurative or imaginative speech. In observing this quality, the poet is said to exhibit fancy. Consider these two expressions, one literal, the other figurative: (a) "You may keep on doing wrong, but some day it will be known just what you have done." This is a literal expression. The words were selected to express exactly what the writer had in mind. This is called the use of the exact phrase. (b) "Time will tell all things." Time, of course, does not speak or write; so this second expression does not use the exact phrase to express its idea. It attributes to time the characteristics of a person and makes an implied comparison between a person speaking and time as a speaker. This quality of words is suggestion or connotation. "Time will tell all things" is a figurative expression which gives dignity and beauty to the style of the writer, appealing to the reader's imagination and to his esthetic sense. In prose we wish to be informed always and often entertained; in poetry the information is secondary, the imaginative effects are of prime importance.

Fancy is seen at its best in Dunbar's "Dawn." Other poets repre-

---

[1] An American statesman, Senator from Massachusetts, (1782-1852).
[2] A Negro abolitionist and orator. A detailed sketch of his life appears on pp. 187-188.

sented in this volume who employ this quality are Evelyn Watson in "Dream World," Naomi Long Witherspoon in "Quest," and Jean Toomer in "Georgia Dusk." The Negro poets who are outstanding as masters of the metaphor or of fancy are Claude McKay, Countee Cullen, and Jean Toomer.

Since prose is the discourse of sophistication and learning, and poetry is the discourse of the feelings, man in developing from savagery to civilization produces written poetry before he produces written prose. That is why this volume begins with folk poetry, the spiritual, and folk rhymes, and then turns to the poetry of known authors.

The American Negro author has often been inspired by having been made conscious of what some of his dark brothers have accomplished in literature in other parts of the world. Early he learned that a Negro slave, Antar, became the epic poet of Arabia. Later he discovered that a Negro, Alexander Pushkin, became the epic poet of Russia. Knowledge of these two writers has inspired many an American Negro to try to write poetry.

There are different types of poetry: the narrative and the lyric. Some rhetoricians place dramatic poetry in a separate class, even though it is essentially narrative. Though the American Negro has the inspiration of Antar and Pushkin, he has not as yet produced an epic poet. Ophelia Robinson, an excerpt of whose poem, "Nat Turner," appears in this volume, has written in the epic style of Longfellow's "Hiawatha." In "The Shroud of Color," Countee Cullen attains the grandeur of the epic style.

The American Negro author has not produced an epic or a metrical romance such as Sir Walter Scott's "The Lady of the Lake" or "Marmion." Countee Cullen could have produced one; but a work of such sustained proportions as an epic or a metrical romance requires leisure. This the Negro in America has not had. He has pursued the creation of literature as an avocation and not as a vocation. It is recalled that Paul Laurence Dunbar ran an elevator for a living and wrote his first poetry between trips. Of living Negro authors only Langston Hughes as a literary artist has lived for years from his literary productions. In a lecture at Stowe Teachers College, Hughes said, "Poetry is fascinating, but a person can not make a living writing poetry in America. He can make a living writing short stories, novels, and dramas, but not by writing poetry. Poetry must remain for his playtime."

The American Negro has, however, produced the other types of poetry. Dunbar has written many metrical tales, two examples of which are "The Party" and "The Rivals." "The Rivals" is included in this volume. The metrical tale and the ballad, which is the shortest of the narrative poems, must each present a story with a point or climax; that is, with an incident that decides the fate of the chief character or chief characters for the better or for the worse. This technique is followed in both "The Party" and "The Rivals." This same technique is observed in Dunbar's "The Wooing" and Cullen's "One Day We Played a Game," and in the humorous ballads of Alice McGee Smart and Ezra W. Turner, "Pa" and "Tell Yo' Ma I Said So," respectively.

As to lyric poetry, the American Negro has produced many examples of each type: the song, the sonnet, the elegy, and the ode. The song as a madrigal is illustrated by Naomi Long Witherspoon's "Quest," Jean Toomer's "Evening Song," and Claude McKay's "Absence" and "To O. E. A." Sonnets are represented by Jean Toomer's "November Cotton Flower" and McKay's "America" and "The Tired Worker." The most versatile sonneteer among American Negro authors is Claude McKay, who has adapted the sonnet to more different moods than any other American poet. Countee Cullen has written several elegies, one of the most appealing of which is his "Threnody for a Brown Girl."

The ode, which is often regarded as the most difficult of the lyrics to write, has not failed to lure the American Negro author. Phillis Wheatley, the first outstanding Negro poet America produced, following the classic style of Alexander Pope, wrote several odes, two of which are included in this volume: "On Virtue" and "His Excellency, General Washington."

Illustrative of humorous poems written by the American Negro are Dunbar's "The Rivals," Smart's "Pa," Reason's "Ma Honey," and Turner's "Tell Yo' Ma I Said So." In each instance, the poem deals with the lowly. The dialect is used to portray the character, not to produce the humor; the humor is produced by the situation and by the reader's contrasting his intelligent response in his imagination and in his everyday experiences with the different response of the character or characters portrayed in the poems.

Some literary critics, in fact most of them, have stressed the genius of Paul Laurence Dunbar in writing dialect poetry. The dialect poems arc well done. However, "Dawn," "Ships That Pass in the Night," "Sunset," "The Wooing," and "When All Is Done" are poems not in dialect of which America may be proud. They are among the best that American poets have produced.

The American Negro poet has made a substantial contribution to American literature. The selections made for this volume will show that, though he at times makes fanciful flights steeped in colorful metaphors, he constantly returns from heaven to earth, conscious of the fact that he is a poet-prophet, protesting against the wrongs he suffers as a Negro. Dunbar in his "Ode to Ethiopia," McKay in "America" and "The Tired Worker," Cullen in "The Shroud of Color," Hughes in "I Am a Negro," and Naomi Long Witherspoon in "To My Country," "Not I Alone," "A Negro in New York," and "City Thought," with the art of masters and the dignity of kings and queens analyze the plight of the Negro in America, express a philosophic hope for justice, and prophesy disaster for any land that will not be motivated by the fact of the brotherhood of man. This theme the American Negro poet treats with consummate art, as he aspires for justice in every phase of life in accordance with the Federal Constitution.

Phillis Wheatley
(1754-1784)

A little slip of a girl, about seven or eight years of age, of very dark complexion, with delicate features, in obedience to the command of a slave trader stood on an auction block to be sold to the highest bidder. Hardly any prospective purchaser of slaves considered her because of her apparent physical weakness; but John Wheatley, a prominent tailor of Boston, Massachusetts, where the sale was taking place, was attracted to her by her innocence and unassuming dignity. Remembering the request of his wife that he purchase her a slave for a companion, he paid the price required, took the little girl by the hand, and led her home.

Mrs. Wheatley named her Phillis and with the help of her daughter, Mary, began at once the literary education of the child. Within eighteen months she was speaking and writing English fluently. At twelve she was reading Latin. By the age of sixteen she was reading the classic Roman poets, Virgil and Horace.

Having read carefully Alexander Pope's *Translation of Homer's Iliad*, Phillis soon mastered his style and imitated him in most of her poems. On various occasions and honoring different persons of note, she produced some of her best poems.

The first edition of her *Poems on Various Subjects* was published in London in 1773. Before 1840, about twelve editions of her poems had been published.

The Wheatleys never treated Phillis as a slave, but always as a member of the family. She was highly acclaimed by the society of Boston and London. By her writing, selections from which follow, and her talented conversation she bore witness to the potential genius of the Negro.

Further details about her life may be found in J. W. Cromwell's *The Negro in Our History* and B. G. Brawley's "The Negro Genius."

ON BEING BROUGHT FROM AFRICA TO AMERICA

'Twas mercy brought me from my PAGAN land,
Taught my benighted soul to understand
That there's a God, that there's a "Saviour" too;
Once I redemption neither sought nor knew.
Some view our sable race with scornful eye,
"Their color is a diabolic die."
Remember, "Christians," "Negroes," black as "Cain,"
May be refined, and join th' angelic train.

A FAREWELL TO AMERICA
To Mrs. S. W.[1]

Adieu, "New England's" smiling meads,
Adieu, the flow'ry plain:

[1] Mrs. Wheatley, who purchased her, taught her, and gave her her freedom.

I leave thine op'ning charms, O spring,
And tempt the roaring main.

In vain for me the flow'rets rise,
And boast their gaudy pride,
While here beneath the Northern skies
I mourn for "health" deny'd.

Celestial maid of rosy hue,
O let me feel thy reign!
I languish till thy face I view,
Thy vanish'd joys regain.

Susannah [1] mourns, nor can I bear
To see the crystal shower,
Or mark the tender falling tear
At sad departure's hour:

Not unregarding can I see
Her soul with grief opprest;
But let no sigh, nor groans for me
Steal from her pensive breast.

In vain the feather'd warblers sing,
In vain the garden blooms,
And on the bosom of the spring
Breathes out her sweet perfumes.

While for "Britannia's" distant shore
We sweep the liquid plain,
And with astonish'd eyes explore
The wide-extended main.

Lo! *Health* appears! celestial dame!
Complacent and serene,
With "Hebe's" [2] mantle o'er her Frame,
With soul-delighting mien.

[1] Mrs. Wheatley.
[2] "Hebe," goddess of youth, cupbearer of the gods.

To mark the vale where "London" lies
With misty vapors crown'd
Which cloud "Aurora's" [1] thousand dyes,
And veil her charms around.

Why, "Phoebus," [2] moves thy car so slow?
So slow thy rising ray?
Give us the famous town to view,
Thou glorious king of day!

For thee, "Britannia," I resign
"New England's" smiling fields;
To view again her charms divine,
What joy the prospect yields!

But thou! Temptation, hence away,
With all thy fatal train
Nor once seduce my soul again,
By thine enchanting strain.

Thrice happy they, whose heav'nly shield
Secures their souls from harms
And fell "Temptation" on the field
Of all its pow'r disarms!

HIS EXCELLENCY, GENERAL WASHINGTON
(1775)

Celestial choir, enthron'd in realms of light,
Columbia's [3] scenes of glorious toils I write.
While freedom's cause her anxious breast alarms,
She flashes dreadful in refulgent arms.
See mother earth her offspring's fate bemoan,
And nations gaze at scenes before unknown;
See the bright beams of heaven's revolving light
Involved in sorrows and the veil of night!

1 "Aurora," goddess of the dawn.
2 "Phoebus," god of the sun.
3 Columbia, the United States of America.

The goddess comes, she moves divinely fair,
Olive and laurel bind her golden hair:
Wherever shines this native of the skies,
Unnumber'd charms and recent graces rise.

Muse! [1] how propitious while my pen relates
How pour her armies through a thousand gates,
As when Eolus [2] heaven's fair face deforms,
Enwrapp'd in tempest and a night of storms;
Astonish'd ocean feels the wild uproar,
The refluent surges beat the sounding shore:
Or thick as leaves in Autumn's golden reign,
Such, and so many, moves the warrior's train.
In bright array they seek the work of war,
Where high unfurl'd the ensign waves in air.
Shall I to Washington their praise recite?
Enough thou know'st them in the fields of fight.
Thee, first in peace and honors,—we demand
The grace and glory of thy martial band.
Fam'd for thy valor, for thy virtues more,
Hear every tongue thy guardian aid implore!

One century scarce perform'd its destined round,
When Gallic [3] powers Columbia's fury found;
And so may you, whoever dares disgrace
The land of freedom's heaven-defended race!
Fix'd are the eyes of nations on the scales,
For in their hopes Columbia's arm prevails.
Anon Britannia droops the pensive head,
While round increase the rising hills of dead.
Ah! cruel blindness to Columbia's state!
Lament thy thirst of boundless power too late.

Proceed, great chief, with virtue on thy side,
Thy ev'ry action let the goddess guide.
A crown, a mansion, and a throne that shine,
With gold unfading, Washington! be thine.

1 Muse, the goddess of lyric poetry, to inspire the poet.
2 Eolus, god of the winds.
3 Gallic, pertaining to France.

AN HYMN TO THE EVENING

Soon as the sun forsook the eastern main
The pealing thunder shook the heav'nly plain;
Majestic grandeur! From the zephyr's wing,
Exhales the incense of the blooming spring,
Soft purl the streams, the birds renew their notes,
And through the air their mingled music floats.

Through all the heav'ns what beauteous dies are spread!
But the west glories in the deepest red:
So may our breasts with every virtue glow,
The living temples of our God below!

Fill'd with the praise of him who gives the light,
And draws the sable curtains of the night,
Let placid slumbers soothe each weary mind,
At morn to wake more heav'nly, more refin'd:
So shall the labors of the day begin
More pure, more guarded from the snares of sin.

Night's leaden sceptre seals my drowsy eyes.
Then cease, my song, till fair *Aurora* rise.

Paul Laurence Dunbar
(June 27, 1872-February 9, 1906)

"There it goes again. The bell!" Paul Laurence Dunbar put his paper and
pencil in a book, closed the safety doors of his elevator, pulled a lever, and
went to the fourth floor to bring a guest of the hotel that employed him
down to the first floor. After letting the passenger out courteously, Dunbar,
the poet of his church and of his high-school class at Dayton, Ohio, where
he was born, returned to the writing of a poem. Thus between rings he wrote
many a lyric.

Such was the humble beginning of the inspired son of Joshua and Matilda
Dunbar: Joshua, who had run away from slavery and settled in Canada
until after the Civil War, and Matilda, a laundress, who while a slave at
Shelbyville, Kentucky had learned to read and write as she played with
white children returning from school with their books. Her genial humor
and deep sense of spiritual and literary values gave encouragement to
Laurence in his courtship of the Muses. To her he was also indebted for

his ideas concerning the life of the slave on the Southern plantation.

It was a hard struggle to publish at his own expense *Oak and Ivy*, his first collection of poems; but liberal white people like Dr. H. A. Tobey of Toledo and William Dean Howells, an outstanding man of American letters, helped him rise to fame and security.

His writings fall into three groups: (1) collections of poetry: *Oak and Ivy* (1893), *Majors and Minors* (1895), *Lyrics of Lowly Life* (1896), *Lyrics of Love and Laughter* (1903), *Complete Poems* (1913); (2) collections of short stories: *Folks from Dixie* (1898), *The Strength of Gideon* (1900), *In Old Plantation Days* (1903); and (3) novels, *Uncalled* (1898), *The Love of Landry* (1900), *The Fanatics* (1901), and *The Sport of the Gods* (1902).

SUNSET [1]

The river sleeps beneath the sky,
    And clasps the shadows to its breast;
The crescent moon shines dim on high;
    And in the lately radiant west
        The gold is fading into gray.
        Now stills the lark his festive lay,
        And mourns with me the dying day.

While in the south the first faint star
    Lifts to the night its silver face,
And twinkles to the moon afar
    Across the heavens' graying space,
        Low murmurs reach me from the town,
        As Day puts on her sombre crown,
        And shakes her mantle darkly down.

SONG [1]

My heart to thy heart,
    My hand to thine;
My lips to thy lips,
    Kisses are wine
Brewed for the lover in sunshine and shade;
Let me drink deep, then, my
    African maid.

Lily to lily,
    Rose unto rose;
My love to thy love
    Tenderly grows.
Rend not the oak and the ivy in twain,
Nor the swart maid from her swarthier swain.

ODE TO ETHIOPIA [1,2]

O Mother Race! to thee I bring
This pledge of faith unwavering,
    This tribute to thy glory.
I know the pangs which thou didst feel,
When Slavery crushed thee with its heel,
    With thy dear blood all gory.
Sad days were those—ah, sad indeed!
But through the land the fruitful seed of better times were
                                growing.

The plant of freedom upward sprung,
Then spread its leaves so fresh and young—
    Its blossoms now are blowing.
On every hand in this fair land,
Proud Ethiope's swarthy children stand
    Beside their fairer neighbor;

[1] From *Complete Poems of Paul Laurence Dunbar.* Copyright, 1896, 1899, 1903, 1905, 1913, by Dodd, Mead & Company, New York.
[2] Ethiopia, a section of northwest Africa, here used to mean the Negro race.

The forests flee before their stroke,
Their hammers ring, their forges smoke,——
    They stir in honest labor.

They tread the fields where honor calls;
Their voices sound through senate halls
    In majesty and power.
To right they cling; the hymns they sing
Up to the skies in beauty ring,
    And bolder grow each hour.

Be proud, my Race, in mind and soul;
Thy name is writ on Glory's scroll
    In characters of fire.
High 'mid the clouds of Fame's bright sky
Thy banner's blazoned folds now fly,
    And truth shall lift them higher.

Thou hast the right to noble pride,
Whose spotless robes were purified
    By blood's severe baptism.
Upon thy brow the cross was laid,
And labor's painful sweat-beads made
    A consecrating chrism.[1]

No other race, or white or black,
When bound as thou wert, to the rack,
    So seldom stooped to grieving;
No other race, when free again,
Forgot the past and proved them men
    So noble in forgiving.

Go on and up! Our souls and eyes
Shall follow thy continuous rise;
    Our ears shall list thy story
From bards who from thy root shall spring,
And proudly tune their lyres to sing
    Of Ethiopia's glory.

1 Chrism, a sacramental ointment.

THE RIVALS [1]

'Twas three an' thirty years ago,
When I was ruther young, you know,
I had my last an' only fight
About a gal one summer night.
'T was me an' Zekel Johnson; Zeke
'N' me'd be'n spattin' 'bout a week,
Each of us tryin' his best to show
That he was Liza Jones's beau.
We couldn't neither prove the thing,
Fur she was fur too sharp to fling
One over fur the other one
An' by so doin' stop the fun
That we chaps didn't have the sense
To see she got at our expense,
But that's the way a feller does,
Fur boys is fools an' allus was.
An' when they's females in the game
I reckon men's about the same.
Well, Zeke an' me went on that way
An' fussed an' quarrelled day by day;
While Liza, mindin' not the fuss,
Jest kep' a-goin' with both of us,
Tell we pore chaps, that's Zeke an' me,
Was jest plum mad with jealousy.
Well, fur a time we kep' our places,
An' only showed by frownin' faces
An' looks 'at well our meanin' boded
How full o' fight we both was loaded.
At last it come, the thing broke out,
An' this is how it come about.
One night ('t was fair, you 'll all agree)
I got Eliza's company,
An' leavin' Zekel in the lurch,
Went trottin' off with her to church.

[1] From *Complete Poems of Paul Laurence Dunbar.* Copyright, 1896, 1899, 1903, 1905, 1913, by Dodd, Mead & Company, New York.

An' jest as we had took our seat
(Eliza lookin' fair an' sweet),
Why, I jest couldn't help but grin
When Zekel come a-bouncin' in
As furious as the law allows.
He'd jest be'n up to Liza's house,
To find her gone, then come to church
To have this end put to his search.
I guess I laffed that meetin' through,
An' not a mortal word I knew
Of what the preacher preached er read
Er what the choir sung er said.
Fur every time I'd turn my head
I couldn't skeercely help but see
'At Zekel had his eye on me.
An' he 'ud sort o'turn an' twist
An' grind his teeth an' shake his fist.
I laughed, fur la! the hull church seen us,
An' knowed that suthin' was between us.
Well, meetin' out, we started hum,
I sorter feelin' what would come.
We'd jest got out, when up stepped Zeke,
An' said, "Scuse me, I'd like to speak
To you a minute." "Cert," said I—
A-nudgin' Liza on the sly
An' laughin' in my sleeve with glee,
I asked her, please, to pardon me.
We walked away a step er two,
Jest to git out o' Liza's view,
An' then Zeke said, "I want to know
Ef you think you're Eliza's beau,
An' 'at I'm going to let her go
Hum with sich a chap as you?"
An' I said bold, "You bet I do."
Then Zekel, sneerin', said 'at he
Didn't want to hender me.
But then he 'lowed the gal was his
An' 'at he guessed he knowed his biz,
An' wasn't feared o' all my kin

With all my friends an' chums throwed in.
Some other things he mentioned there
That no born man could no ways bear
Er think o' ca'mly tryin' to stan'
Ef Zeke had be'n the bigges' man
In town, an' not the leanest runt
'At time an' labor ever stunt.
An' so I let my fist go "bim,"
I thought I'd mos' nigh finished him.
But Zekel didn't take it so.
He jest ducked down an' dodged my blow
An' then come back at me so hard,
I guess I must 'a' hurt the yard,
Er spilet the grass plot where I fell,
An' sakes alive it hurt me; well,
It wouldn't be'n so bad, you see,
But he jest kep' a-hittin' me.
An' I hit back an' kicked an' pawed,
But 't seemed 't was mostly air I clawed,
While Zekel used his science well
A-makin' every motion tell.
He punched an' hit, why, goodness lands,
Seemed like he had a dozen hands.
Well, afterwhile they stopped the fuss,
An' some one kindly parted us.
All beat an' cuffed an' clawed an' scratched,
An' needin' both our faces patched,
Each started hum a different way;
An' what o' Liza, do you say,
Why, Liza—little humbug—dern her,
Why, she'd gone home with Hiram Turner.

THE WOOING [1]

A youth went faring up and down,
  Alack and well-a-day.

[1] From *Complete Poems of Paul Laurence Dunbar.* Copyright, 1896, 1899, 1903, 1905, 1913, by Dodd, Mead & Company, New York.

He fared him to the market town,
    Alack and well-a-day.
And there he met a maiden fair,
With hazel eyes and auburn hair;
His heart went from him then and there,
    Alack and well-a-day.

She posies sold right merrily,
    Alack and well-a-day;
But not a flower was fair as she,
    Alack and well-a-day.
He bought a rose and sighed a sigh,
"Ah, dearest maiden, would that I
Might dare the seller too to buy!"
    Alack and well-a-day.

She tossed her head, the coy coquette,
    Alack and well-a-day.
"I'm not, sir, in the market yet,"
    Alack and well-a-day.
"Your love must cool upon a shelf;
Tho' much I sell for gold and pelf,
I'm yet too young to sell myself,"
    Alack and well-a-day.

The youth was filled with sorrow sore,
    Alack and well-a-day.
And looked he at the maid once more,
    Alack and well-a-day.
Then loud he cried, "Fair maiden, if
Too young to sell, now as I live,
You're not too young yourself to give,"
    Alack and well-a-day.

The little maid cast down her eyes,
    Alack and well-a-day.
And many a flush began to rise,
    Alack and well-a-day.

"Why, since you are so bold," she said,
"I doubt not you are highly bred,
So take me!" and the twain were wed,
    Alack and well-a-day.

DAWN [1]

An angel, robed in spotless white,
Bent down and kissed the sleeping Night.
Night woke to blush; the sprite was gone.
Men saw the blush and called it Dawn.

LITTLE BROWN BABY [1]

Little brown baby wif spa'klin' eyes,
    Come to yo' pappy an' set on his knee.
    What you been doin', suh—makin' san' pies?
    Look at dat bib—you's ez du'ty ez me.
Look at dat mouf—dat's merlasses, I bet;
    Come hyeah, Maria, an' wipe off his han's
Bees gwine to ketch you an' eat you up yit,
    Bein' so sticky and sweet—goodness lan's!

Little brown baby wif spa'klin' eyes,
    Who's pappy's darlin' an' who's pappy's chile?
Who is it all de day nevah once tries
    Fu' to be cross, er once loses dat smile?
Whah did you get dem teef? My, you's a scamp!
    Whah did dat dimple come f'om in yo' chin?
Pappy do' know you—I b'lieves you's a tramp,
    Mammy, dis hyeah's some ol' straggler got in!

Let's th'ow him outen de do' in de san',
    We do' want stragglers a-layin' 'roun' hyeah;
Let's gin him 'way to de big buggah-man;
    I know he's hidin' erroun' hyeah right neah.

[1] From *Complete Poems of Paul Laurence Dunbar*. Copyright, 1896, 1899, 1903,
1905, 1913, by Dodd, Mead & Company, New York.

Buggah-man, buggah-man, come in de do',
Hyeah's a bad boy you kin have fu' to eat.
Mammy an' pappy do' want him no mo',
    Swaller him down f'om his haid to his feet!

Dah, now, I t'ought dat you'd hug me up close.
    Go back, ol' buggah, you sha'n't have dis boy.
He ain't no tramp, ner no straggler, of co'se;
    He's pappy's pa'dner an' playmate an' joy.
Come to yo' pallet now—go to yo' res';
    Wisht you could allus know ease an' cleah skies;
Wisht you could stay jes' a chile on my breas'—
    Little brown baby wif spa'klin' eyes!

SHIPS THAT PASS IN THE NIGHT [1]

Out in the sky the great dark clouds are massing;
    I look far out into the pregnant night,
Where I can hear a solemn booming gun
    And catch the gleaming of a random light,
That tells me that the ship I seek is passing, passing.

My tearful eyes my soul's deep hurt are glassing;
    For I would hail and check that ship of ships.
I stretch my hands imploring, cry aloud,
    My voice falls dead a foot from mine own lips,
And but its ghost doth reach that vessel, passing, passing.

O Earth, O Sky, O Ocean, both surpassing,
    O heart of mine, O soul that dreads the dark!
Is there no hope for me? Is there no way
    That I may sight and check that speeding bark
Which out of sight and sound is passing, passing?

WHEN ALL IS DONE [1]

When all is done, and my last word is said,
And ye who loved me murmur,
    "He is dead,"
Let no one weep, for fear that I should know,
And sorrow too that ye should sorrow so.

When all is done and in the oozing clay,
Ye lay this cast-off hull of mine away,
Pray not for me, for, after long despair,
The quiet of the grave will be a prayer.

For I have suffered loss and grievous pain,
The hurts of hatred and the world's disdain,
And wounds so deep that love, well-tried and pure,
Had not the pow'r to ease them or to cure.

When all is done, say not my day is o'er,
And that thro' night I seek a dimmer shore:
Say rather that my morn has just begun,—
I greet the dawn and not a setting sun,
            When all is done.

James Weldon Johnson

James Weldon Johnson, educator, poet, essayist, novelist, librettist, lawyer, diplomat, and reformer, was born June 17, 1871 at Jacksonville, Florida. His versatility was amazing. The path that led from student days in the public schools of Jacksonville to his position as Professor of Creative Literature at Fisk University and Exchange Professor in this same capacity at New York University was strewn with many honors.

With his brother, J. Rosamond, a musician, he collaborated in the writing and production of several musical comedies, which made Broadway and toured the country successfully. One of the most famous of these was "Red Moon." The Johnson brothers also wrote the popular song, "Lift Every Voice and Sing," which begins most of the exalted programs given by Negroes. James Weldon was also librettist for the opera *Goyescas,* which was produced at the Metropolitan Opera House in 1915.

As Consul to Venezuela and Nicaragua, as Field Secretary for many years for the National Association for the Advancement of Colored People, Johnson served well his country and his age. Here was the scholar-poet, equally at home in the dialect or the classic style. An automobile accident during the summer of 1938 ended this brilliant career.

Among his publications were the following: *The Autobiography of an Ex-Colored Man* (1912), *Fifty Years and Other Poems* (1917), *God's Trombones* (1927), *Black Manhattan* (1930), *Saint Peter Relates an Incident of the Resurrection Day* (1930), *The Book of American Negro Poetry* (1921), and two books of American Negro spirituals in collaboration with his brother. His is certainly the poetry of dignity and restraint; yet he touched the hearts of the highest and the lowest.

O BLACK AND UNKNOWN BARDS [1]

O black and unknown bards of long ago,
How came your lips to touch the sacred fire?
How, in your darkness, did you come to know
The power and beauty of the minstrel's lyre?
Who first from midst his bonds lifted his eyes?
Who first from out the still watch, lone and long,
Feeling the ancient faith of prophets rise
Within his dark-kept soul, burst into song?

Heart of what slave poured out such melody
As "Steal away to Jesus"? On its strains
His spirit must have nightly floated free,
Though still about his hands he felt his chains.

[1] From *Saint Peter Relates an Incident,* by James Weldon Johnson. Copyright, 1917, 1921, 1935, by James Weldon Johnson. Reprinted by permission of The Viking Press, Inc., New York.

Who heard great "Jordan roll"? Whose starward eye
Saw chariot "swing low"? And who was he
That breathed that comforting, melodic sigh,
"Nobody knows de trouble I see"?

What merely living clod, what captive thing,
Could up toward God through all its darkness grope,
And find within its deadened heart to sing
These songs of sorrow, love, and faith, and hope?
How did it catch that subtle undertone,
That note in music heard not with the ears?
How sound the elusive reed so seldom blown,
Which stirs the soul or melts the heart to tears?

Not the great German master in his dream
Of harmonies that thundered amongst the stars
At the creation, ever heard a theme
Nobler than "Go down, Moses." Mark its bars,
How like a mighty trumpet-call they stir
The blood. Such are the notes that men have sung
Going to valorous deeds; such tones there were
That helped make history when Time was young.

There is a wide, wide wonder in it all,
That from degraded rest and servile toil
The fiery spirit of the seer should call
These simple children of the sun and soil.
O black slave singers, gone, forgot, unfamed,
You—you alone, of all the long, long line
Of those who've sung untaught, unknown, unnamed,
Have stretched out upward, seeking the divine.

You sang not deeds of heroes or of kings;
No chant of bloody war, no exulting pean
Of arms-won triumphs; but your humble strings
You touched in chord with music empyrean.

You sang far better than you knew: the songs
That for your listeners' hungry hearts sufficed
Still live,—but more than this to you belongs:
You sang a race from wood and stone to Christ.

O SOUTHLAND [1]

O Southland! O Southland!
    Have you not heard the call,
The trumpet blown, the word made known
    To the nations, one and all?
The watchword, the hope-word,
    Salvation's present plan?
A gospel new, for all—for you:
    Man shall be saved by man.

O Southland! O Southland!
    Do you not hear today
The mighty beat of onward feet,
    And know you not their way?
'Tis forward, 'tis upward,
    On to the fair white arch
Of freedom's dome, and there is room
    For each man who would march.

O Southland, fair Southland!
    Then why do you still cling
To an idle age and a musty page,
    To a dead and useless thing?
'Tis springtime! 'Tis work-time!
    The world is young again!
And God's above, and God is love,
    And men are only men.

O Southland! my Southland!
    O birthland! do not shirk

1 From *Saint Peter Relates an Incident,* by James Weldon Johnson. Copyright, 1917, 1921, 1935, by James Weldon Johnson. Reprinted by permission of The Viking Press, Inc., New York.

The toilsome task, nor respite ask,
  But gird you for the work.
Remember, remember
    That weakness stalks in pride;
That he is strong who helps along
    The faint one at his side.

TUNK [1]

Look heah, Tunk—now ain't it awful! T'ought I sont you off to school.
Don't you know dat you is growin' up to be a reglah fool?
Whah's dem books dat I's done bought you? Look heah, boy, you
    tell me quick,
Whah's dat Webster blue-black spellah an' dat bran' new 'rifmatic?
W'ile I'm t'inkin' you is lahnin' in de school, why bless ma soul!
You off in de woods a-playin'. Can't you do like you is tol'?
Boy, I tell you, it's jes' scan'lous d'way dat you is goin' on;
An' you sholy go'n' be sorry, jes' as true as you is bo'n.
Heah I'm tryin' hard to raise you as a credit to dis race,
An' you tryin' heap much harder fu' to come up in disgrace.
Dese de days w'en men don't git up to de top by hooks an' crooks,
Tell you now, dey's got to git der standin' on a pile o' books.
W'en you sees a black man goin' to de fiel' as soon as light,
Followin' a mule across it f'om de mawnin' tel de night,
Wukin' all his life fu' vittles, hoein' 'tween de cott'n rows,
W'en he knocks off ole an' tiah'd, ownin' nut'n but his ragged clo'es,
You kin put it down to ignunce, aftah all what's done an' said,
You kin bet dat dat same black man ain't got nut'n in his head.
Ain't you seed dem w'ite men set'n' in der awfice? Don't you know
Dey goes dere 'bout nine each mawnin'? Bless you' soul, dey's out
    by fo'.
Dey jes' does a little writin'; does dat by some easy means;
Gals jes' set an' play pianah on dem printin'-press muchines.
Chile, dem men knows how to figgah, how to use dat little pen,
An' dey knows dat blue-black spellah f'om beginnin' to de en'.
Dat's de 'fect of education; dat's de t'ing what's gwine to rule;
Git dem books, you lazy rascal! Git back to yo' place in school.

[1] *Ibid.*

James Weldon Johnson

LIFT EVERY VOICE AND SING [1,2]

Lift every voice and sing
Till earth and heaven ring,
    Ring with the harmonies of Liberty;
Let our rejoicing rise
High as the list'ning skies,
Let it resound loud as the rolling sea;
Sing a song full of the faith that the dark past has taught us,
Sing a song full of the hope that the present has brought us;
Facing the rising sun
Of our new day begun,
Let us march on till victory is won.

Stony the road we trod,
Bitter the chast'ning rod
    Felt in the days when hope unborn had died;
Yet with a steady beat,
Have not our weary feet
Come to the place for which our fathers sighed?
We have come over a way that with tears has been watered,
We have come treading our path thro' the blood of the slaughtered,
Out from the gloomy past,
Till now we stand at last
Where the white gleam of our bright star is cast.

God of our weary years,
God of our silent tears,
    Thou who hast brought us thus far on the way;
Thou who has by Thy might
Led us into the light,
Keep us forever in the path, we pray,
Lest our feet stray from the places, our God, where we met Thee,
Lest our hearts drunk with the wine of the world, we forget Thee;

1 Music by J. Rosamond Johnson, words by James Weldon Johnson. This has often
been called the Negro National Anthem.
2 Copyright 1900 by Joseph W. Stern & Co. Renewal copyright 1927 by Edward B.
Marks Music Company. Copyright assigned 1932 to Edward B. Marks Music Corporation. Used by permission.

Shadowed beneath Thy hand,
May we forever stand,
True to our God, true to our Native Land!

William Stanley Braithwaite

On December 6, 1878, when the Reconstruction after the Civil War had both the North and the South confused and when the genius of the Negro was still being questioned, there was born in Boston, Massachusetts a child of promise, William Stanley Braithwaite. With a love for beauty that showed itself in his early childhood, he became sensitive also to the rhythms of life. It was not strange, therefore, that while he was attending the Boston Latin School he should develop a special interest in poetry.

Here ended his formal education. Nature, travel, personal contacts, and books then became his teachers.

In 1904 appeared his first collection of poems, *Lyrics of Life and Love;* in 1908 he published *The House of Falling Leaves,* from which have been taken the poems for this volume.

For a number of years, he served as literary editor of the *Boston Daily Transcript,* during which time he annually edited an anthology of magazine verse. Thus he came to be regarded as the great critic of poetry in America.

In 1918 he was awarded three honors. Atlanta University conferred upon him the honorary degree of Master of Arts; Talladega College in Alabama bestowed upon him the degree of Doctor of Literature; and at a special meeting of the National Association for the Advancement of Colored People at Providence, Rhode Island, Hon. R. Livingstone Beeckman, Governor of Rhode Island, presented him the Spingarn Medal [1] for outstanding achievement in literature.

In 1944 he retired from the position of professor of creative literature at Atlanta University.

He was what might be called a pure poet; that is, he wrote poetry not for any moral purpose or for propaganda. Like Edgar Allan Poe, he pursued his literary art for art's sake. The struggles of his race for equality and the strivings of the common man to obtain economic freedom and security found no place in his poetry. As a poet, he worked only as an apostle of beauty.

[1] Awarded each year by the National Association for the Advancement of Colored People to a Negro who has achieved in an unusual manner.

SONG: TODAY AND TOMORROW [1]

Today and tomorrow, and the days that come after,
    Springtime and summer and two seasons more;
The night full of tears and the day full of laughter,
    And dreams that come in and go out of the door.
O Time that is fleeting too fast for our capture,
    While the heart of our dreams beholds it pass by—
The yearning and burning, the desire and the rapture,
    Till we home to the earth and we home to the sky.

O harvest of dreams! when the sowing is over
    And fulfillment of growth gives over all plying—
Ah, down the long sunset of life the heart-rover
    Turns twilight to weeping and darkness to sighing.
We gather the harvest of dreams and we store them
    Deep down in our hearts for the hunger that craves
When springtime and summer—the laughter that bore them
    Sails away like a ship that we watch on the waves.

THE ETERNAL SELF [1]
To Vere Goldthwaite

This earth is but a semblance and a form—
An apparition poised in boundless space;
This life we live so sensible and warm,
Is but a dreaming in a sleep that stays
About us from the cradle to the grave.
Things seen are as inconstant as a wave
That must obey the impulse of the wind;
So in this strange communicable being
There is a higher consciousness confined—
But separate and divine, and foreseeing.

Our bodies are but garments made of clay
That is a smothering weight upon the soul—

But as the sun, conquering a cloudy day,
Our spirits penetrate to Source and Goal.
That intimate and hidden quickening
Bestowing sense and color with the Spring,
Is felt and known and seen in the design
By unsubstantial Self within the portal
Of this household of flesh, that doth confine
Part of the universally immortal.

Beyond the prison of our hopes and fears,
Beyond the undertow of passion's sea—
And stronger than the strength earth holds in years,
Lives man's subconscious personality.
O world withheld! seen through the hazy drift
Of this twilight of flesh, when sleep shall lift,
I shall go forth my own true self at last,
And glory in the triumph of my winning
The road that joins the Future and the Past,
Where I can reach the Ending and Beginning!

Claude McKay

Genius is generally versatile. In Claude McKay, the sweet singer, first of
Jamaica, then of America, and finally of the world, this trait of universality, uniqueness, and variegated art is readily seen. As poet, essayist, novelist, or writer of the short story, he was always an artist. Educated by his
elder brother, a schoolmaster and a freethinker, whose library included
the works of Ernst Haeckel, Thomas Huxley, and Matthew Arnold, it was
natural for him to become an apostle of freedom and a rebel against his
age.

Arriving in the United States in 1912, he entered Tuskegee Institute;
but as its spirit was industrial and his was academic and literary, he pushed
on towards Kansas State University, where he remained for two years.
Being a true poet, he could not stop there long; the Wanderlust caught him
and he rambled on to England, France, Russia, and Germany, after many
years returning to America. When the fire subsided, he joined the Catholic
Church. He is now connected with the Catholic Youth Organization of
Chicago.

Though he worked as a porter, a houseman, longshoreman, barman, and waiter, he never ceased writing. Among the magazines that published his writings were *The Crisis, Seven Arts Magazine, Pearson's,* and *The Liberator.* Some of his books are: Collections of poems, *Songs of Jamaica* (1911), *Spring in New Hampshire, Harlem Shadows* (1922); novels, *Home to Harlem* (1928), *Banjo* (1929); collection of short stories, *Gingertown* (1932); and a collection of essays, *Harlem, the Negro Metropolis.*

AMERICA [1]

Although she feeds me bread of bitterness,
And sinks into my throat her tiger's tooth,
Stealing my breath of life, I will confess
I love this cultured hell that tests my youth!
Her vigor flows like tides into my blood,
Giving me strength erect against her hate.
Her bigness sweeps my being like a flood.
Yet as a rebel fronts a king in state,
I stand within her walls with not a shred
Of terror, malice, not a word of jeer.
Darkly I gaze into the days ahead,
And see her might and granite wonders there,
Beneath the touch of Time's unerring hand,
Like priceless treasures sinking in the sand.

THE TIRED WORKER [1]

O whisper, O my soul! The afternoon
Is waning into evening, whisper soft!
Peace, O my rebel heart! for soon the moon
From out its misty veil will swing aloft!
Be patient, weary body, soon the night
Will wrap thee gently in her sable sheet,
And with a leaden sigh thee wilt invite
To rest thy tired hands and aching feet.
The wretched day was theirs, the night is mine;
Come, tender sleep, and fold me to thy breast.

1 From *Harlem Shadows,* by Claude McKay. Copyright, 1922, by Harcourt, Brace, and Company, Inc., New York.

But what steals out the gray clouds red like wine?
O dawn! O dreaded dawn! O let me rest,
Weary my veins, my brain, my life! Have pity!
No! Once again the harsh, the ugly city.

ABSENCE [1]

Your words dropped into my heart like pebbles into a pool
Rippling around my breast and leaving it melting cool.

Your kisses fell sharp on my flesh like dawn-dews from the limb
Of a fruit-filled lemon tree when the day is young and dim.

Like soft rain-christened sunshine, as fragile as rare gold lace,
Your breath, sweet-scented and warm, has kindled my tranquil face.

But a silence vasty-deep, oh deeper than all these ties,
Now, through the menacing miles, brooding between us lies.

And more than the songs I sing, I await your written word,
To stir my fluent blood as never your presence stirred.

TO O.E.A.[1]

Your voice is the color of a robin's breast,
    And there's a sweet sob in it like rain—still rain in the night.
Among the leaves of the trumpet-tree, close to his nest,
    The pea-dove sings, and each note thrills me with strange delight
Like the words, wet with music, that well from your trembling throat.
    I'm afraid of your eyes, they're so bold,
    Searching me through, reading my thoughts, shining like gold.
But sometimes they are gentle and soft like the dew on the lips of the
                                                    eucharis [2]
Before the sun comes warm with his lover's kiss.
    You are sea-foam, pure with the star's loveliness,

1 From *Harlem Shadows,* by Claude McKay. Copyright, 1922, by Harcourt, Brace,
and Company, Inc., New York.
2 Eucharis, a type of lily.

Not mortal, a flower, a fairy, too fair for the beauty-shorn earth.
All wonderful things, all beautiful things, gave of their wealth to your
birth.
Oh, I love you so much, not recking of passion, that I feel it is wrong!
But men will love you, flower, fairy, non-mortal spirit burdened with
flesh,
Forever, life-long.

Anne Spencer

Anne Spencer, whom many regard as the greatest of the Negro women
poets, was born at Bramwell, West Virginia, in 1882. She received her
formal education at the Virginia Seminary in Lynchburg. In later years,
at her Alma Mater as a teacher and adviser she became the ideal of many
students.

Her poetry shows greater terseness and maturity than that of most of
our poets, men or women.

Her poems have appeared in the *Crisis, Opportunity,* and many other
magazines, and in Braithwaite's *Anthology of Magazine Verse.*

The poems included in this volume are reprinted with the permission of
the author.

DUNBAR

Ah, how poets sing and die!
Make one song and Heaven takes it;
Have one heart and Beauty breaks it;
Chatterton, Shelley, Keats and I
Ah, how poets sing and die!

LINES TO A NASTURTIUM
(*A Lover Muses*)

Flame-flower, Day-torch, Mauna Loa,
I saw a daring bee, today, pause, and soar
Into your flaming heart;

Then did I hear crisp crinkled laughter
As the Furies after tore him apart?
    A bird, next, small and humming,
Looked into your startled depths and fled . . .
Surely, some dread sight, and dafter
        Than human eyes as mine can see,
Set the stricken air waves drumming
        In his flight.

    Day-torch, Flame-flower, cool-hot Beauty
I cannot see, I cannot hear your flutey
Voice lure your loving swain,
But I know one other to whom you are in beauty
Born in vain:
Hair like the setting sun,
Her eyes a rising star,
Motions gracious as reeds by
        Babylon, bar
All your competing;
Hands like, how like, brown lilies sweet,
Cloth of gold were fair enough to touch her feet. . . .
Ah, how the senses flood at my repeating,
As once in her firelit heart I felt the Furies
        Beating, beating.

Leslie Pinckney Hill

Leslie Pinckney Hill, who was born at Lynchburg, Virginia, has a distinguished career as an educator and a poet. He attended the grade schools
of Lynchburg; high school at East Orange, New Jersey; and did his college
work at Harvard University. He taught at Tuskegee Institute from 1904
to 1907, and from 1907 to 1913 was principal of Manassas, Virginia, Industrial School. Since 1913 Mr. Hill has been president of the Cheyney
Training School for Teachers, at Cheyney, Pennsylvania.

    In 1921 "The Wings of Oppression" was published by the Stratford
Company of Boston. In 1928 the Christopher Publishing Company of

Boston published his poetic historical drama, *Toussaint L'Ouverture,* which
is in five parts.

His poems appearing in this volume are reprinted with the permission
of the author.

FREEDOM

O FREEDOM, let thy perfect work be wrought
In us, the children of a chastened race,
Long, long ago in thy benignant face
Our fathers saw "the glass." They meekly brought
Their shackled limbs in faith to thee, and sought
Thy heart with prayer; and thou didst rend apace
The bonds of men who leaned upon thy grace,
Their spirits with a tuneful patience fraught,
We call upon thee now no more in chains
Such as our fathers wore—from these we're freed—
But clanging still the fetters of the soul,
"The gleam" we follow weakly, for we need
The Freedom of a sturdy self-control.

SUMMER MAGIC

So many cares to vex the day,
So many fears to haunt the night,
My heart was all but weaned away
From every lure of old delight.
Then summer came, announced by June,
With beauty, miracle and mirth,
She hung aloft the rounding moon,
She poured her sunshine on the earth,
She drove the sap and broke the bud,
She set the crimson rose afire,
She stirred again my sullen blood,
And waked in me a new desire.
Before my cottage door she spread
The softest carpet nature weaves,

And deftly arched above my head
A canopy of shady leaves.
Her nights were dreams of jeweled skies,
Her days were bowers rife with song,
And many a scheme did she devise
To heal the hurt and soothe the wrong.
For on the hill or in the dell,
Or where the brook went leaping by
Or where the fields would surge and swell
With golden wheat or bearded rye,
I felt her heart against my own,
I breathed the sweetness of her breath,
Till all the cark of time had flown,
And I was lord of life and death.

THE TEACHER

Lord, who am I to teach the way
To little children day by day,
So prone myself to go astray?

I teach them KNOWLEDGE, but I know
How faint they flicker and how low
The candles of my knowledge glow.

I teach them POWER to will and do,
But only now to learn anew
My own great weakness through and through.

I teach them LOVE for all mankind
And all God's creatures, but I find
My love comes lagging far behind.

Lord, if their guide I still must be,
Oh, let the little children see
The teacher leaning hard on Thee.

Ophelia Robinson

Ophelia Robinson, the seventh of ten children, was born in Saint Louis, Missouri, May 27, 1897, the daughter of Richard S. and Ophelia Jones Robinson. She received her formal education in the public schools of Saint Louis and at Northwestern University and the University of Chicago. She was one of the first teachers to be selected for a scholarship to study Intergroup Education in a Workshop at the University of Chicago.

At the Sumner High School, she was president of the Girls Gymnasium Club. At present she teaches physical education at the Simmons Demonstration School.

As a child in the grades, she began to write poetry, and writing poetry remains her hobby. She is the first Negro in America to write an epic poem. Her "Nat Turner" is a poem of forty pages with a sustained, dignified style. Its prologue is reprinted here.

NAT TURNER [1]
Prologue

I shall tell you how Nathaniel
How the sage, devout, young prophet
Gave his life to save his people
Gave to them his time, his talents,
Gave to them his youth, his courage
Gave his all for love of freedom
That his people should not suffer,
Should not wear the yoke of bondage.

Even as the Hebrew Children
Found a savior in their Moses;
Even as the ancient Grecians
Found a hero in Achilles;
As the brave ill-fated Trojans
Placed their hope, their faith in Hector;
As the Indians famine-ridden
Looked for aid to Hiawatha;

[1] Reprinted with the permission of the author.

So did God's most swarthy Children
Find their savior, this Nathaniel,
Trust in him for strength and courage,
Foresight, faith, and fearless action.
And Nathaniel gave them gladly,
Never for one moment failed them.

BLACK BOY [1]

Crisp and curly hair has he,
Eyes that twinkle dev'lishly;
Snowy teeth that slash a smile
Free of evil, free from guile.

Tall and slender, supple, lithe,
Cheerful, carefree, handsome, blithe;
Rippling muscles, agile feet,
Nimble fingers, clothing neat.

At the door of life he stands
Eager, waiting her demands.
Success to him without alloy,
Success and honor, sleek, black boy.

Floretta Howard

Floretta Howard, poet and playwright, was born in St. Louis, Missouri.
She was educated in the public schools of St. Louis and the University of
Southern California. She is a teacher of Speech in the public schools of
St. Louis and founder of the Floretta Howard School of Expression for
Tots and 'Teensters, now in its thirteenth year.

"Round the Neighborhood" and "On a Colored Doll" are reprinted
with the permission of the author.

[1] Reprinted with the permission of the author.

'ROUND THE NEIGHBORHOOD

There's Tony, he's the Fruit Man's boy
    With sallow skin—black hair,
And Tommie, he's the Banker's child,
    He's blond—his skin is fair;
And Chick, the Chinese Laundry boy,
    With slanting eyes—he's yellow,
And me, I'm dark—my hair is rough,
    Yet, I'm a regular fellow;
We're in a gang, and have real fun,
Yet, each a different race,
What difference does it make to us,
    What color's on our face?

ON A COLORED DOLL

I have nine pretty smiling dolls,
    And which do I like the best?
No—I like the one with the pompadour,
    But, still, you haven't guessed!
My Raggedy Ann is very sweet,
    And I like the funny old clown,
    But the prettiest one, and the one I love,
    Is this cunning big doll of brown!
Yes, Dolly Dimple's a nice one, too,
    With the frilly grown-up gown,
But Pansy is just like my own dear friends,
    She's my own little self of brown!

Lorenzo D. Blanton

Lorenzo D. Blanton, poet and writer of short stories, was educated at the State University of Iowa and the University of Chicago. His short stories have appeared in various magazines.

I WONDER [1]

Sometimes amidst the yelping, screaming thunder
Of toppling edifices of ancient wonder,
Of lazy bridges now leaping high in the sky,
Then writhing convulsively in anguish to die
On the sweet bosom of some happy stream,
Unmindful of the war's nightmarish dream—
Sometimes amidst the ruins when peering under
Some splintered, dusty beams, I begin to wonder
When martial feet no longer tread on land
Made soft and green by Nature's bounteous hand
And mansions newly born to rear each head
To mark in chiseled stone the honored dead,
If Man could not just let his hatreds die
Among those ruins—there to forever lie!

Langston Hughes

In *"The Big Sea,"* his autobiography, Langston Hughes tells how he began to write poetry. His grammar-school class at Lincoln, Illinois had two Negro members: a girl and Langston. After the class officers were elected, the children looked around for a poet; however, there was no one in the class who looked like a poet. Believing that all Negroes could sing and dance and thereby had some sense of rhythm, they unanimously elected Langston class poet. He had never written a poem. He proceeded thus: he wrote one stanza for each of eight teachers and an especially good stanza for his favorite teacher. He wrote that his teachers were the finest in the world and his class the best that had ever graduated. At graduation his poem was loudly applauded. This was the begin-

[1] From *Sing, Laugh, Weep*. Copyright, 1944, by The Scribes, St. Louis, Mo.

ning of Hughes' career as a poet. It led to unexpected heights.

He was born in Joplin, Missouri, of well-educated parents, but was educated in the public schools of Lawrence, Kansas and Lincoln, Illinois and then the Central High School of Cleveland, Ohio. Later he attended Columbia University and Lincoln University at Oxford, Pennsylvania. For a while he worked in the office of Carter G. Woodson, editor of the *Journal of Negro History.* Among his distinguished ancestors is John Mercer Langston, who served as a congressman from Virginia and was the first dean of the Law School of Howard University.

Lured by the sea, into which through disgust he threw his books, he traveled extensively in Africa and Europe.

Among his publications are the following: Collections of poems, *The Weary Blues* (1926), *Fine Clothes to the Jew* (1927), and *The Dream Keeper* (1932); a novel, *Not Without Laughter* (1930), which won the Harmon Gold Award; and a collection of short stories, *The Ways of White Folks* (1934). He also wrote *The Mulatto,* a play which was produced on Broadway for a long run.

DREAMS [1]

Hold fast to dreams
For if dreams die,
Life is a broken-winged bird
That can not fly.

Hold fast to dreams
For when dreams go
Life is a barren field
Frozen with snow.

JOY [1]

I went to look for Joy,
Slim, dancing Joy,
Gay, laughing Joy,
Bright-eyed Joy—
And I found her

1 Reprinted from *The Dream Keeper and Other Poems,* by Langston Hughes, by permission of Alfred A. Knopf, Inc. Copyright, 1932, by Alfred A. Knopf, Inc.

Driving the butcher's cart
In the arms of the butcher boy!
Such company, such company,
As keeps this young nymph, Joy!

NIGHT AND MORN [1]

Sun's a settin',
This is what I'm gonna sing:
I feel de blues a comin',
Wonder what the blues'll bring?
Sun's a risin',
This is gonna be ma song.
Sun's a risin',
This is gonna be ma song:
I could be blue but
I been blue all night long.

THE WEARY BLUES [1]

Drowning a drowsy syncopated tune,
Rocking back and forth to a mellow croon,
      I heard a Negro play.
Down on Lenox Avenue the other night
By the dull pallor of an old gas light
      He did a lazy sway.
      He did a lazy sway
To the tune o' those Weary Blues.
With his ebony hands on each ivory key
He made that poor piano moan with melody.
      O Blues!
Swaying to and fro on his rickety stool
He played that sad raggy tune like a musical fool.
      Sweet Blues!
Coming from a black man's soul.
      O Blues!

[1] Reprinted from *The Dream Keeper and Other Poems*, by Langston Hughes, by permission of Alfred A. Knopf, Inc. Copyright, 1932, by Alfred A. Knopf, Inc.

In a deep strong voice with a melancholy tone
I heard that Negro sing, that old piano moan—
   "Ain't got nobody in all this world,
   Ain't got nobody but maself.
   I's gwine to quit ma frownin'
   And put ma troubles on de shelf."
Thump, thump, thump, went his foot on the floor.
He played a few chords, then he sang some more—
   "I got de Weary Blues
   And I can't be satisfied.
   Got de Weary Blues
   And can't be satisfied—
   I ain't happy no mo'
   And I wish that I had died."
And far into the night he crooned that tune.
The stars went down and so did the moon.
The singer stopped playing and went to bed.
While the Weary Blues echoed through his head,
He slept like a rock or a man that's dead.

MOTHER TO SON [1]

Well, son, I'll tell you:
Life for me ain't been no crystal stair.
It's had tacks in it,
And splinters,
And boards torn up,
And places with no carpet on the floor—
Bare.

But all the time
I'se been a-climbin' on,
And reachin' landin's,
And turnin' corners
And sometimes goin' in the dark
Where there ain't no light.

1 Reprinted from *The Dream Keeper and Other Poems,* by Langston Hughes, by permission of Alfred A. Knopf, Inc. Copyright, 1932, by Alfred A. Knopf, Inc.

So, boy, don't you turn back.
Don't you set down on the steps
'Cause you find it's kinder hard.
Don't you fall now—
For I'se still goin', honey,
I'se still climbin'
And life for me ain't been no crystal stair.

John Adolph Turner   •

John Adolph Turner, the poet, was educated in the schools of St. Louis,
Missouri, and East St. Louis, Illinois. A few years ago he published a collection of lyrics called *Bright Gleams*. "Rain," which appears in that collection, is reprinted with the author's permission.

RAIN

Rain . . . rain . . . rain,
    Like a heart deep racked with pain—
    As a musical note,
    From a lyre remote.
It comes, and goes again.

Rain . . . rain . . . rain,
    Like a tom-tom's loud refrain—
    With a rhythmical beat
    It seems to repeat
The prayers we raise in vain.

Rain . . . rain . . . rain,
    Like tears forced down by the chain—
    As in slavery time
    They sought to decline
From making known their pain.

Rain . . . rain . . . rain,
  Like tears I have shed in vain—
  With a whimsical frown
  I seek to kneel down
And ask God to explain! explain!

Arthur W. Reason

Arthur W. Reason, though busy as the principal of the L'Ouverture School
in St. Louis, Missouri, always has time to recite an original poem at church
teas, at the programs sponsored by various culture clubs, and at informal
home gatherings. He was one of the leaders that organized The Scribes, a
club devoted exclusively to encouraging people to appreciate and to write
poetry.

He was born at Leesburg, Florida, and was educated at Oberlin College
and some of our leading universities, the last of which was the University of Illinois.

His poems have appeared in *World's Fair Anthology, America Speaks,
Songs and Lyrics,* and *United We Sing.*

WHY WORRY? [1]

Why should I worry when clouds are dark
Or fear today on my ship to embark?
Why should I worry when torrents fall
Or dread to answer my Master's call?

Why should I worry when day is done
Because I boast no crowns I've won?
Why should I worry 'midst deepest strife
When God, I know, will save my life?

Why should I worry when I've done my best
To live with my soul when laid to rest?
Why should I worry when I've played the game
To build and serve with stalwart frame?

1 From *Sing, Laugh, Weep.* Copyright, 1944, by The Scribes, St. Louis, Mo.

I'll not worry nor fear through the years
For worry brings only the tears;
The love that flows, the joys that shine
Will ever light this life of mine.

MA HONEY [1]

I luvs ma honey and ma money too
And I'se so happy I dunno what to do;
I'm gwine to hol' her close and tight
And keep ma 'oman if I has to fight.

I gives ma gal ev'ry cent I make
And does ma best jes' fer her sake;
She am the sweetes' gal in de lan'
And when she smiles her face is gran'.

I'se a lonesome guy when she's away,
But when she's near I'm happy and gay;
With her in ma arms ma heart's at ease——
She may spend ma money jes' as she please.

Sterling A. Brown

Sterling A. Brown, professor of English at Howard University and distinguished both as a poet and as a literary critic, was born in Washington, D. C., May 1, 1901. He is a product of the public schools of Washington, Williams College, and Harvard University. Recently he has served as visiting professor of English at New York University and the University of Minnesota.

His poetry is of two types: that which follows the folk style, using the folk patterns and folk rhythms, and that which follows the classic style. As Franz Liszt took folk tunes of Hungary and worked them up into great rhapsodies, so Brown used the folk poetry of the American Negro and developed it into masterpieces that maintain the freedom, the lilt, the simplicity, and the humorous fervor of the original and yet under his touch have become his own works of art.

[1] From *Sing, Laugh, Weep*. Copyright, 1944, by The Scribes, St. Louis, Mo.

He published *Southern Road,* his collection of poems, in 1932. This work was followed by two essays: *The Negro in American Fiction* and *Negro Poetry and the Drama.*

SOUTHERN ROAD [1]

(A work song that was sung between the blows of a
sledge hammer, when there were no electric drills)

Swing dat hammer——hunh——
Steady, bo';
Swing dat hammer——hunh——
Steady, bo';
Ain't no rush, bebby,
Long ways to go.

Burner tore his——hunh——
Black heart away;
Burner tore his——hunh——
Black heart away;
Got me life, bebby,
An' a day.

Gal's on Fifth Street——hunh——
Son done gone;
Gal's on Fifth Street——hunh——
Son done gone;
Wife's in de ward, bebby,
Babe's not bo'n.

My ole man died——hunh——
Cussin me;
My ole man died——hunh——
Cussin me;
Ole lady rocks, bebby,
Huh misery.

Doubleshackled——hunh——
Guard behin';

Doubleshackled——hunh——
Guard behin';
Ball and chain, bebby,
On my mind

.   .   .   .

Chain gang nevah——hunh——
Let me go;
Chain gang nevah——hunh——
Let me go;
Po' los' boy, bebby,
Evahmo'.

RETURN [1]

I have gone back in boyish wonderment,
To things that I foolishly put by . . .
Have found an alien and unknown content
In seeing how some bits of cloud-filled sky
Are framed in bracken pools; through chuckling hours
Have watched the antic frogs, or curiously
Have numbered all the unnamed, vagrant flowers,
That fleck the unkempt meadows, lavishly.
Or where a headlong toppling stream has stayed
Its racing, lulled to quiet by the song
Bursting from out the thick-leaved oaken shade,
There I have lain while hours sauntered past—
I have found peacefulness somewhere at last,
Have found a quiet needed for so long.

THOUGHTS OF DEATH [1]

Thoughts of death
Crowd over my happiness
Like dark clouds
Over the silver sickle of the moon.

[1] From *Southern Road*, by Sterling A. Brown. Copyright, 1932, by Harcourt, Brace and Company, Inc., New York.

Death comes to some
Like a grizzled gangster
Clubbing in the night;
To some
Like an obstinate captain
Steadily besieging barriers;
To some like a brown adder
Lurking in violet-speckled underbrush;
To some
Like a gentle nurse
Taking their toys and stroking their hot brows.
Death will come to you, I think,
Like an old shrewd gardener,
Culling his rarest blossom. . . .

Alice McGee Smart

In the pursuit of her dreams Alice McGee Smart became a poet; in her search for truth she became a social scientist. She has traveled extensively in the Orient, in the Caribbean Islands, and in Europe. Not satisfied with the magic touch of American universities, she did post-graduate work at the Universities of London and Berlin. Twice she has at the request of the Liberian government gone there to do research in education. She is now Professor of Geography at Stowe Teachers College.

She is the author of a book of travel, *Black America Abroad.*

THE STREET CALLED PETTICOAT LANE [1]

I walked thro' the street called Petticoat Lane on a Sunday
                                          morning,
Where the rich, the poor, the crippled, the mime
Rubbed elbows together to Big Ben's chime
In Petticoat Lane on Sunday morning.
"Bargains cheap, best in the street,
No'ere in London can you beat

[1] From *Sing, Laugh, Weep.* Copyright, 1944, by The Scribes, St. Louis, Mo.

Petticoat Lane on Sunday morning";
Above the din the hawkers cry,
Unheeding the jeers of the passersby
Who, sated with leisure but lacking in verve,
Seek something to feed the jaded nerve
In Petticoat Lane on Sunday morning.
Merchant, barber, beggar, rogue
Have a common ground for a livelihood
In Petticoat Lane on Sunday morning;
But the wealthy folk who look on and guy
And say "poor devils" and pass them by
Still go searching the world around
For something the ne'er-do-well has found
In Petticoat Lane on Sunday morning.
For hunger and cold go hand in hand
To foster the brotherhood of man
In Petticoat Lane on Sunday morning;
There is no quest for revelry,
Wits too dulled at night to play,
Dreading the dawn of another day;
Merchant, beggar, barber, rogue—
All unite for the common good
In trying to earn a livelihood
Down Petticoat Lane on Sunday morning.

PA [1]

I went up to New York las' week
To see my daughter, Mary,
But after jes' two days of it
I come home in a hurry.

Ma asked me why I didn't stay
De two weeks lak I planned,
But, Deacon, I jes' tell you, suh,
'Twas more'n I could stand.

[1] From *Sing, Laugh, Weep.* Copyright, 1944, by The Scribes, St. Louis, Mo.

Lak I told Ma when I gits back,
De City, hit's all right;
De trees an' parks an' flowers too,
Dey mak a purty sight.

But some o' dose new-fangled things
Which Mary raves about
Hit seems to me 'twould better be
If dey would do widout.

Her house was high up in de air
An' I was mad wid rage
When she sed, "Faw-ther, step inside,"
Den put me in a cage.

Now what could've come o'er de chile
To make her act so queer?
I'd allus been jes' plain ol' Pa
An' now 'twas "Faw-ther, dear."

" 'Twill tek you to the 'ficiency,"
She sed, den tried to preen,
While I jes' stood agapin', wundrin'
What de gal could mean.

"Do hurry, Faw-ther, ef you please,"
Jes' tryin' so hard to smile;
Den up we shot so quick an' fast
It tuk my breath awhile.

An' den de cage flew open wide
Widout no mortal hand;
In truth dere warn't no sign of knob—
I was too scairt to stand.

Jes' think of hit now, Deacon White,
Me ridin' in a cage
Dat shuts and ope's all by hit-self—
Yes, me at my old age.

By all de virgins it is true,
Although hit 'pears a lie:
Hit oped an' shut all by hit-self,
Right 'fore my naked eye.

I could-a stood de cage all right
'Til I went to see de zoo
An' foun' dat same contraption used
Fur apes an' monkeys, too.

What was dat 'ficiency, you ax?
Why dat was Mary's house;
But 'twarn't room enuf in dere
Fur me to change my blouse.

Dere warn't a sign o' bed no whar
Fur me to sit or lie,
An' me so tired from de bus ride
I thought I'd surely die.

At las' night came, den Mary said,
"I guess no one will call;
We'll go to bed now, Faw-ther, dear,"
Den pushed agen de wall.

De hull side wall went slidin' up
An' out a bed did roll;
When I got in de thing, my feet
Hung out lak some flag pole.

We went to a eatin' place
Dey called some kind of "mat,"
Whah I went 'roun' an' 'roun' glass doors
An' lost my Sunday hat.

De thing dat got me most het up
Was when we went downtown,
An' Mary she jes' 'sisted dat
I ride beneath de groun'.

Now I'se a Christian, Deacon White,
Fuh Hebben I sho' must strive;
But I ain't gonna he'p de debbil out
By being buried alive.

Countee Cullen

Like Keats and Shelley, Countee Cullen followed the classic style in poetry.
Almost like a meteor, he came and disappeared. Born in New York City
March 30, 1903, the son of a Methodist minister, he had an excellent religious background for his work. In the public schools of New York City
and at New York University, his teachers readily recognized that he had
poetic genius. By the age of twenty-one he had become a great American
poet. In 1925 he won the Bynner Intercollegiate Poetry Contest; the next
year he received the Harmon Gold Award, the first prize, for signal
achievement in literature. Among his collections of poems are *Color*
(1925), *Copper Sun* (1927), and *The Black Christ* (1929). *Caroling
Dusk,* his anthology, was published in 1929. He also published one novel,
One Way to Heaven. He died in 1945.

TO YOU WHO READ MY BOOK [1]

Soon every sprinter,
   However fleet,
Comes to a winter
   Of sure defeat:
Though he may race
   Like the hunted doe,
Time has a pace
   To lay him low.

Soon we who sing,
   However high,
Must face the Thing
   We cannot fly.

[1] From *Color,* by Countee Cullen. Copyright, 1925, by Harper & Brothers, New York.

Yea, though we fling
    Our notes to the sun,
Time will out-sing
    Us every one.

All things must change
    As the wind is blown;
Time will estrange
    The flesh from the bone.
The dream shall elude
    The dreamer's clasp,
And only its hood
    Shall comfort his grasp.

A little while,
    Too brief at most,
And even my smile
    Will be a ghost.
A little space,
    A finger's crook,
And who shall trace
    The path I took?

Who shall declare
    My whereabouts;
Say if in the air
    My being shouts
Along light ways,
    Or if in the sea,
Or deep earth stays
    The germ of me?

Ah, none knows, none,
    Save (but too well)
The Cryptic One
    Who will not tell.
This is my hour
    To wax and climb,
Flaunt a red flower
    In the face of time.

And only an hour
    Time gives, then snap
Goes the flower,
    And dried is the sap.
Juice of the first
    Grapes of my vine,
I proffer your thirst
    My own heart's wine.

Here of my growing
    A red rose sways,
Seed of my sowing,
    And work of my days.
(I run, but time's
    Abreast with me;
I sing, but he climbs
    With my highest C.)

Drink while my blood
    Colors the wine,
Reach while the bud
    Is still on the vine—

Then . . .
    When the hawks of death
Tear at my throat
    Till song and breath
Ebb note by note,
    Turn to this book
Of the mellow word
    For a singing look
At the stricken bird.

Say, "This is the way
    He chirped and sung,
In the sweet heyday
    When his heart was young.
Though his throat is bare,
    By death defiled,

Song labored there
  And bore a child."

When the dreadful Ax
  Rives me apart,
When the sharp wedge cracks
  My arid heart,
Turn to this book
  Of the singing me
For a springtime look
  At the wintry tree.

Say, "Thus it was weighed
  With flower and fruit,
Ere the Ax was laid
  Unto its root.
Though the blows fall free
  On a gnarled trunk now,
Once he was a tree
  With a blossomy bough."

BLACK MAJESTY [1]
A Sonnet

(After reading John W. Vandercook's chronicle of sable glory) [2]

These men were kings, albeit they were black,
Christophe and Dessalines and L'Ouverture;
Their majesty has made me turn my back
Upon a plaint I once shaped to endure.
These men were black, I say, but they were crowned
And purple-clad, however brief their time.
Stifle your agony; let grief be drowned;
We know joy had a day once and a clime.

1 From *The Black Christ and Other Poems,* by Countee Cullen. Copyright, 1929, by Harper & Brothers, New York.
2 Vandercook wrote *Black Majesty,* a book which describes the activities of the three rulers of Haiti, the Negro republic—Toussaint L'Ouverture, Jean Jacques Dessalines, and Henri Christophe.

Dark gutter-snipe, black sprawler-in-the-mud,
A thing man did a man may do again.
What answers filter through your sluggish blood
To these dark ghosts who knew so bright to reign?
"Lo, I am dark, but comely," Sheba [1] sings.
"And we were black," three shades reply, "but kings."

LOVE'S WAY [2]

Love is not love demanding all, itself
Withholding aught; love's is the nobler way
Of courtesy, that will not feast aware
That the beloved hungers, nor drink unless
The cup be shared down to the last sweet dregs.
Renunciatory never was the thorn
To crown love with, but prodigal and proud!
Too proud to test the debtor of the one
Dear passion most it dotes upon, always
Love rehabilitates unto the end.
So let it be with us; the perfect faith
We each to other swear this moment leaves
Our scales harmonious, neither wanting found
Though weighed in such strict balances. So let
It be with us always. I am too proud
To owe you one caress; you must not drop
Beholden to my favor for one least
Endearing term. Should you reveal some stretch
Of sky to me, let me revive some note
Of music lost to you. This is love's way,
That where a heart is asked gives back a heart.

[1] Refers to the Queen of Sheba, who visited Solomon, king of the Israelites. I Kings
10:1-13.
[2] From *Copper Sun,* by Countee Cullen. Copyright, 1927, by Harper & Brothers,
New York.

ONE DAY WE PLAYED A GAME [1]
(*Yolande: Her Poem*)

One day we lay beneath an apple tree,
Tumultuous with fruit, live with the bee,
And there we played a gay, fantastic game
Of our own making, called Name me a Name.
The grave was liberal, letting us endow
Ourselves with names of lovers who by now
Are dust, but rarer dust for loving high
Than they shall be who let the red flame die . . .
Crouched sphinx-wise in the grass, you hugged your knees,
And called me "Abelard;" I, "Heloise,"
Rejoined, and added thereto, "Melisande;"
Then "Pelleas," I heard, and felt a hand
Slide into mine; joy would not let us speak
Awhile, but only sit there cheek to cheek,
Hand clasping hand . . . till passion made us bold;
"Tristan," you purred to me . . . I laughed, "Isolde."
"King Ninus, I," I cried; snared in a kiss
You named yourself my dark Semiramis.
"Queen Guinevere," I sang; you, "Lancelot."
My heart grew big with pride to think you'd not
Cried "Arthur," whom his lovely queen forgot
In loving him whose name you called me by . . .
We two grew mad with loving then, and I
With whirlpool rapture strained you to my breast;
"First love! First love!" I urged, and "Adam!" blessed
My urgency. My lips grew soft with "Eve,"
And round with ardor purposing to leave
Upon your mouth a lasting seal of bliss. . . .
But midway of our kissing came a hiss
Above us in the apple tree; a sweet
Red apple rolled between us at our feet,
And looking up we saw with glide and dip,
Cold supple coils among the branches slip.

[1] From *Copper Sun,* by Countee Cullen. Copyright, 1927, by Harper & Brothers, New York.

"Eve! Eve!" I cried, "Beware!" Too late. You bit
Half of the fruit away . . . The rest of it
I took, assuring you with misty eyes,
"Fare each as each, we lose no Paradise."

Georgia Douglas Johnson

Out of cultured Atlanta, Georgia, the city
dotted with Negro colleges and universities—
Clark, Morris Brown, Spelman, Morehouse,
Gammon, and Atlanta—went Georgia Douglas Johnson, to establish a home that would
attract people of the greatest refinement in
the capital of our Nation. Inspired by the
training she had received in the public
schools of Atlanta, her native city, and by
further studies at Atlanta University and
Oberlin College, Georgia continued to write
poetry as of other years. The discovery of
her talent caused the élite of Washington
to come to her salons as to a shrine. Like a
high priestess, she led her guests to the
sacred altars of the Muses. Poets, musicians,
painters, dramatists, orators came, not only
artists but also lovers of the arts who were
just admirers. They came and found welcome there. It seemed that all
who entered her doors drank deep of the Pierian Spring.[1] Washington
liked the sincere simplicity and the grace and unaffected beauty of her
verses, her person, and her personality.

She has published three volumes of poems: *The Heart of a Woman*
(1918), *Bronze* (1922), and *An Autumn Love Cycle* (1928).

The poems that follow are reprinted with the permission of the author.

FOREGATHER [2]

Nor white nor black shall habitate the earth,
But like a rainbow man shall web and span

[1] A fountain in Pieria, Thessaly, sacred to the Muses, and believed to communicate
poetic inspiration.
[2] Copyright, 1935, by *Opportunity, Journal of Negro Life.*

The turning globe. Tho eagle eyes may scan
The mingled colors of its living girth
None may assail the equity of birth;
False values vanish, this shall be the plan,—
The mark, the count, the goal to any man
Who runs with courage on the ring of earth.

And war shall lift her fingers from the land,
Men shall go forth like children, hand in hand
Vaunting the vision of the recent blind
Rapt with the vista of the cloudless mind
They shall foregather and again recall
The trail lost somewhere since the primal fall.

THE HEART OF A WOMAN

The heart of a woman goes forth with the dawn,
As a lone bird, soft winging, so restlessly on,
Afar o'er life's turrets and vales does it roam
In the wake of those echoes the heart calls home.

The heart of a woman falls back with the night,
And enters some alien cage in its plight,
And tries to forget it has dreamed of the stars,
While it breaks, breaks, breaks on the sheltering bars.

GOOD-BYE

Let's say, "Good-bye,"
Nor wait Love's latest breath
Poised now so lightly on the wing of Death,
While yet within our eyes one fervent gleam
Remains to hallow this, a passing dream:
Yes, yes, "Good-bye,"
For it is best to part
While Love's low light still burns
Within the heart!

Frederick W. Bond

Frederick W. Bond, poet, dramatist, essayist, journalist, obtained his first training in the elementary schools of his home town, Windsor, North Carolina. The rest of his formal education he obtained at Howard and Columbia Universities. He taught for some time at Johnson C. Smith University and West Virginia State College. He is now professor of English at Stowe Teachers College.

Among his publications are the following: a textbook, *Speech Construction; The Negro and the Drama,* and *The Negro,* of which he is the editor.

TO A WHIPPOORWILL [1]

Lyrical Poet, victor of winter's cold,
Where hast thou slumbered all winter?
Within that melodic voice you'd withhold
Music with the charm of a chorister;
Hast thou hibernated with the mockingbird,
Or failed to sing because of ice and snow?
It may be thou hast dwelt with another herd,
Or flown to a Southern bungalow,
The wren and sparrow oft did come,
Though they refused to chirp or sing.
Please perch by my lair as a chum
And there be sure to rest and cling.
As I shall nearly in a trance be
Enthralled with thy unadulterated song.

[1] From *Sing, Laugh, Weep.* Copyright, 1944, by The Scribes, St. Louis, Mo.

Ezra W. Turner

Ezra W. Turner, poet and educator, received his training at Lincoln University, Jefferson City, Missouri, and the University of Minnesota. For a number of years he served as principal of the Sumner High School of Cairo, Illinois, and the Lincoln School at Richmond Heights, Missouri. His poems have appeared in various newspapers and magazines.

TELL YO' MA I SAID SO [1]

Co' Mandy, wha' you get dat dress?
I sw'ar, you look de ve'y best
Of any gal dat's in dis town
An' you can go a-sailin' 'round
Jes' lak yo' mammy use' tu do
When she was 'bout de age o' you:
     You tell yo' ma I said so.

An' Mandy, I can see right now
Dat someone sho' done luhnt you how
To fix dat haih; Lawd! ain't it straight?
Why, ev'ry time I pass yo' gate,
I specs to see you standin' thaih
All wropped up in that shinin' haih:
     You tell yo' ma I said so.

An' wha' you get dat smilin' face
Dat seems to light up all de place?
De Lawd done sho'ly blest you, chile,
To give you sech a winnin' smile;
It makes me look 'way back an' see:
De way yo' mammy smiled at me:
     Sho', tell yo' ma I said so.

[1] From *Sing, Laugh, Weep.* Copyright, 1944, by The Scribes, St. Louis, Mo.

Yes, dat was yeahs an' yeahs ago;
I wasn't ha'f so ol' er slo'
As I is now; no, I was spry,
But ev'y time yo' ma was nigh
It seems a mighty load was hung
Half down my th'oat an' on my tongue:
  Yes, tell yo' ma I said so.

Yo' mammy use' to lead de choir
An' she could hang huh voice up higher
Than all de rest dat tried to sing;
An' when she opened up 'twould bring
De ve'y teahdrops rollin' down;
Dat's why she married Reve'n Brown;
  You evah heah huh say so?

I nevah shall fo'get de day
Yo' pappy led dat gal away;
Somethin' inside me jes' went out
Lak stahs when dahs a cloud about;
An' all dese yeahs I've moped eroun',
Trying to live my troubles down:
  Yes, tell yo' ma I said so.

Yo' mammy is a widow now,
But dat don't make no diff'ence how
She hol' huh head an' lift huh eyes
Lak somethin' out o' Paradise:
The bigges' joy in life I get
Is knowin' we're both livin' yet:
  You tell yo' ma I said so.

An' Mandy, I ain't po' as dirt
If I does weah a hick'ry shirt,
Cuz I been wuhkin' all my days
Jes' lak de bee dat hums an' lays
His honey up. I give Gawd thanks
Dat I got money in three banks:
  You tell yo' ma I said so.

Evelyn Watson

"Here is a poem by Evelyn Watson," said her fifth grade teacher. "It is called 'My Doll.' "

"I hope you continue to write poetry, because you have the poet's love for beauty," was the encouraging remark of her teacher.

Evelyn Watson was born and educated in the public schools and the Illinois State Normal School of Carbondale, Illinois. Upon graduating from college, she taught in the grade school at Harrisburg, Illinois. For several years after leaving Harrisburg, she taught English and French at the Herrin Township High School of Colp, Illinois.

In 1939 she began to teach English and French at Douglass University in Saint Louis. Later she was made its Provost. She has also won distinction as a teacher of the Bible.

DREAM WORLD [1]

The shades of eve are falling fast,
I settle down, my thoughts to rest.
No sound of birds to mar the calm—
No stifling heat—just evening balm—
My thoughts will turn to you;

Will turn to you, and dream and soar
And wish this beastly war were o'er,
And you were home again.
I'll dream of all the things we've done;
I'll count them over one by one;
And gloat o'er those that brought me fun—
And maybe shed a tear.
I'll count them over one by one;
And gloat o'er those that brought me fun—
And maybe shed a tear.

[1] Reprinted with the permission of the author.

My thoughts will turn to you and see
On a green island by the sea
That ephemeral castle fair and tall,
Where hand in hand we'll gaily stroll
Down a long shining hall.

In dreams I'll hear the echoes burst
With all the sounds of thrilling mirth;
And all the beauties of this earth
I'll see within its walls.

And happiness and peace are there,
With all the sounds of thrilling
Contentment—not a frown—
Where love and fellowship abound
Few troubles can be found.

Alas! I'm back to earth again,
My thoughts have hit a snag;
For when reality creeps in
My spirit's bound to lag.

But just the same I'll always seek
The land that's bright and fair,
And find in it my happiness,
Because I know you're there.

Jean Toomer

Jean Toomer, poet and writer of the short story, was born in Washington, D. C., in 1894. He was educated in the public schools of Washington, the University of Wisconsin, and the College of the City of New York. He is the author of *Cane*, from which the following selections are taken.

NOVEMBER COTTON FLOWER [1]

Boll-weevil's coming, and the winter's cold,
Made cotton-stalks look rusty, seasons old,
And cotton, scarce as any southern snow,
Was vanishing; the branch, so pinched and slow,
Failed in its function as the autumn rake;
Drouth fighting soil had caused the soil to take
All water from the streams; dead birds were found
In wells a hundred feet below the ground—
Such was the season when the flower bloomed.
Old folks were startled, and it soon assumed
Significance. Superstition saw
Something it had never seen before:
Brown eyes that loved without a trace of fear,
Beauty so sudden for that time of year.

GEORGIA DUSK [1]

The sky, lazily disdaining to pursue
    The setting sun, too indolent to hold
    A lengthened tournament for flashing gold,
Passively darkens for night's barbecue,

A feast of moon and men and barking hounds,
    An orgy for some genius of the South
    With blood-hot eyes and cane-lipped scented mouth,
Surprised in making folk-songs from soul sounds.

The sawmill blows its whistle, buzz-saws stop,
    And silence breaks the bud of knoll and hill,
    Soft settling pollen where plowed lands fulfill
Their early promise of a bumper crop.

Smoke from the pyramidal sawdust pile
    Curls up, blue ghosts of trees, tarrying low

[1] From *Cane*, by Jean Toomer. Copyright, 1923, by Liveright Publishing Corporation, New York.

Where only chips and stumps are left to show
The solid proof of former domicile.

Meanwhile, the men, with vestiges of pomp,
    Race memories of king and caravan,
    High-priests, an ostrich, and a juju-man,
Go singing through the footpaths of the swamp.

Their voices rise . . . the pine trees are guitars,
    Strumming, pine-needles fall like sheets of rain . . .
    Their voices rise . . . the chorus of the cane
Is caroling a vesper to the stars . . .

O singers, resinous and soft your songs
    Above the sacred whisper of the pines,
    Give virgin lips to cornfield concubines,
Bring dreams of Christ to dusky cane-lipped throngs.

EVENING SONG [1]

Full moon rising on the waters of my heart,
Lakes and moon and fires,
Cloine tires,
Holding her lips apart.

Promises of slumber leaving shore to charm the moon,
Miracle made vesper-keeps,
Cloine sleeps,
And I'll be sleeping soon.

Cloine, curled like the sleepy waters where the moon-waves
                            start
Radiant, resplendently she gleams,
Cloine dreams,
Lips pressed against my heart.

Arna Bontemps
(See page 269.)

THE RETURN [1]

I

Once more, listening to the wind and rain,
Once more, you and I, and above the hurting sound
Of these comes back the throbbing of remembered rain,
Treasured rain falling on dark ground.
Once more, huddling birds upon the leaves
And summer trembling on a withered vine.
And once more, returning out of pain,
The friendly ghost that was your love and mine.

II

Darkness brings the jungle to our room:
The throb of rain is the throb of muffled drums.
Darkness hangs our room with pendulums
Of vine and in the gathering gloom
Our walls recede into a denseness of
Surrounding trees. This is a night of love
Retained from those lost nights our fathers slept
In huts; this is a night that must not die.
Let us keep the dance of rain our fathers kept
And tread our dreams beneath the jungle sky.

III

And now the downpour ceases.
Let us go back once more upon the glimmering leaves
And as the throbbing of the drums increases
Shake the grass and dripping boughs of trees.
A dry wind stirs the palm; the old tree grieves.

Time has charged the years: the old days have returned.

1 Reprinted with the permission of the author.

Let us dance by metal waters burned
With gold of moon, let us dance
With naked feet beneath the young spice trees.
What was that light, that radiance
On your face?—something I saw when first
You passed beneath the jungle tapestries?

A moment we pause to quench our thirst
Kneeling at the water's edge, the gleam
Upon your face is plain: you have wanted this.
Let us go back and search the tangled dream
And as the muffled drum-beats throb and miss
Remember again how early darkness comes
To dreams and silence to the drums.

IV

Let us go back into the dusk again,
Slow and sad-like following the track
Of blowing leaves and cool white rain
Into the old gray dream, let us go back.
Our walls close about us; we lie and listen
To the noise of the street, the storm and the driven birds.
A question shapes your lips, your eyes glisten
Retaining tears, but there are no more words.

HOMING [1]

Sweet timber land
Where soft winds blow
The high green tree
And fan away the fog!
Ah fragrant stream
Where thirsty creatures go
And strong black men
Hew the heavy log!

[1] Reprinted with the permission of the author.

Oh broken house
Crumbling there alone,
Wanting me!
Oh silent tree
Must I always be
A wild bird
Riding the wind
And screaming bitterly?

DAY-BREAKERS [1]

We are not come to wage a strife
   With swords upon this hill.
It is not wise to waste the life
   Against a stubborn will.
Yet would we die as some have done:
Beating a way for the rising sun.

Naomi Long Witherspoon

Naomi Long Witherspoon, poet and journalist, was born at Norfolk, Virginia. She published a book of poems while in high school. In her senior year she was Editor-in-Chief of the *Maroon and White,* her high-school yearbook at Sumner High School, St. Louis, Mo. She graduated from Virginia State College in 1945. At present she is an associate editor of the *Michigan Chronicle* of Detroit.

    Her poems that follow were written especially for this anthology. She is one of the promising young American poets. Her *Songs to a Nightingale* was published in 1941.

QUEST

I will track you down the years,
   Down the night

[1] Reprinted with the permission of the author.

'Til my anguish falls away,
    Star by star,
And my heart spreads feathered wings
    Where you are.

I will find you; never fear—
    Make you mine!
Think that you have bound me fast
    To the earth,
I will rise to sing you yet,
    Song of mirth.

I will let you think you won,
    Perfect dream,
'Til I creep from dark and toil
    To your side,
Hold you to my heart and sleep,
    Satisfied.

I will track you down the sky,
    Down the blue
'Til my song becomes the sun
    Of the years
And the golden April rains
    Are my tears.

THE POET DESERTS HIS IVORY TOWER

O sing no more of pretty, useless things
And weep no more for skies no longer blue;
The feathered bird that flies on lovely wings
Is not for you.

Let towers, white and gleaming in the sun,
Be but a memory of faded dreams;
Their gods are sadly leaving, one by one,
(Or so it seems).

Here is a nobler shrine, a higher god
More needed, more admired, though unsung—
He suffers with the fallen of the sod
Whose heads are hung.

He works with grimy hands for those who bleed;
He gives a vision to the hopeless blind;
He fights, his pen a weapon, for the need
Of all mankind.

O sing no more the once-bright similes.
Remember now the hungry, beaten throng,
The hopeless, the defeated ones—To these
You owe your song!

NOT I ALONE

Because I am not just I alone,
One individual creating momentary impressions
That are soon forgotten;
Because, instead, I am an entire people,
Baffled, confused, misunderstood,
And the weight and obligation of clarity
And enlightenment are heavy on my shoulders,
I must speak and act and think
Not only for myself but for my people.

Because not riots nor revolutions can do as much,
In bitter years of bloodshed and hatred,
As I can do in a brief moment of being myself—
Being my best self by which I would be characterized;
Because if I fail in destroying the myth of differences—
The myths of barbarism and filth and laziness,
And vulgarity and ignorance and all the contemptible
Meanings they attach to my name—
If I fail to prove them wrong in my simplest act or word,
Then books have failed and sermons have failed,
And councils for the advancement of my people have failed.

Because none of these things is so powerful a key
To the solution of the great American problem
As the appearance and conduct which I exhibit,
Not as an individual only, but as the symbol of an entire race,
I must hold my head higher and walk straighter
And think clearer and speak more with my mind in my words,
For the weight is heavy on my shoulders
And I cannot ignore it.

CITY THOUGHT

Is this my house, I ask?
Is this my fine white house in a great,
        wicked, sinful city,
        Standing alone, fortified, barricaded
        against—what?
Is this my pure, white, untouched
        house, watchful of being tainted,
        afraid of being tainted, guarding
        against being tainted?
Oh, my own love, my city street,
        gray and dirty!
Oh, my vagrant thoughts wandering
        like gray pigeons on a city street!
My pigeons are young, but they are
        fearless and undaunted;
They do not mind the brown grasses
        that wither at October's breath;
They do not mind the fallen leaves
        that cling in damp puddles
        on the gray pavement;
They do not mind the sheen of sullen
        clouds that the sky wears,
        through which, after a recent
        rain, a timid autumn blueness
        tries to break.
They do not mind the trees that stand
        stripped and pitifully naked in the
        brisk wind.

These pigeons, they fear nothing; they
       shrink from nothing; they flee
       from nothing, screaming.
The driver on a busy street is irritated
       by the pigeons; he is eager to go
       somewhere, to be by a warm fire
       of an autumn evening. He does
       not like the stubborn pigeons
       boldly refusing to let him pass.
My pigeons flap their wings at
       security and a cozy fire, and
       turn away indignantly into
       the busy street.
My fine white house could easily
       shelter them, but they will not
       have it. They are curious little
       rebels digging their talons into
       life, breaking it, looking to
       see what is contained within
       the crushed shell; and they
       will not have the house.
What good is my house, then, if my
       thoughts will not take refuge
       in it?
What use have I of a sturdy house
       if my soul will not stay by the
       fire?
I ask myself, then, is it really MY
       house that stands so serenely
       mocking the world?
Is it really MY soul that keeps
       its undefiled windows
       lighted with so calm and
       patient a lamp?

Gwendolyn Brooks

Gwendolyn Brooks, who was born in Topeka, Kansas in 1917, came to Chicago when quite a little girl. Inspired by her nursery rhymes, she began to form her own little rhymes. As she pursued her studies at Englewood High School and at the Wilson Junior College of Chicago, she continued to court the poetic Muse. As her poems appeared in various magazines, she began to win prizes. In 1945 *Mademoiselle*, a woman's magazine, named her as one of the most distinguished women of the year. In 1946 the American Academy of Arts and Letters gave her a distinguished award. Recognizing her ability, the Guggenheim Foundation awarded her a fellowship in 1946 and in 1947. And in 1950 her collection of poems entitled *Annie Allen*, which tells the story of a woman as daughter, wife, and mother, was awarded the Pulitzer Prize.

LOVE NOTE [1]

I: Surely

Surely you stay my certain own, you stay
My you. All honest, lofty as a cloud,
Surely I could come now and find you high,
As mine as you ever were; should not be awed,
Surely your word would pop as insolent
As always: "Why, of course, I love you, dear."
Your gaze, surely, ungauged as I could want.
Your touches, that never were careful, what they were.
Surely——But I am very off from that.
From surely. From indeed. From decent arrow
That was my clean naïveté and my faith.
This morning men deliver wounds and death.
They will deliver death and wounds tomorrow.
And I doubt all. You. Or a violet.

[1] From *A Street in Bronzeville*, by Gwendolyn Brooks. Copyright, 1945, by **Gwendolyn Brooks Blakely**. Reprinted by permission of Harper & Brothers, New York.

THE PROGRESS [1]

And still we wear our uniforms, follow
The cracked cry of the bugles, comb and brush
Our pride and prejudice, doctor the sallow
Initial ardor, wish to keep it fresh.
Still we applaud the President's voice and face.
Still we remark on patriotism, sing,
Salute the flag, thrill heavily, rejoice
For death of men who too saluted, sang.
But inward grows a soberness, an awe,
A fear, a deepening hollow through the cold.
For even if we come out standing up
How shall we smile, congratulate: and how
Settle in chairs? Listen, listen. The step
Of iron feet again. And again   wild.

Rosa Paul Brooks

"What a beautiful song!" remarked a friend, who heard Rosa Paul Brooks
play and sing a song, the words and music of which she had just written.
"Well, I like that myself," Rosa responded. "I wrote it for the opera
'Dixie Love.'" She was collaborating with Mrs. Zelle Cole Hunton, another composer of St. Louis, in producing this operetta, which has drawn
crowds each time it has been produced in St. Louis.
Rosa Paul Brooks is from Nashville, Tennessee.

WINTER'S MORN [2]

Sullen and dark as an angry mood
     That envelops a treacherous soul,
The grey mist hangs in the brooding sky
     While dark clouds menacingly roll.

[1] From *A Street in Bronzeville,* by Gwendolyn Brooks. Copyright, 1945, by Gwendolyn
Brooks Blakely. Reprinted by permission of Harper & Brothers, New York.
[2] From *Poetic Meditations,* by Rosa Paul Brooks. Copyright, 1945, by Rosa Paul
Brooks.

Cold and dreary the fog and mist
    Fill the air with a deathly chill,
And barren trees rise out of the dark
    Like spectres grim and still.

No confronting ray or sun can shine
    Through clouds so sombre that roll
Upward as though the hand of fate
    Unfolds some mighty scroll.

The mist and fog of hate can freeze
    The hearts like the winter's cold;
Like barren trees in the cold, grey dawn
    Life becomes ugly and old.

NOT WANTED [1]

Gee, I'm so disgusted, I feel like I could cry,
I believe I'll eat some wooly worms and go right out and die.
I've got a baby brother, and believe me he's a fright,
His nose is all unjointed, and he cries all day and night.

The way he bawls and hollers, Pa says it is a sin:
I heard Pa ask Ma if she was sticking pins in him.
Ma says the angels brought him down from heaven to play
                        with me.
I know she must be teasing, 'cause the angels don't know me.
I think they would have told me they were coming, now don't
                        you?
And then I could have asked them about the things that he
                        could do.
Pshaw! He can't play with me, 'cause he can't even walk;
He hasn't any teeth; and say—he don't know how to talk.

I wish the angels had-a brought a little dog or cat,
I'd rather have a bird that sings, or a rubber ball and bat,
'Cause I don't want that baby, he's no good and that's a fact,
And I just wish the angels would come down and take him
                        back.

[1] From *Poetic Meditations,* by Rosa Paul Brooks. Copyright, 1945, by Rosa Paul Brooks.

PART III

Letters

Introduction   The letter early became a literary form used by the American Negro. He used it in communicating with his friends, as did Phillis Wheatley, Benjamin Banneker, and Frederick Douglass, for example. The letter gives one a chance to be informal, to drop some conventions and write with an intimacy which reveals the soul.

The letter also may be an historical document. It often records many an important historical event of a particular period. For instance, the letter written by Phillis Wheatley which is included in this volume reveals some aspects of her character not shown by her poems. Her poems will show that she believed in God; but her treatment of God in her poems is formal, conventional. This is not true of the same theme in her letter. In her letter, we readily become aware of the sincerity and the fervor of her faith in God; here her treatment of God is spontaneous.

Her letter also illustrates the manner in which messages were sent in her day, not by a professional postal carrier, but by an occasional traveler.

Similarly the letter of Frederick Douglass to Harriet Beecher Stowe, the distinguished author of *Uncle Tom's Cabin,* is an historical document. It shows that Frederick Douglass and Harriet Beecher Stowe were friends. It shows the generosity and the vision of both. It shows also Douglass's understanding not only of the American Negro, but of the American situation. In 1853, about six years before the birth of Booker T. Washington, the great Negro champion of industrial education, Frederick Douglass, in replying to a request of Mrs. Stowe as to how best she might help the free Negro, suggested that she use her influence with her friends in America and in England to establish an industrial college, where free Negroes might learn trades.

This letter depicts the difficulties the free Negro faced at that time in getting employment. It also demonstrates Douglass's correct prognostication of what the future would be. It shows that he was wise in expecting the Negro to start at the bottom and gradually work his way to the top. It is a document that is not only biographical, but historical and sociological as well.

The excerpt that John W. Cromwell gives from a letter of Benjamin Banneker to Thomas Jefferson, which is included in the section on Biography and Autobiography, is also an historical and a sociological document.

Besides, it is interesting to observe how well these three writers, under the greatest of handicaps, mastered the English language. The style of each, though showing different characteristics, is simple but at the same time elegant.

Phillis Wheatley
(See page 21.)

To Arbour Tanner, in Newport. To the care of
Mr. Pease's Servant, Rhode Island.

Boston, July 19th, 1772

My Dear Friend,——I rec'd your kind epistle a few days ago; much disappointed to hear that you had not rec'd my answer to your first letter. I have been in a very poor state of health all the past winter and spring, and now reside in the country for the benefit of its more wholesome air. I came to town this morning to spend the Sabbath with my master and mistress. Let me be interested in your prayers that God would please to bless to me the means us'd for my recovery, if agreeable to his holy will. While my outward man languishes under weakness and pain, may the inward be refresh'd and strengthen'd more abundantly by him who declar'd from heaven that his strength was made perfect in weakness! May he correct our vitiated taste, that the meditation of him may be delightful to us. No longer to be so excessively charm'd with fleeting vanities: but pressing forward to the fix'd mark for the prize. How happy that man who is prepar'd for that night wherein no man can work! Let us be mindful of our high calling, continually on our guard, lest our treacherous hearts should give the adversary an advantage over us. O! who can think without horror of the snares of the Devil. Let us, by frequent meditation on the eternal Judgment, prepare for it. May the Lord bless to us these thoughts, and teach us by his Spirit to live to him alone, and when we leave this world may we be his. This may be our happy case, is the sincere desire of, your affectionate friend, and humble serv't,

Phillis Wheatley

I sent the letter to Mr. Whitwell's who said he wou'd forward it.

Frederick Douglass
(See page 187.)

(See page 187.)

Rochester, New York
March 8, 1853

My dear Mrs. Stowe:

You kindly informed me, when at your house a fortnight ago, that you designed to do something which should permanently contribute to the improvement and elevation of the free Colored people in the United States. You especially expressed an interest in such of this class as had become free by their own exertions, and desired most of all to be of service to them. . . .

I answer, first, not by establishing for our use high schools and colleges. Such institutions are, in my judgment, beyond our immediate occasions and are not adapted to our present most pressing wants. High schools and colleges are excellent institutions, and will in due season be greatly subservient to our progress; but they are the result, as well as they are the demand, of a point of progress which we as a people have not yet attained.

Accustomed as we have been to the rougher and harder modes of living, and of gaining a livelihood, we cannot and we ought not to hope that in a single leap from our low condition, we can reach that of *Ministers, Lawyers, Doctors, Editors, Merchants,* etc. These will doubtless be attained by us; but this will only be when we have patiently and laboriously, and I may add successfully, mastered and passed through the intermediate gradations of agriculture and the mechanic arts. Besides, there are (and perhaps this is a better reason for my view of the case) numerous institutions of learning in this country, already thrown open to Colored youth. To my thinking, there are quite as many facilities now afforded to the Colored people as they can spare the time, from the sterner duties of life, to appropriate judiciously. In their present condition of poverty, they cannot spare their sons and daughters two or three years at boarding-schools or colleges, to say nothing of finding the means to sustain them while at such institutions.

I take it, therefore, that we are well provided for in this respect; and that it may be fairly inferred from the fact that the facilities for our education, so far as schools and colleges in the Free States are concerned, will increase quite in proportion with our future wants. Colleges have been open to Colored youth in this country during the last dozen years. Yet few, comparatively, have acquired a classical education; and even this few have found themselves educated far above a living condition, there being no methods by which they could turn their learning to account. Several of this latter class have entered the ministry; but you need not be told that an educated people is needed to sustain an educated ministry. There must be a certain amount of cultivation among the people, to sustain such a ministry. At present we have not that cultivation amongst us; and, therefore, we value in the preacher strong lungs rather than high learning. I do not say that educated ministers are not needed amongst us, far from it! I wish there were more of them! But to increase their number is *not* the largest benefit you can bestow upon us.

We have two or three Colored lawyers in this country; and I rejoice in the fact; for it affords very gratifying evidence of our progress. Yet it must be confessed that, in point of success, our lawyers are as great failures as our ministers. White people will not employ them to the obvious embarrassment of their causes, and the Blacks, taking their *cue* from the Whites, have not sufficient confidence in their abilities to employ them. Hence educated Colored men, among the Colored people, are at a very great discount. It would seem that education and emigration go together with us, for as soon as a man rises amongst us, capable, by his genius and learning, to do us great service, just so soon he finds that he can serve himself better by going elsewhere. In proof of this, I might instance the Russwurms, the Garnetts, the Wards, the Crummells, and others, all men of superior ability and attainments, and capable of removing mountains of prejudice against their race by their simple presence in the country; but these gentlemen, finding themselves embarrassed here by the peculiar disadvantages to which I have referred, disadvantages in part growing out of their education, being repelled by ignorance on the one hand, and prejudice on the other, and having no taste to continue a contest against such odds, have sought more congenial climes, where they can live more peaceable and quiet lives. I regret their election, but I cannot blame them; for with an equal amount of education, the hard lot which was theirs, I might follow their example. . . .

What can be done to improve the condition of the free people of Color in the United States? The plan which I humbly submit in answer to this inquiry (and in the hope that it may find favor with you, and with the many friends of humanity who honor, love, and cooperate with you) is the establishment in Rochester, New York, or in some other part of the United States equally favorable to such an enterprise, of an *Industrial College* in which shall be taught several important branches of the mechanic arts.

This college shall be opened to Colored youth. I will pass over the details of such an institution as I propose . . . Never having had a day's schooling in all my life, I may not be expected to map out the details of a plan so comprehensive as that involved in the idea of a college. I repeat, then, that I leave the organization and administration of the institution to the superior wisdom of yourself and the friends who second your noble efforts. The argument in favor of an Industrial College (a college to be conducted by the best men, and the best workmen which the mechanic arts can afford; a college where Colored youth can be instructed to use their hands, as well as their heads; where they can be put in possession of the means of getting a living whether their lot in after life may be cast among civilized or uncivilized men; whether they choose to stay here, or prefer to return to the land of their fathers) is briefly this: Prejudice against the free Colored people in the United States has shown itself nowhere so invincible as among mechanics. The farmer and the professional man cherish no feeling so bitter as that cherished by these. The latter would starve us out of the country entirely.

At this moment I can more easily get my son into a lawyer's office to study law than I can into a blacksmith's shop to blow the bellows and to wield the sledge-hammer. Denied the means of learning useful trades, we are pressed into the narrowest limits to obtain a livelihood. In times past we have been the hewers of wood and drawers of water for American society, and we once enjoyed a monopoly in menial employments, but this is so no longer. Even these employments are rapidly passing away out of our hands. The fact is (every day begins with the lesson, and ends with the lesson) that Colored men must learn trades; must find new employments, new modes of usefulness to society; or that they must decay under the pressing wants to which their condition is rapidly bringing them.

We must become mechanics; we must build as well as live in houses; we must make as well as use furniture; we must construct bridges as well as pass over them, before we can properly live with or be respected by our fellow men. We need mechanics as well as ministers. We need workers in iron, clay, and leather. We have orators, authors,

and other professional men, but these reach only a certain class, and
get respect for our race in certain select circles. To live here as we
ought, we must fasten ourselves to our countrymen through their
every-day, cardinal wants. We must not only be able to black boots,
but to make them. At present we are, in northern States, unknown as
mechanics. We give no proof of genius or skill at the county, State, or
national fairs. We are unknown at any of the great exhibitions of the
industry of our fellow-citizens, and being unknown we are uncon-
sidered.

The fact that we make no show of our ability is held conclusive
of our inability to make anything, hence all the indifference and con-
tempt with which incapacity is regarded fall upon us, and that too
when we have had no means of disproving the infamous opinion of
our natural inferiority. I have, during the last dozen years, denied before Americans that we are an inferior race; but this has been done
by arguments based upon admitted principles rather than by the pre-
sentation of facts. Now firmly believing, as I do, that there are skill,
invention, power, industry, and real mechanical genius among the
Colored people, which will bear favorable testimony for them, and
which only need the means to develop them, I am decidedly in favor
of the establishment of such a college .

.   .   .   .

The most telling, the most killing refutation of slavery is the pre-
sentation of an industrious, enterprising, thrifty, and intelligent free
black population. Such a population I believe would rise in the Northern States under the fostering care of such a college as that proposed.

.   .   .   .

Allow me to say in conclusion that I believe every intelligent
Colored man in America will approve and rejoice at the establishment
of some such an institution as that now suggested. There are families,
having boys nearly grown up, whose minds are tossed by day and by
night with the anxious inquiry, What shall I do with my boys? Such an
institution would meet the wants of such persons.

.   .   .   .

The noble and good of all classes would see in the effort an excellent motive, a benevolent object, temperately, wisely, and practically manifested.

I am, most truly, your grateful friend

Frederick Douglass

Mrs. H. B. Stowe
Mrs. Harriet Beecher Stowe

Alrutheus Ambush Taylor

Alrutheus Ambush Taylor, historian, essayist, and educator, was born in Washington, D. C. He obtained the degree of Bachelor of Arts from the University of Michigan and the degrees of Master of Arts and Doctor of Philosophy from Harvard University. At present he is Dean of Fisk University. Among his publications are the following: *The Negro Congressman a Generation After, The Negro in South Carolina During Reconstruction,* and *The Negro in the Reconstruction of Virginia.*

The great soul of Dean Taylor, which is every day expressed in his relations with the students at Fisk University, is readily and fervently revealed in the following letter to his children, which is reprinted with Dean Taylor's permission.

FISK UNIVERSITY
Nashville 8, Tennessee

A. A. TAYLOR, *Dean*   *December 25, 1945*

My dear Children,

Today we celebrate the anniversary of the birth of Jesus Christ, the great Galilean whose advent into this world nearly two thousand years ago became one of the great facts of history. You know, as well as I, the relation of this outstanding event to the Christian tradition. And you know the significance and the universality of the Christmas observance among the peoples of the earth.

Consistent with the spirit and the meaning of Christmas, it gives me great joy to greet you and to express sentiments appropriate to the season. Moreover, I am greatly privileged to convey to you a Christmas gift which bears in truth the love and the sincerest hopes of the giver. My gift is a wish—a momentous wish, that I humbly pray God to help you to achieve.

My gift, my wish, is complex and multiple, but unified. It is concerned chiefly with your acquisition and your development of characteristics and qualities which form a foundation for living the good life.

May you acquire a liberal education and a sound training, develop good judgment and a discriminating sense of selflessness, sustain the excellent character that is an outstanding feature of your lives, maintain and protect your health and accept the challenge of a cause so worthy as to merit your consecrated service and your most effective effort. Above all, may you dedicate your lives to the support and the promotion of Christianity and of democracy as potent forces capable of making this world a place of freedom and of happiness for mankind.

This wish is at once the supreme present gift that I can offer you and the greatest future legacy that I can bequeath to you. May God bless you and lead you to accept it.

With love and devotion,

Father

PART IV

Biography and Autobiography

Introduction   As literary forms, biography and autobiography logically come under narration and should be taught as examples of this form of discourse. The biography is an account of the life of a person written by someone else; the autobiography, on the other hand, is the author's account of himself. From the point of view of technique, the biography and the autobiography may be regarded as stories without plot, since the chief events of the lives of the persons subject to literary treatment are presented in chronological order. In the case of the story with plot, the events are not presented in their chronological order. The very nature of plot, for the literary artist, is planning. He will follow chiefly the chronological order, but some prior events he will relate after he has related events that actually occurred after these. He does this rearranging in order to keep the attention and the interest of the reader, arousing his curiosity and holding him in suspense. This curiosity, if it is sufficiently aroused, will make the reader want to continue reading a story. This technique will be discussed at greater length and illustrated in the introduction to the short-story as a literary form.

Banjo, by Claude McKay, is an example of a novel without plot. All the incidents are related in chronological order. Jessie Fauset's *The Chinaberry Tree,* on the other hand, from which an excerpt appears in this book, is an example of a novel with plot. Its events are not related in chronological order. The author of *The Chinaberry Tree* begins in the middle of her story with a situation that is the culmination of many years, a situation that at once arouses the curiosity of the reader, causing him to wonder how that crisis came about; for *The Chinaberry Tree* does begin with a crisis. Having presented an important crisis, which is the result of happenings of many years, Jessie Fauset then proceeds to relate the important events of those years that produced the crisis presented at the opening of the novel. This rearrangement of the chief events of a story is what is meant by plot.

The biographer, or one writing his autobiography, may use this literary device of plot in an anecdote, which is an incident in a person's life, like that of Booker T. Washington's examination for admission to Hampton Institute or his first vacation. He could not use plot for the entire biography. However, if one writes a biographical novel, which would bring into the story both the actual and the fictitious, he could organize the entire story into a plot. This was done by Charles Dickens in *David Copperfield* and by William Makepeace Thackeray in *Pendennis*.

For biography or autobiography to become the highest type of literature, the writer has to do more than relate merely the important incidents of one's life. He needs to present the setting, the physical as well as the social setting, that served as the environment for the events of a life. The biographer, as a literary artist, must, therefore, intersperse his work with both physical and impressionistic description of the persons that move in the life-story. In addition to this, he must, as far as he can, set forth the motives of his subject and interpret that life in terms of the age in which the individual lived, stating the influence of the age upon this individual and the influence of this individual upon his age. Such a biography, which interweaves history, psychology, and sociology with the story of a life, attains the sublime of literature.

Similarly, he who writes an account of his own life, if he expects it to become the best in literature, must observe the same principles and standards as must the biographer. A biography is never perfect, because no biography contains all the incidents of a person's life. James Boswell's *Life of Samuel Johnson,* according to most literary critics, is the greatest biography ever written. The material he put into this work is the result of daily contacts with Dr. Johnson over a period of many years; but since Boswell was not with Johnson every hour of those years, there are important events of Johnson's life that do not appear in Boswell's work. Thus it is not a perfect biography; however, it does, so far as is humanly possible, approach perfection.

There also is no perfect autobiography. This happens because a writer will omit certain events in his life. It fails further because the writer does not see himself as others see him. At the same time he can tell the motives that inspired him to action; he can well describe his deeper feelings, which he often hides from even his closest friends. Therefore, to have the best possible account of a life there must be both the biography and the autobiography: the biography for the objective story and the autobiography for the subjective, each serving as a supplement to the other.

The need of both biography and autobiography to give a proper account of a life is well illustrated by several accounts of the life of Frederick Douglass, regarded by most of his dark brothers as the greatest Negro America has produced. Excellent biographies of Douglass were written by Charles W. Chesnutt, the lawyer and novelist, Booker T. Washington, the educator, and Harriet Beecher Stowe, the humanitarian. Chesnutt stresses the courage, the vision, and the statesmanship of the great orator. Washington stresses his patience, his faith and common sense. Mrs. Stowe stresses his great attainment in spite of handicaps. Early in her *Men of Our Times,* she says, "Frederick Douglass had as far to climb to come to the place where the poorest White boy is born, as that White boy has to climb to become President of the Nation and take his place among the kings and judges of the earth." The facts of Douglass' life are about the same in all three accounts, but the emphasis, the interpretation, is different in each.

The autobiography, *The Life and Times of Frederick Douglass,* is different from these biographies. Douglass stresses the hard conditions of slavery. He emphasizes his identification with the masses of his people. As a slave and as a free man, he identified himself with these, the oppressed. Though he attained the greatest heights, he never forsook his people. He emphasizes the fact that he rose to greatness as a

Negro. His inner feelings, the hurts, the pains, his motives, the strivings of his soul—of these Douglass himself was the best interpreter. Thus biography and autobiography both serve a definite purpose.

The Negro author has made a representative contribution to biography, of which some of the outstanding examples are the following: Richard Allen, *Life and Times;* John W. Cromwell, *The Negro in American History;* Elizabeth Ross Haynes, *Unsung Heroes;* John Mercer Langston, *From the Virginia Plantation to the National Capitol;* and Langston Hughes, *The Big Sea.*

Alexander Pope, the English poet of the eighteenth century, realizing that man is most interested in man, wrote, "The proper study of mankind is man." The greatest champion of biography is Thomas Carlyle, the Scotch essayist and historian, who in his "Heroes and Hero-Worship" wrote: "The history of the world is simply the history of the few great men who have lived in it." The biographical and autobiographical selections in this volume are sufficient to enable the student to become acquainted with the technique of the literary artist who chooses biography or autobiography as his vehicle of expression, and varied enough for the student to discern the great possibilities of this appealing medium.

John W. Cromwell

John W. Cromwell, educator, for many years principal of the Benjamin Banneker School of Washington, D. C., was a pioneer Negro historian. While he was secretary of The American Negro Academy, an organization of Negro scholars and professional people of Washington, he published in 1914 *The Negro in American History*. This was just one year before W. E. B. DuBois published his *The Negro* and also one year before Carter G. Woodson organized The Association for the Study of Negro Life and History. Both DuBois and Woodson have done monumental work in this field.

"Benjamin Banneker" is reprinted with the permission of Mr. Cromwell's children, Dr. Otelia Cromwell and John W. Cromwell, Jr. The chapter is reproduced just as it came from the pen of their father.

BENJAMIN BANNEKER

A little more than one hundred years ago a black prince arrived on the shores of the Chesapeake Bay. He came by compulsion, not by choice; he was brought here a slave. That he was no ordinary black is attested by the fact that he clung to his heathen gods and refused to work for those who had him in control; yet he was of noble mien, dignified and possessed of rare intelligence, even retaining to the last the name which he brought with him from Africa—Banneker.[1]

In the same year in which William Penn established his colony on the banks of the Delaware, an English peasant woman having accidentally spilled a can of milk—so the story goes—was charged with and found guilty of stealing. As her punishment she was transported to Maryland, where she was bound to service for seven years, a mild sentence for the offense, because she could read. A thrifty woman she was and bought a small farm on which she subsequently placed Banneker, the exiled black African prince.

Though he would not work, Banneker touched the heart of Molley Welsh, who liberated and married him.

Four children were born of this union, one of whom, Mary Banneker, was married about the year 1730 to Robert, a native African slave, who on being baptized in the Episcopal faith was formally given his freedom. Robert, like many a one of his race of whom there is unfortunately no record, did not take the name of the white people who had claimed him a slave, but called himself Banneker, after his wife, the daughter of the African prince.

Their oldest offspring, Benjamin Banneker, was born November 9, 1731, just about three months before George Washington. In the year 1737 Robert Banneker, his father, purchased for the sum of seventeen thousand pounds of tobacco a farm of one hundred acres. It was in a primeval wilderness, though only ten miles from Baltimore, then a village of less than thirty houses. Roads were few, houses were miles and miles apart, schools and churches were exceedingly scarce, the steam whistle had not yet echoed through the valleys nor across the

[1] Banaky.

plains of that primitive country; yet there were a few private schools, and to one of these the lad Benjamin was sent.

Here he was a most apt student and had received instruction as far as "double position," as it was then called, proficiency in which even a century later was regarded as a test of arithmetical skill; and today, as compound proportion, by which name it is now known, it is a source of great perplexity to pupils in our advanced grammar schools. This was the limit of the educational training which Banneker received, but it must have been most thorough, for as the sequel proved it was the foundation upon which he built so well as to take rank with the greatest scientific men of his times, to achieve a world-wide distinction for skill as mathematician and astronomer that one hundred years have not obliterated. Apart from his studies, his life was not eventful, yet it is deserving of all emulation. The oldest, and only son, among four children, he assiduously gave his service on his farm even after he had attained his majority. Upon the death of the father in 1757 (which fact is learned from an entry in Benjamin's Bible), the full responsibility of the management of the farm fell upon him, the household duties being performed by Benjamin's mother, whose vigor of body remained until she was quite advanced in years. It is said of her agility that even when over seventy years of age it was a common thing for her to run down the barn yard fowls which were desired for the table or for market.

In those days the country stores were the centers of information and social contact. Here the planters brought their corn, their wheat, their tobacco, for sale or for exchange; here the latest news from London, Boston, or Philadelphia was obtained. The country store also contained the post office at which letters were received or dispatched in the weekly or monthly mail. Here the weekly newspaper, of which there were only two at that time in the colony, was read by the most intelligent and the affairs of the day discussed. Banneker, himself a landed proprietor, was frequently at the store during these gatherings, at which his intelligent conversation, his quiet and dignified manner, and his accurate information on current affairs made him a unique but welcome visitor. He did not resort there to the neglect of his farm, for it was thoroughly well-kept, his orchards abounded in fruit, his cattle were sleek and fat, his storehouse was well filled with grain and tobacco.

It was in his early manhood, in about 1753, that Banneker, having only seen a watch, with it for a model constructed a wooden clock all the parts of which—the wheels, the springs, the balances—were the result of his own ingenuity, skill, patience, and perseverance. This is said to be the first clock constructed in America which was made entirely in this country. For more than twenty years it kept good time, an example of the cunning workmanship of the sable artificer.

An event of very great significance in the quiet neighborhood of Banneker's home was the erection in 1772 of the flour mills of what is now Ellicott City. The machinery, so crude and antiquated by present standards, was more than a nine days' wonder in those far-off days. Among others, Banneker, delighted even after the novelty had worn off, lingered to study it, to understand its philosophy, and to enlarge the sphere of his knowledge of mechanics. The establishment of these mills was not only an event designed to advance the material interests of this neighborhood. It was a means to him of great intellectual development.

The proprietors, the Ellicotts, became warmly attached to him, especially because of the strong personal friendship that grew up between him and George Ellicott. Mr. Ellicott saw in Banneker an intellect that not only was ever grasping after the truth, but one capable of an almost infinite development. Though Banneker was black he was to Ellicott, to use a favorite expression of Frederick Douglass, "a kinsman, a clansman, a brother beloved."

One day in 1787 George Ellicott loaned Banneker Mayer's Tables, Ferguson's *Astronomy,* Leadbeater's Lunar Tables and some astronomical instruments, which only those far advanced in mathematics could comprehend, telling Banneker at the time that at the earliest opportunity he (Ellicott) would explain them to him. Banneker took them and retired to the seclusion of his cottage, where without any aid save that which God had given he made himself so familiar with the contents of the volumes as to detect errors in their calculations. You can imagine Ellicott's surprise to find on next meeting the philosopher that his services as instructor were not needed. Banneker, possessing "the cunning-warded keys" that open every door in one's pursuit of knowledge, at the mature age of fifty-six entered zealously upon the study of astronomy, closely observing all the natural phenomena of his neighborhood, as well as the movement of the heavenly bodies, making records, still in existence, that spread his fame far and wide.

The time required for his study and investigations so trenched upon that required for the work of the farm that the necessity of utilizing his scientific knowledge led him in part to consider the feasibility of compiling an ephemeris, or almanac, for the states of Pennsylvania, Delaware, Maryland, and Virginia. For this work he had advanced far towards the construction of tables of logarithms for the necessary calculations when Mr. Ellicott presented him with a set.

Many observers who saw Banneker asleep during the day in his cottage, which on a knoll commanded a fine view of the surrounding country, declared him to be a worthless, good-for-nothing fellow, a victim to an old propensity for intoxicating liquors; but it was untrue, for when

> Nature let her curtain down,
> And pinned it with a star,

they might have seen Banneker, enveloped in the ample folds of his cloak, reclining on the ground, his eyes watching the heavenly bodies and determining their laws. In these days of observatories this would be unnecessary; but Banneker was his own observatory and telescope —he built the roadbed on which he trod to success.

His patience and determination won. He solved the problems confronting him, if not to his own satisfaction at least to that of mankind. When his almanac was nearly ready for publication he was prevented from carrying out his purpose by a most fortunate combination of circumstances.

The United States Government had begun with Washington's inauguration in 1789, but there was yet no permanent official home. In keeping with a provision of the Constitutional Convention, Maryland and Virginia had ceded to the central government certain territory, known as the Federal Territory, to be used as the Nation's Capital, but its exact boundaries had not been fixed. Andrew Ellicott was commissioned to survey the boundaries, and Benjamin Banneker was invited as a man of scientific attainments and professional skill to assist in the work. He accepted the invitation and shared in fixing the boundaries of the District, in the selection of the site of the Capitol Building, in locating an eligible spot for the Executive Mansion, the Treasury, and other buildings. So satisfactory was his work and so agreeable a companion was he that despite prevailing customs the Commissioners invited him again and again to a seat during their meals at the same table with themselves, but he was content to occupy a seat at a side table in the same dining room.

Banneker, having completed his engagement at the Federal Territory with which he was very well pleased, as he recounted to his friends, addressed himself to the publication of his almanac.

That I may not be accused of exaggeration or giving undue praise, I quote from J. H. B. Latrobe's Memoir before the Maryland Historical Society:

The first almanac which Banneker prepared fit for publication was for the year 1792. By this time his acquirements had become generally known, and among others who took an interest in him was James McHenry, Esquire. Mr. McHenry wrote a letter to Goddard and Angell, then the almanac publishers in Baltimore. . . .

In their editorial notice Messrs. Goddard and Angell say, "They feel gratified in the opportunity of presenting to the public, through their press, what must be considered as an extraordinary effort of genius; a complete and accurate Ephemeris for the year 1792 calculated by a sable descendent of Africa." And they further say, that "they flatter themselves that a philanthropic public in this enlightened era, will be induced to give their patronage and support to this work, not only on account of its intrinsic merits (it having met the approbation of several of the most distinguished astronomers of America, particularly the celebrated Mr. Rittenhouse), but from similar notices to these which induce the editors to give this calculation the preference" (mark the words—the preference) "the ardent desire for drawing modest merit from obscurity and controverting the long-established, ill-bred prejudice against the blacks."

The Mr. McHenry referred to was a division surgeon of the Revolutionary War, a trusted friend of General Washington, a member of the Constitutional Convention of 1787 and a Cabinet officer under

both Washington and John Adams. David Rittenhouse was the celebrated astronomer and statesman who wrote the constitution of
Pennsylvania, and a professor of the University of Pennsylvania. Like
Banneker he had at an early age constructed a clock and for several
years was the most noted clock maker in America.

The endorsement of two such men standing in the very first professional and political rank is sufficient to establish the standing and
claim of this great, this monumental work of Banneker. For ten years
his almanac was the main dependence of the farmers of Maryland,
Delaware, and the adjacent States, which demonstrated its utility; in
fact it was discontinued only with the inability of Mr. Banneker, on
account of old age, to undergo the intellectual labor incidental to its
further publication.

In the publication of his almanac, Banneker was not unmindful
of the service rendered to the race of which he was a part. It was an
opportunity that he did not shrink from seizing and improving. Before
the first copy was received from the printers, he prepared a complete
autographed copy and sent it, accompanied by a letter, to Thomas
Jefferson, then United States Secretary of State—a most remarkable letter, a most manly appeal through Jefferson to the American
people on behalf of a class of people who had rendered most valuable
service to the country. The entire letter deserves to be read again and
again for its courteous manner, its nobility of thought, its dignified
utterances, as well as for its eloquence. We have space for only a
few extracts:

> Sir, I hope I may safely admit in consequence of the report which
> hath reached me, . . . that you are measurably friendly and well-
> disposed toward us and that you are willing to lend your aid and
> assistance to our relief from those many distresses and numerous
> calamities to which we are reduced. . . . I apprehend you will
> readily embrace every opportunity to eradicate that train of absurd
> and false ideas and opinions which so generally prevail with respect
> to us; and that your sentiments are concurrent with mine, which are,
> that one Universal Father hath given being to us all; that He hath
> not only made us all of one flesh, but he hath also, without partiality,
> afforded to us all the same faculties, and that however variable we
> may be in society and religion, however diversified in situation or
> color, we are all of the same family and stand in the same relation
> to Him.

He next makes an argument that it is the duty of all who profess the obligations of Christianity to extend their power and influence for the relief of every part of the human race.

Notwithstanding the privileges freely accorded to him personally, Banneker keenly felt the force of the prejudice against the race as a class. He says:

> I freely and cheerfully acknowledge that I am of the African race, and in that color which is natural to them, of the deepest dye, and it is under a sense of the most profound gratitude to the Supreme Ruler of the universe, I now confess I am not under that state of tyrannical and inhuman captivity to which many of my brethren are doomed, but that I have abundantly tasted of the fruition of those blessings which proceed from that free and unequalled liberty with which you are favored, and which I hope you will willingly allow you have received from the immediate hands of that Being from whom proceedeth every good and perfect gift.

And so he makes argument after argument, and then apologizing for the length of the letter he concludes as follows:

> I ardently hope that your candor and generosity will plead with you in my behalf when I make known to you that it was not originally my design; but that having taken up my pen in order to direct to you as a present a copy of an almanac which I have calculated for the succeeding year, I was unexpectedly and unavoidably led thereto.
>
> This calculation, sir, is the product of my arduous study in this my advanced stage of life; for having long had unbounded desire to become acquainted with the secrets of nature, I have had to gratify my curiosity herein through my own assiduous application to astronomical study, in which I need not recount to you the many difficulties and disadvantages which I have had to encounter.
>
> And although I had almost declined to make my calculations for the ensuing year, in consequence of that time which I had allotted therefor being taken up at the Federal Territory, by the request of Mr. Andrew Ellicott, yet finding myself under engagements to printers of this State, to whom I had communicated my design on my return to my place of residence, I industriously applied myself thereto which I hope I have accomplished with correctness and accuracy, a copy of which I have taken the liberty to direct to you and which I humbly request you will favorably receive; and although you may have the opportunity of perusing it after its publication, yet, I chose to send it to you in manuscript previous thereto, that thereby you might not only have an earlier inspection, but that you might also view it in my own handwriting.

Jefferson's reply is brief, but characteristic.

Philadelphia, August 31, 1791

Sir: I thank you sincerely for your letter of the 19th instant and for the almanac it contained. Nobody wishes more than I do to see such proofs as you exhibit that nature has given to our black brethren talents equal to those of the other colors of men and that the appearance of a want of them is owing only to the degraded condition of their existence both in Africa and America. I can add with truth, that no one wishes more ardently to see a good system commenced for raising the conditions, both of their body and mind to what it ought to be, as fast as the imbecility of their present existence, and other circumstances which cannot be neglected, will admit.

I have taken the liberty of sending your almanac to Monsieur de Condorcet, Secretary of the Academy of Science at Paris, and members of the Philanthropic Society, because I considered it a document to which your color had a right, for their justification against the doubts which have been entertained of them.

I am, with great esteem, sir,

Your most obedient servant,
Thomas Jefferson

What of Banneker as a social being? He never married. So thoroughly devoted was he to science that the tender passion, love, never gained the mastery. He loved to live by himself, prepared his own food and washed his own clothes, and in other domestic necessities his wants were supplied by his sisters who lived near by.

A few anecdotes will shed a light on other traits in his character.

When he was no longer actively engaged in agriculture, he divided his holdings into smaller tenancies, but the tenants were not regular in their payments and they considered it a personal affront when he called on them for his rent; nevertheless, he was determined to provide for his maintenance, so he sold his land for an annuity based on the market value of the land and his expectancy of life, reserving a residence for himself for life. He lived eight years longer than his calculations, and therefore got not only the value of his land but a handsome advance on it.

Reference has been made to his abundant orchards. His pear trees were especially noted, and the smaller boys of those days, the great-grandfathers of those who live in our midst to-day, would steal the fruit while the old gentleman was intent on his astronomical calculations. Once when some boys were more persistent or bolder than usual he arose, left his table and coming to the door said, "Boys, you are perfectly welcome to one-half of the fruit if you will leave me the other." With that he returned to his room and resumed his studies. When he had occasion to come once more to the door, he found that the boys had left him the leaves.

He was a musician. Like that other great son of Maryland of three generations later, Frederick Douglass, he was a good violinist. Nothing was more common than to find him under his favorite tree at evening tide playing his violin.

He was not a member of any church, but the spirit of reverence for the Father of all pervades much of his writings. He frequently attended the meetings of the Society of Friends, during which he leaned on his staff in the spirit of humility and devotion.

There was nothing to indicate the slightest trace of white blood in his appearance. "In size and personal appearance," says one who remembered him as he appeared in the later years of his life, "the statue of Franklin at the library in Philadelphia as seen from the street is a perfect likeness of him. This likeness is heightened because he wore a superfine drab broadcloth suit made in the old style, plain coat with a straight collar, and long waistcoat and a broad-brimmed hat."

The excessive mental application, kept up with intensity for a score of years, told on his vigorous constitution and he became a victim to a complication of disorders, but his indomitable will added years to his life. He could not forego the pleasure of communing with nature under the open sky. It was during one of his walks one bright autumnal Sunday afternoon of 1804 that he complained of not feeling well; he returned to his cabin, became speechless, and in a few hours passed from contemplation of the terrestrial to an enjoyment of prospects celestial.

His surviving relatives promptly carried out the injunction he had given, of taking over to Mr. Ellicott all his books, mathematical instruments, and papers, as well as the oval table on which he made his calculations, almost as soon as the breath had left his body.

Two days later the last funeral rites were held. While these were in progress a fire consumed his house and everything that remained in it, including the wooden clock that first evidenced his mechanical skill and inventive genius.

Today his name is not more than a tradition; no headboard or other monument marks his final resting place, if even it be known.

In the Chautauqua for September, 1899, Gabriella Jacobs in winding up an article on "The Black Astronomer," says:

> Neither the site of his birthplace nor his grave was ever marked by a memorial. He was buried on the hillside near to his own property, but by a strange irony of fate, the exact location of his grave is now unknown.

She says in concluding:

> A public-school building for colored pupils in Washington, D. C., known as the Banneker School, is believed to be the only monument to the genius of the Negro who at the dawn of the nineteenth century foreshadowed the advancement of his race which marks the century's close.

Frederick Douglass
(See page 187.)

ESCAPE FROM SLAVERY [1]

In the first narrative of my experience in slavery, written nearly forty years ago, and in various writings since, I have given the public what I considered very good reasons for withholding the manner of my escape. In substance these reasons were, first, that such publication at any time during the existence of slavery might be used by the master against the slave, and prevent the future escape of any who might adopt the same means that I did. The second reason was, if possible, still more binding to silence—for publication of details would certainly have put in peril the persons and property of those

[1] From *The Life and Times of Frederick Douglass.* Reprinted by permission of Haley Douglass.

who assisted. Murder itself was not more sternly and certainly pun-
ished in the State of Maryland than was aiding and abetting the
escape of a slave. Many colored men, for no other crime than that of
giving aid to a fugitive slave, have, like Charles T. Torrey, perished
in prison. The abolition of slavery in my native State and throughout
the country, and the lapse of time, render the caution hitherto observed
no longer necessary. But, since the abolition of slavery, I have sometimes thought it well enough to baffle curiosity by saying that while
slavery existed there were good reasons for not telling the manner
of my escape, and since slavery had ceased to exist there was no reason
for telling it.

I shall now, however, cease to avail myself of this formula, and,
as far as I can, endeavor to satisfy this very natural curiosity. I should
perhaps have yielded to that feeling sooner, had there been anything
very heroic or thrilling in the incidents connected with my escape, for
I am sorry to say I have nothing of that sort to tell; and yet the courage
that could risk betrayal and the bravery which was ready to encounter
death if need be, in pursuit of freedom, were essential features in the
undertaking. My success was due to address rather than to courage;
to good luck rather than to bravery. My means of escape were provided for me by the very men who were making laws to hold and
bind me more securely in slavery. It was the custom in the State of
Maryland to require of the free colored people to have what were
called free papers. This instrument they were required to renew very
often, and by charging a fee for this writing, considerable sums from
time to time were collected by the State. In these papers the name, age,
color, height, and form of the free man were described, together with
any scars or other marks upon his person which could assist in his
identification.

This device of slaveholding ingenuity, like other devices of wicked-
ness, in some measure defeated itself—since more than one man
could be found to answer the same general description. Hence many
slaves could escape by personating the owner of one set of papers;
and this was often done as follows: A slave nearly or sufficiently
answering the description set forth in the papers, would borrow or

hire them till he could by their means escape to a free state, and then, by mail or otherwise, return them to the owner. The operation was a hazardous one for the lender as well as for the borrower. A failure on the part of the fugitive to send back the papers would imperil both the fugitive and his friend. It was therefore an act of supreme trust on the part of a freeman of color thus to put in jeopardy his own liberty that another might be free. It was, however, not infrequently bravely done, and was seldom discovered.

I was not so fortunate as to sufficiently resemble any of my free acquaintances as to answer the description of their papers. But I had one friend—a sailor—who owned a sailor's protection, which answered somewhat the purpose of free papers—describing his person and certifying to the fact that he was a free American sailor. The instrument had at its head the American eagle, which at once gave it the appearance of an authorized document. This protection did not, when in my hands, describe its bearer very accurately. Indeed, it called for a man much darker than myself, and close examination of it would have caused my arrest at the start. In order to avoid this fatal scrutiny on the part of the railroad official, I had arranged with Isaac Rolls, a hackman, to bring my baggage to the train just on the moment of starting, and jumped upon the car myself when the train was already in motion. Had I gone into the station and offered to purchase a ticket, I should have been instantly and carefully examined, and undoubtedly arrested. In choosing this plan upon which to act, I considered the jostle of the train, and the natural haste of the conductor in a train crowded with passengers, and relied upon my skill and address in playing the sailor as described in my protection to do the rest.

One element in my favor was the kind feeling which prevailed in Baltimore and other seaports at the time, towards "those who go down to the sea in ships." "Free trade and sailors' rights" expressed the sentiment of the country just then. In my clothing I was rigged out in sailor style. I had on a red shirt and a tarpaulin hat and black cravat, tied in sailor fashion, carelessly and loosely about my neck. My knowledge of ships and sailor's talk came much to my assistance, for

I knew a ship from stem to stern, and from keelson to cross-trees, and could talk sailor like an "old salt."

On sped the train, and I was well on the way to Havre de Grace before the conductor came into the Negro car to collect tickets and examine the papers of his Black passengers. This was a critical moment in the drama. My whole future depended upon the decision of this conductor. Agitated I was while this ceremony was proceeding, but still, externally at least, I was apparently calm and self-possessed. He went on with his duty—examining several colored passengers before reaching me. He was somewhat harsh in tone and peremptory in manner until he reached me, when, strangely enough, and to my surprise and relief, his whole manner changed. Seeing that I did not readily produce my free papers, as the other colored persons in the car had done, he said to me in a friendly contrast with that observed towards the others: "I suppose you have your free papers?" To which I answered, "No, sir; I never carry my free papers to sea with me."

"But you have something to show that you are a free man, have you not?"

"Yes, sir," I answered; "I have a paper with the American eagle on it, that will carry me round the world." With this I drew from my deep sailor's pocket my seaman's protection, as before described. The merest glance at the paper satisfied him, and he took my fare and went on about his business.

This moment of time was one of the most anxious I ever experienced. Had the conductor looked closely at the paper, he could not have failed to discover that it called for a very different looking person from myself, and in that case it would have been his duty to arrest me on the instant and send me back to Baltimore from the first station. When he left me with the assurance that I was all right, though much relieved, I realized that I was still in great danger: I was still in Maryland, and subject to arrest at any moment.

I saw on the train several persons who would have known me in any other clothes, and I feared they might recognize me, even in my sailor "rig," and report me to the conductor, who would then subject me to a closer examination, which I knew well would be fatal to me.

Though I was not a murderer fleeing from justice, I felt, perhaps, quite as miserable as such a criminal. The train was moving at a very high rate of speed for that time of railroad travel, but to my anxious mind, it was moving far too slowly. Minutes were hours, and hours were days during this part of my flight.

After Maryland I was to pass through Delaware—another slave State, where slave-catchers generally awaited their prey, for it was not in the interior of the State, but on its borders, that these human hounds were most vigilant and active. The borderlines between slavery and freedom were the dangerous ones for the fugitives. The heart of no fox or deer, with hungry hounds on his trail, in full chase, could have beaten more anxiously or noisily than did mine from the time I left Baltimore till I reached Philadelphia. The passage of the Susquehanna River at Havre de Grace was at that time made by ferry-boat, on board of which I met a young colored man by the name of Nichols, who came very near betraying me.

He was a "hand" on the boat, but instead of minding his business, he insisted upon knowing me, and asking me dangerous questions as to where I was going, and when I was coming back, etc. I got away from my old and inconvenient acquaintance as soon as I could decently do so, and went to another part of the boat. Once across the river I encountered a new danger.

Only a few days before I had been at work on a revenue cutter, in Mr. Price's shipyard, under the care of Captain McGowan. On the meeting at this point of the two trains, the one going South stopped on the track just opposite to the one going North, and it so happened that this Captain McGowan sat at a window where he could see me very distinctly, and would certainly have recognized me had he looked at me but for a second.

Fortunately, in the hurry of the moment, he did not see me, and the trains soon passed each other on their respective ways. But this was not the only hair-breadth escape. A German blacksmith, whom I knew well, was on the train with me, and looked at me very intently, as if he thought he had seen me somewhere before in his travels. I really believe he knew me, but had no heart to betray me. At any rate he saw me escaping and held his peace.

The last point of imminent danger, and the one I dreaded most, was Wilmington. Here we left the train and took the steamboat for Philadelphia. In making the change I again apprehended arrest, but no one disturbed me, and I was soon on the broad and beautiful Delaware, speeding away to the Quaker City. On reaching Philadelphia in the afternoon I inquired of a colored man how I could get on to New York. He directed me to the Willow Street Depot, and thither I went, taking the train that night. I reached New York Tuesday morning, having completed the journey in less than twenty-four hours. Such is briefly the manner of my escape from slavery—and the end of my experience as a slave.

Booker T. Washington

Booker Taliaferro Washington, educator, historian, orator, and essayist, was born in 1858 or 1859, a slave, near Hale's Ford, Franklin County, not far from Lynchburg, Virginia. He secured his education at Hampton Normal and Industrial Institute, working as a janitor for his board. For two years after his graduation he taught at Malden, West Virginia, return-

ing to Hampton as an instructor in 1879. In 1881 he was appointed organizer of Tuskegee Institute at Tuskegee, Alabama, remaining as its principal until his death in 1915. Mr. Washington, to promote the interests of this school and to establish better understanding between whites and Negroes, delivered many addresses throughout the United States. He was the great champion of industrial education and the accumulation of wealth by people of the colored race.

Among his publications are the following: *Up from Slavery, Speeches of Booker T. Washington, The Life of Frederick Douglass, The Future of the American Negro, The Story of My Life and Work,* and *The Man Farthest Down.*

HELPING OTHERS [1]

At the end of my first year at Hampton I was confronted with another difficulty. Most of the students went home to spend their vacation. I had no money with which to go home, but I had to go somewhere. In those days very few students were permitted to remain at the school during vacation. It made me feel very sad and homesick to see the other students preparing to leave and starting for home. I not only had no money with which to go home, but I had none with which to go anywhere.

In some way, however, I had gotten hold of an extra, second-hand coat which I thought was a pretty valuable coat. This I decided to sell, in order to get a little money for travelling expenses. I had a good deal of boyish pride, and I tried to hide, as far as I could, from the other students the fact that I had no money and nowhere to go. I made it known to a few people in the town of Hampton that I had this coat to sell, and, after a good deal of persuading, one colored man promised to come to my room to look the coat over and consider the matter of buying it. This cheered my drooping spirits considerably. Early the next morning my prospective customer appeared. After looking the garment over carefully, he asked me how much I wanted for it. I told him I thought it was worth three dollars. He seemed to agree with me as to price, but remarked in the most matter-of-fact way: "I tell you what I will do; I will take the coat, and I will pay you five cents, cash down, and pay you the rest of the money just as soon as I can get it." It is not hard to imagine what my feelings were at this time.

With this disappointment I gave up all hope of getting out of the town of Hampton for my vacation work. I wanted very much to go where I might secure work that would at least pay me enough to purchase some much-needed clothing and other necessities. In a few days practically all the students and teachers had left for their homes, and this served to depress my spirits even more.

After trying for several days in and near the town of Hampton, I finally secured work in a restaurant at Fortress Monroe. The wages, however, were very little more than my board. At night, and between meals, I found considerable time for study and reading; and in this direction I improved myself very much during the summer.

When I left school at the end of my first year, I owed the institution sixteen dollars that I had not been able to work out. It was my greatest ambition during the summer to save money enough with which to pay this debt. I felt that this was a debt of honor, and that I could hardly bring myself to the point of even trying to enter school again till it was paid. I economized in every way that I could think of—did my own washing, and went without necessary garments—but still I found my summer vacation ending and I did not have the sixteen dollars.

One day, during the last week of my stay in the restaurant, I found under one of the tables a crisp, new ten-dollar bill. I could hardly contain myself, I was so happy. As it was not my place of business I felt it to be the proper thing to show the money to the proprietor. This I did. He seemed as glad as I was, but he coolly explained to me that, as it was his place of business, he had a right to keep the money, and he proceeded to do so. This, I confess, was another pretty hard blow to me. I will not say that I became discouraged, for as I now look back over my life I do not recall that I ever became discouraged over anything that I set out to accomplish. I have begun everything with the idea that I could succeed, and I never had much patience with the multitudes of people who are always ready to explain why one cannot succeed. I have always had a high regard for the man who could tell me how to succeed. I determined to face the situation just as it was. At the end of the week I went to the treasurer of the Hampton Institute, General J. F. B. Marshall, and told him frankly my condition. To my gratification he told me that I could reënter the institution, and that he would trust me to pay the debt when I could. During the second year I continued to work as a janitor.

The education that I received at Hampton out of the textbooks was but a small part of what I learned there. One of the things that impressed itself upon me deeply, the second year, was the unselfishness of the teachers. It was hard for me to understand how any individuals could bring themselves to the point where they could be so happy in working for others. Before the end of the year, I think I began learning that those who are happiest are those who do the most for others. This lesson I have tried to carry with me ever since.

.   .   .   .

Perhaps the most valuable thing that I got out of my second year was an understanding of the use and value of the Bible. Miss Nathalie Lord, one of the teachers, from Portland, Maine, taught me how to use and love the Bible. Before this I had never cared a great deal about it, but now I learned to love to read the Bible, not only for the spiritual help which it gives, but on account of it as literature. The lessons taught me in this respect took such a hold upon me that at the present time, when I am at home, no matter how busy I am, I always make it a rule to read a chapter or a portion of a chapter in the morning, before beginning the work of the day.

Whatever ability I may have as a public speaker I owe in a measure to Miss Lord. When she found out that I had some inclination in this direction, she gave me private lessons in the matter of breathing, emphasis, and articulation. Simply to be able to talk in public for the sake of talking has never had the least attraction for me. In fact, I consider that there is nothing so empty and unsatisfactory as mere abstract public speaking; but from my early childhood I have had a desire to do something to make the world better, and then to be able to speak to the world about that thing.

.   .   .   .

At the end of my second year at Hampton, by the help of some money sent me by my mother and brother John, supplemented by a small gift from one of the teachers at Hampton, I was enabled to return to my home in Malden, West Virginia, to spend my vacation. . . . My mother and the other members of the family were, of course, much rejoiced to see me and to note the improvement that I had made during my two years' absence. The rejoicing on the part of all classes of the colored people, and especially the older ones, over my return, was almost pathetic. I had to pay a visit to each family and take a meal with each, and at each place tell the story of my experience at Hampton. In addition to this I had to speak before the church and Sunday School, and at various other places. The thing that I was most in search of, though, work, I could not find. There was no work on account of the strike.[1] . . .

Toward the end of the first month, I went to a place a considerable distance from my home, to try to find employment. I did not succeed, and it was night before I got started on my return. When I had gotten within a mile or so of my home I was so completely tired out that I could not walk any farther, and I went into an old, abandoned house to spend the remainder of the night. About three o'clock in the morning my brother John found me asleep in this house, and broke to me, as gently as he could, the sad news that our dear mother had died during the night.

This seemed to me the saddest and blankest moment in my life. For several years my mother had not been in good health, but I had no idea, when I parted from her the previous day, that I should never see her alive again. Besides that, I had always had an intense desire to be with her when she did pass away. One of the chief ambitions which spurred me on at Hampton was that I might be able to get to be in a position in which I could better make my mother comfortable and happy. She had so often expressed the wish that she might be permitted to live to see her children educated and started out into the world.

In a very short time after the death of my mother our little home was in confusion. My sister Amanda, although she tried to do the best she could, was too young to know anything about keeping house, and my stepfather was not able to hire a housekeeper. Sometimes we had food cooked for us, and sometimes we did not. I remember that more than once a can of tomatoes and some crackers constituted a meal. Our clothing went uncared for, and everything about our home was soon in a tumble-down condition. It seems to me that this was the most dismal period of my life.

My good friend Mrs. Ruffner always made me welcome at her home, and assisted me in many ways during this trying period. Before the end of the vacation she gave me some work, and this, to-

[1] A coal strike.

gether with work in a coal mine at some distance from my home, enabled me to earn a little money.

At one time it looked as if I would have to give up the idea of returning to Hampton, but my heart was so set on returning that I determined not to give up going back without a struggle. I was very anxious to secure some clothes for the winter, but in this I was disappointed, except for a few garments which my brother John secured for me. Notwithstanding my need of money and clothing, I was very happy in the fact that I had secured enough money to pay my travelling expenses back to Hampton.

W. Montague Cobb

Sometimes it is difficult to predict what an undergraduate will do. This was true of the long-distance runner, W. Montague Cobb, famous as an athlete in high school and college. After getting his preparatory training in the public schools of Washington, D. C., his native city, he went to Amherst College in Massachusetts, from which he received his Bachelor's and Master's degrees. The degree of Doctor of Medicine from Howard University was not sufficient; he next went to Western Reserve University, Cleveland, Ohio, from which he obtained the degree of Doctor of Philosophy in Anatomy.

A few years ago when he began a study of the collection of human skeletons at Western Reserve University, Washington University Medical School of St. Louis requested that Dr. Cobb include its collection of skeletons in his study.

Among his publications are *The First Negro Medical Society* (1884-1939) and many scientific articles in medical journals and in the *Journal of Physical Anthropology*.

DANIEL HALE WILLIAMS—PIONEER AND INNOVATOR [1]

Daniel Hale Williams (1856-1931), charter member of the American College of Surgeons, is becoming a tradition as the pioneer Negro

[1] From the *Journal of the National Medical Association*. Reprinted with the permission of the author.

surgeon. He is best known to the medical world and to the Negro people for his repair of a stab wound in which he sutured the pericardium, an operation which he affirmed in a carefully worded statement was "the first successful or unsuccessful case of suture of the pericardium that has ever been recorded." The enthusiasm of interested persons for directing attention to medical contributions by Negroes has resulted in wide publicity for this surgical repair as the first operation on the human heart, although only the sac in which the heart lies, and not the heart itself, was involved. Recent bibliographic research indicates, however, although Williams is not mentioned, that before Dr. Williams sutured the pericardium of James Cornish on July 10, 1893, no surgeon had operated upon either the human heart or the pericardium.

In present perspective, the emergency operation which brought Dr. Williams acclaim has greater significance than for its priority. It symbolized the courage, confidence, and competence which characterized an entire career. Here was a man called upon, without time for special preparation, to apply his surgical skill to a potentially fatal wound and about the most vital organ in the body. He did not hesitate, though he ventured where none had trod before. His account of his treatment is that of one who had mastered anatomy, technique, and physiologic principles and knew well how to apply them. Moreover, in the subsequent checking of his procedure by duplication of the wound on cadavera, we see the objective mind of the scientist at work, the quality of mind that has given to surgery men like Parr, Hunter, and Cushing.

This same courageous, assured ability is manifest in another dramatic phase of the too little known career of our distinguished surgeon.

Dr. Williams was Surgeon-in-Chief of Freedmen's Hospital at a time when the Negro public had not become accustomed to Negro physicians, as obtains today in many places, and had not learned to have full confidence in them. This was even more true in the case of the Negro surgeon. Many dreaded to cross the threshold of a hospital, any hospital. Often the mere thought of an operation tended to strike terror into the heart of a prospective subject and his relatives, and the approach of medical attendants could provoke screams.

Dr. Williams took the boldest and most thoroughgoing step possible for one who would combat this irrational fear. He threw open the doors of his operating room once a week to the public and said in effect, "Come watch us work, observe conditions, and see for yourselves that there is nothing to be afraid of."

It required courage thus to thrust aside convention. Only confidence would invite critical public inspection of the equipment, arrangements, routine, and decorum in the operating room. Surgical performance before all comers under definitely adverse circumstances bespeaks a cool competence which none ever dared deny.

For a number of Sunday afternoons at two o'clock, it was the privilege of any layman interested to watch a skilled Negro surgical team at work. The operations were performed in the amphitheater which had been built on to the rear of the old medical building. This building housed the Howard University medical, dental, and pharmaceutical schools, and the hospital administrative offices and internes. The patients were brought through a closed passageway from and to one of the adjacent frame hospital buildings. This surgical amphitheater was later used as the anatomical theater until the new medical building was opened in 1927. When the old building was remodeled, the site of Dr. Williams' historic experiment became part of the present dental infirmary.

It was not to be expected that so startling an innovation as public operations would fail to arouse powerful opposition. This opposition, indeed, appears eventually to have forced an end to what can be interpreted as a noble and far-sighted effort in public education.

We are thoroughly familiar with the custom of inviting the public in to see all the details of preparation of various products like food, pharmaceuticals, and cigarettes. One can watch, for example, the processing of meat from hoof to dealer, of vaccine from culture to phial, and of tobacco from leaf to sealed package. Some modern hotels have built their kitchens fully exposed to the view of diners, so that all may witness their cleanliness in the handling of food. One has to be sure that everything is above reproach to do this kind of thing.

In practically all of the Renaissance anatomical theaters, after which most surgical amphitheaters were patterned until very recent date, the public was usually permitted to witness the anatomical demonstration from the last two or three rows. A very large number of pictures by European artists attest the fact that surgical operations in Europe, from the fifteenth century to modern times, were by no means private proceedings. Modern magazines have been very successful in portraying the full details of surgical operations and surgical care in ways which add greatly to public enlightenment and enhance the prestige of the medical profession.

As to the objections to Dr. Williams' measure that it involved an invasion of the right of the patient to privacy, and that it constituted unethical self-advertisement, it may be answered first, that except for the small aperture in the sheets over the site of incision, there is practically no exposure of a patient prepared for a major operation. The patient is not recognizable to spectators. On the other hand, a layman should be greatly impressed with the professional dignity and extreme care for the patient which marks any properly conducted operation. No brief need be made for public operations as a general practice, but it must be admitted that Dr. Williams took the most direct and forceful means possible to destroy the public fear he faced. The charge of self-aggrandizement is petty, secondary, and impossible of verification, but if it could be proved true it would not detract from the fact of an excellence which invited critical attention of all comers.

Unfortunately, we do not have any statement of the objectives of the open surgical amphitheater by Dr. Williams himself, nor a comprehensive account of the reactions produced. It is to be hoped that biographic research may bring to light something of value in this connection. The few local witnesses available for any of these operations report the surgeon to have been a careful, undemonstrative worker and of few words, who impressed with his competence.

Details of the opposition also are not at hand. It is said that the performance of a curettage at one of the open periods was severely criticized as improper, and that the superintendent of nurses and operating room nurses finally refused to co-operate, bringing the series to a close. Available evidence is inadequate for appraisal of these aspects of the case. Basic issues are often beclouded by secondary considerations, but there is no room for doubt that Dr. Williams was a surgeon of significant stature.

The profession needs more men of his caliber with intelligence, skill, and the courage to pioneer and innovate. The Negro people can ill afford to temporize with mediocrity in high professional place. In 1943, Mr. Cornish, the patient of the famous operation, was presented at a memorial program to Dr. Williams. He had survived the surgery more than half a century and his surgeon more than a decade. May the memory of the surgeon's good works survive him indefinitely as an inspiration for medical progress.

Ralph W. Bullock

Ralph W. Bullock, biographer, is the National Boys' Work Secretary of the National Council of the Young Men's Christian Association.

CHARLES CLINTON SPAULDING [1]

From plowboy to president of a two and a quarter million dollar corporation is the story of the career of Charles Clinton Spaulding, president of the institution which he built up through years of patient work in a section where only distrust of Negro business enterprise had formerly prevailed.

Born on a small North Carolina farm, he manages today the largest going insurance company within the race, a company which paid $729,833 to policyholders last year [1926] while increasing its surplus to an amount exceeding $100,000. The company maintains an agency force of 450 workers in twelve states, with headquarters in its $250,000 modern, seven-story office building in Durham, North Carolina.

Charles Clinton Spaulding was born in Clarkton, North Carolina,

[1] From *In Spite of Handicaps,* by Ralph W. Bullock. Copyright, 1927, by Association Press, New York.

August 1, 1874. As soon as he was old enough to do a day's work in the field he was sent out with the rest of the boys to take his turn at the plow. But dissatisfaction with the dull routine of farm life early manifested itself, and at an early age he sought permission to join an uncle who was a graduate of the Leonard Medical College and was then practicing in Durham.

The late Dr. A. M. Moore was the uncle. Young Spaulding's first job in Durham was as a dishwasher in a hotel for ten dollars a month. He was soon promoted to be head bellboy and then side waiter, but finding that he could not attend school while holding down these jobs he took a position as a cook for Judge R. W. Winston, whom he served for two years while going to school.

Upon graduation from the Whitted graded school in 1898, he accepted a job as manager of a grocery company into which twenty-five of Durham's leading colored citizens had put ten dollars each. The company got into financial straits, the other members withdrew their investments, and then Spaulding was left with bare shelves and a $300 indebtedness. It took him five years to work out of it.

Just at this time Dr. Moore and John Merrick decided to make a second effort to launch an insurance company, and Spaulding was called in to help. With such funds as they could spare he managed the company, while serving as office boy, janitor, agent, and manager. He sold all the policies, collected all the premiums, and kept the records. Out of his travels over the state grew the structure of the North Carolina Mutual Life Insurance Company, founded in 1898.

Last year the company collected more than $2,000,000 in income. Its balance sheet shows assets of $300,000 in real estate, $900,000 in first mortgages to Negroes on real estate valued at more than $2,000,000, more than $200,000 in policy loans, and $350,000 in approved stocks and bonds. The cash item is $100,000.

Examiners of the insurance departments of three states have concurred in a report that the North Carolina Mutual Life Insurance Company is the only mutual life insurance company of any size in the entire state of North Carolina which is managed and owned exclusively by and for its policyholders.

Under President Spaulding are Dr. Clyde Donnell, medical director,

E. R. Merrick, treasurer, J. M. Avery, vice-president, and R. L. Mac-Dougald, vice-president, all of whom are members of the Company's board of directors.

Mr. Spaulding has mapped out a program of social service which stretches far beyond the ordinary routine functions of a business corporation. Employment is provided for hundreds, while, through its control of capital, it has been able, within the limits of safe investment and of sound financial policy, to finance the building of homes, the development of industries, and the general uplift of the race.

The organization of the medical department under Mr. Spaulding includes at the home office a morbidity, mortality, and life-extension service, while in the field a staff of 500 workers cooperate in the prevention of disease and premature death.

The life of Charles Clinton Spaulding tells a story of grim perseverance that lifted a boy from plow-hand on a farm to the presidency of a giant industry, simply because he refused to be downed. When his grocery venture failed and left him with a $300 indebtedness, he simply gathered himself together, started over again, and used the failure as a new point of departure for a career that was to prove far more remunerative and socially useful than his success as a grocery man could possibly have been.

Zora Neale Hurston
(See page 10.)

BACKSTAGE AND THE RAILROAD [1]

There is something about poverty that smells like death. Dead dreams dropping off the heart like leaves in a dry season and rotting around the feet; impulses smothered too long in the fetid air of under-

[1] From *Dust Tracks on a Road*, by Zora Neale Hurston. Copyright, 1942, by J. B. Lippincott Company, Philadelphia.

ground caves. The soul lives in a sickly air. People can be slave ships in shoes.

This wordless feeling went with me from the time I was ten years old until I achieved a sort of competence around twenty. Naturally, the first five years were the worst. Things and circumstances gave life a most depressing odor.

The five years following my leaving the school at Jacksonville were haunted. I was shifted from house to house of relatives and friends and found comfort nowhere. I was without books to read most of the time, except where I could get hold of them by mere chance. That left no room for selection. I was miserable, and no doubt made others miserable around me, because they could not see what was the matter with me, and I had no part in what interested them.

I was in school off and on, which gave me vagrant peeps into the light, but these intervals lacked peace because I had no guarantee that they would last. I was growing and the general thought was that I could bring in something. This book-reading business was a hold-back and an unrelieved evil. I could not do very much, but look at so-and-so. She was nursing for some good white people. A dollar a week and most of her clothes. People who had no parents could not afford to sit around on school benches wearing out what clothes they had.

One of the most serious objections to me was that having nothing, I still did not know how to be humble. A child in my place ought to realize I was lucky to have a roof over my head and anything to eat at all. And from their point of view, they were right. From mine, my stomach pains were the least of my suffering. I wanted what they could not conceive of. I could not reveal myself for lack of expression, and then for lack of hope of understanding, even if I could have found the words. I was not comfortable to have around. Strange things must have looked out of my eyes like Lazarus after his resurrection.

So I was forever shifting. I walked by my corpse. I smelt it and felt it. I smelt the corpses of those among whom I must live, though they did not. They were as much at home with theirs as death in a tomb.

Gradually, I came to the point of attempting self-support. It was a glorious feeling when it came to me. But the actual working out of the thing was not so simple as the concept. I was about fourteen then.

For one thing, I really was young for the try. Then my growth was retarded somewhat so that I looked younger than I really was. Housewives would open the door at my ring and look me over. No, they wanted someone old enough to be responsible. No, they wanted someone strong enough to do the work, and so on like that. Did my mother know I was out looking for work? Some times in bed at night I would ask myself that very question and wonder.

But now and then someone would like my looks and give me a try. I did very badly because I was interested in the front of the house, not in the back. No matter how I resolved, I'd get tangled up with their reading matter, and lose my job. It was not that I was lazy, I just was not interested in dusting and dishwashing. But I always made friends with the children if there were any. That was not intentional. We just got together somehow. That would be fun, but going out to play did not help much on jobs.

One woman liked me for it. She had two little girls, seven and five. I was hired as an upstairs maid. For two or three days things went on very well. The president of the kitchen was a fat, black old woman who had nursed the master of the house and was a fixture. Nobody is so powerful in a Southern family as one of these family fixtures. No matter who hires you, the fixture can fire you. They roam all over the house bossing everybody from the boss on down. Nobody must upset Cynthia or Rhoda or Beckey. If you can't get along with the house president you can't keep the job.

And Miz Cally was President in Full in this house. She looked at me cut-eye first thing because the madam had hired me without asking her about it. She went into her grumble just as soon as I stuck my head in the kitchen door. She looked at me for a moment with her hands on her hips and burst out, "Lawd a'mercy! Miz Alice must done took you to raise! She don't need no more young'uns around de place. Dis house needs a woman to give aid and assistance."

She showed her further disapproval by vetoing every move I made. She was to show me where to find the aprons, and she did. Just as soon as I pulled open the drawer, she bustled me right away from it with her hips.

"Don't you go pulling and hauling through my drawers! I keeps things in they place. You take de apron I give you and git on up dem stairs."

I didn't get mad with her. I took the apron and put it on with quite a bit of editing by Sister Cally, and went on up the back stairs. As I emerged on the upper floor, two pairs of gray-blue eyes were ranged on me.

"Hello!" said the two little girls in chorus. "Hello!" I answered back. "You going to work for us?" the taller one asked, and fell in beside me.

"Yeah." Maybe I cracked a smile or something, for both of them took a hand on either side and we went on into the room where Mrs. Alice was waiting for me to show me what to do and how to do it.

She was a very beautiful woman in her middle twenties, and she was combing out her magnificent hair. She looked at me through the looking-glass, and we both started to grin for some reason or another.

She showed me how to clean up and make beds. There were three rooms up there, but she told me not to try to do too much at a time. Just keep things looking sort of neat. Then she dressed and left the house. I got things straightened out with Helen and Genevieve acting as convoy at every step. Things went all right till I got to the bathroom, then somehow or other we three found ourselves in a tussle, screaming, laughing, splashing water and tussling, when a dark shadow filled up the door. Heinz could have wrung enough vinegar out of Cally's look to run his pickle works.

"You going 'way from here!" she prophesied, and shook her head so vigorously that her head rag wagged. She was going to get me gone from there!

"No!" screamed Helen, the littlest girl, and held on to me.

"No! No! No!" Genevieve shrieked.

"Humph! You just wait till yo' daddy come home!" Cally gloomed. "I ain't never seen no sich caper like dis since I been borned in dis world." Then she stumped on back downstairs.

"Don't you go," Genevieve begged. "I like you."

"Me too, I like you too," Helen chorused. "If you go home, we'll go with you."

I had to wait on the table at dinner that night, with my apron too long for me. Mrs. Alice and the children were giving a glowing account of me. The boss glanced at me tolerantly a time or two. Helen would grab hold of my clothes every time I passed her chair, and play in the vegetable dishes when I offered them to her, until her father threatened to spank her hands, but he looked up at me and smiled a little. He looked to me like an aged old soul of thirty-five or so.

Cally kept on cracking the kitchen door to see how I was getting along in there, and I suspect to give the boss a view of her disapproving face.

Things rocked on for a week or two. Mrs. Alice went out more and more to bridge clubs and things like that. She didn't care whether I made up the rooms or not so long as the children were entertained. She would come in late in the afternoon and tell Cally to run upstairs and straighten up a bit.

"What's dat gal been doing?" Cally would growl. Dat gal she was talking about had been off to the park with the children, or stretched out on the floor telling stories or reading aloud from some of their story books. Their mother had been free to go about her business, and a good time was had by all—except Cally.

Before a month passed, things came to a head: Cally burst into the dining-room one night and flew all over the place. The boss had to get somebody to do his cooking. She was tired of doing all the work. She just wasn't going to cook and look after things downstairs and then troop upstairs and do the work somebody else was getting paid for. She was old. Her joints hurt her so bad till she couldn't rest of nights. They really needed to get somebody to help.

Mrs. Alice sat there stark, still and quiet. The boss looked at her, then at old Cally, and then at me.

Finally, he said, "I never meant for you to work yourself down like that, Aunt Cally. You've done more than your share."

" 'Deed, Gawd knows I is!" Cally agreed belligerently, rolling her white eyeballs in my direction.

"Isn't Zora taking care of the upstairs? I thought that was what she was hired for," the boss asked, and looked at his wife.

"Taking care of what?" Cally snorted. " 'Deed, I ain't lying, Mr. Ed. I wouldn't tell a lie on nobody——"

"I know you wouldn't, Auntie," he soothed.

"Dat gal don't do a living thing round dis house but play all day long wid these young 'uns. Den I has to scuffle up dem stairs and do round, cause effen I didn't, dis here place would be like a hawg-pen. Dat's what it would. I has to go and do it, Mr. Ed, else it wouldn't never git done. And I'm sick and tired. I'm gwine 'way from here!"

"Naw, Cally, you can't do it. You been with me all my life, and I don't aim to let you go. Zora will have to go. These children are too big now to need a nurse."

What did he say that for? My public went into sound and action. Mrs. Alice was letting a tear or two slip. Otherwise she was as still as stone. But Helen scrambled out of her chair with her jaws latched back to the last notch. She stumbled up against me and swung on. Genevieve screamed, "No!" in a regular chant like a cheer leader, and ran to me, too. Their mother never raised her head. The boss turned to her.

"Darling, why don't you quiet these children?" he asked gently.

"No! No! No! Zora can't go!" my cheering squad yelled, slinging tears right and left.

"Shut up!" the boss grated at the children and put his hand on the table and scuffled his feet as if he meant to rush off for the hairbrush. "I'll be on you in one more minute! Hush!"

It was easy to see that his heart was not in any spanking. His frown was not right for it. The yelling kept right on. Cally flounced on back to the kitchen, and he got up and hauled the children upstairs. In a minute he called his wife and shut the bedroom door.

Well, then, I didn't have a job any more. I didn't have money either, but I had bought a pair of shoes.

But I was lucky in a way. Somebody told the woman I was staying with about another job, so I went to see about it, and the lady took me. She was sick in bed, and she had a little girl three years old, but this child did not shine like Helen and Genevieve. She was sort of old-looking in the face.

I didn't like that house. It frowned at me just as soon as I crossed the doorsill. It was a big house with plenty of things in it but the rooms just sat across the hall from each other and made gloomy faces back and forth.

I was soon out of a job again. I got out of many more. Sometimes I didn't suit the people. Sometimes the people didn't suit me. Sometimes my insides tortured me so that I was restless and unstable. I just was not the type. I was doing none of the things I wanted to do. I had to do numerous uninteresting things I did not want to do, and it was tearing me to pieces.

I wanted family love and peace and a resting place. I wanted books and school. When I saw more fortunate people of my own age on their way to and from school, I would cry inside and be depressed for days, until I learned how to mash down on my feelings and numb them for a spell. I felt crowded in on, and hope was beginning to waver.

PART V

The Essay

Introduction   In the year 1580, Michel de Montaigne published two volumes of *Essais*. These were expository compositions in which the author expressed his opinion upon various subjects, such as friendship, love, revenge, and dignity. This literary form created by Montaigne has been in vogue ever since. Following his illustrious beginning, there have been many distinguished essayists, among them Sir Francis Bacon, Thomas Babington Macaulay, Henry David Thoreau, Ralph Waldo Emerson, Charles Lamb, William Hazlitt, and Matthew Arnold. Since the Negro has had to struggle for physical freedom and intellectual freedom with greater persistency than other groups in America, he has had to think more about this problem than any other. As a result, he has regularly used the essay as a favorite literary form to express to the world his desire for equality of opportunity as vouched for by the Federal Constitution.

The American Negro has produced many controversial essayists of great power. Among the most noted of these are David Walker, Kelly Miller, and W. E. B. Du Bois. The two collections of essays by Du Bois, *Souls of Black Folk* and *Darkwater,* are as artistic as the best essays of any nation, race, or language. These essays are simple and yet profound; the language at times rises to the beauty and dignity of the best poetry. They lure the reader with an elusive charm because of their felicitous phrasing.

The Negro race has produced also good critical essayists. William Stanley Braithwaite, in his prefaces to his *Anthologies of Magazine Verse* and in his essay, "The Negro in American Literature," James Weldon Johnson in his Preface to the first edition of *The Book of American Negro Poetry,* and Benjamin G. Brawley in *The Negro in American Literature and Art,* prove themselves eminently to be masters of this literary form.

To aid the student, the writer will give a brief analysis of this type of composition. What is an essay? An essay is generally a prose type of composition in which the author presents facts concerning a particular subject and at the same time gives his opinion concerning that subject. If no opinion is expressed, there is no essay. In addition to this requirement, the essay is a type of composition that is supposed to be read silently, since it appeals chiefly to the intellect rather than to the emotions. The aim of the essay is not to entertain but to give information. These facts determine the style of the essay.

Since this is a literary form that is to be read silently, the fundamental principle that guides the essayist is clarity. The kinds of paragraphs that especially lend themselves to clearness are those developed by definition of the important terms, by use of examples, by cause and effect, and by particulars and details. In causal relation the paragraphs are developed from cause to effect, from effect to cause, and from effect to effect. These are the types of paragraphs that predominate in the essay, because they are peculiarly suited to making ideas clear. The essayist may use one of these methods of paragraph development, or in a single paragraph he may use a combination of methods.

A few of the paragraphs of Du Bois's essay in this volume, "Of the Faith of the Fathers," may be used as examples to illustrate this technique. For instance, the first paragraph is developed by a combination of methods, particulars, and comparison and contrast, with particulars or details dominating the paragraph. The next paragraph is also developed by a combination of methods, particulars, and examples, with examples dominating the thought. The third paragraph is a combination of cause and effect, particulars, and comparison and contrast. The next paragraph is developed from cause to effect. Finally, the paragraph beginning with the words "Moreover, the religious growth of millions of men" is developed from effect to cause. Note the predominance of particulars, examples, and cause and effect; the comparison and contrast, as a type of development, is subordinate or incidental.

The sentences of the essay are almost entirely declarative and just occasionally imperative, interrogative, or exclamatory, because the declarative sentence is the sentence best suited to conveying information; and the conveying of information is the chief purpose of the essay. The imperative sentence, the interrogative, and the exclamatory are designed to arouse the emotions, especially the imperative and the exclamatory sentences. The interrogative sentence is occasionally used to stimulate thinking, as is done by Du Bois in the fourth paragraph of "Of the Faith of the Fathers." The stirring of the emotions is the province of the speech, the address, or the oration; the essayist makes his appeal to the intellect.

Rhetorically, the sentences of the essay are naturally loose rather than periodic, with rare use of the balanced sentence. It is true that the style of Thomas De Quincey is chiefly periodic, which is unusual for the essayist. To make this point clear, the writer will explain for the student these three types of sentences. Examples of the loose and the periodic sentences are taken from Kelly Miller's essay appearing in this book, "The Farm—The Negro's Best Chance."

LOOSE SENTENCES

The vast majority of Negroes in the United States are engaged in agriculture, and in domestic and personal service.

Slavery was not continued in the North, because slave labor was too unprofitable in manufacturing pursuits.

The rigorous climate made their maintenance too expensive and crowding too many together in one plant tended to make their status insecure.

Definition.   The loose sentence is a sentence that places its main thought at the beginning or near the beginning. The italics show the main thought of each of the sentences listed above. By placing the main thought at the beginning of the sentence, the essayist has done his best to make his thought clear. If a reader cannot grasp the thought of a writer when he places the main idea at the beginning of the sentence, he certainly will not understand the thought if it is placed elsewhere in the sentence. Note that, in the case of the loose sentence, the reader might stop at two or more points in the sentence and yet have a complete thought. In the second sentence, for instance, the reader would get a complete thought if he stopped with the word "continued," "North," or "unprofitable."

PERIODIC SENTENCES

Broadly speaking, *manufacture, mechanical pursuits, trade and transportation are monopolized by white work folk*.

At the time the Negro was introduced into America, *agriculture constituted practically 100 per cent of all gainful occupations*.

In the border states of Missouri, Kentucky, Maryland, Delaware, and West Virginia, where cotton culture is of relatively small importance, *the Negro is an industrial asset of diminishing value*.

Definition. A comparison of these sentences, as to structure, with the loose sentences taken from this same essay shows a reversal of technique. In the periodic sentence the main thought is held in suspense until the reader comes to the end. By placing the main thought at the end of a sentence, the writer tends to arouse or increase the curiosity or interest of the reader. Thus the periodic sentence may be defined as one that holds the main thought in suspense until the reader comes to the end or nearly to the end. Generally the main thought is reached only at the end of the sentence.

BALANCED SENTENCES

Work in the *day; rest* at *night*.

Life is as *shallow* as foam; *death,* as *deep* as eternity.

A *glutton lives to eat;* but a *wise man eats to live*.

Definition. A perusal of these three sentences will cause one to note that each sentence is composed of two independent clauses. He will further observe that each sentence is constructed with contrasting thought: *work* and *rest; day* and *night; life* and *death; shallow* and *deep; glutton* and *wise man: lives to eat* and *eats to live*. A balanced sentence, therefore, may be defined as a sentence composed of two independent clauses—and only two—with ideas in contrast. It may contain dependent clauses, but never more than two independent clauses. This type of sentence is used only sparingly by the essayist; but it is used extensively by the orator.

TYPES OF ESSAYS

There are several classifications of the essay. According to one of these there are two kinds of essays: the formal and the informal. All the essays in this volume are formal. The essays of Emerson, Lowell, Carlyle, Macaulay, are formal. The formal essay is the essay with a logical procedure. According to this type, the writer will pass from one division to another of his subject and not return to a previous division that he has already discussed to give it further elaboration. On the other hand, the informal essay proceeds not logically but psychologically. It proceeds according to the moods of the essayist. After treating a division of a subject and discussing another division of the thought, the writer of the informal essay may return to a previous division and give it additional treatment.

The most distinguished master of the informal essay is Charles Lamb, the English humorist, who lived from 1775 to 1834. The best example of this type is his essay, "Old China." This begins and ends with a discussion of the author's joy as aroused by his ownership of chinaware; but that is not the theme of the essay. Instead of writing an essay on chinaware, he discusses at length his pleasures as a poor man contrasted with his joys as a man with a competence who is not compelled to stint. The essay proceeds according to his moods. He relates his personal experiences. He becomes familiar with his reader as he uses a conversational style. Since this is the method of the informal essayist, this type of essay has also been called the conversational essay, the familiar essay, or the personal.

The classification just considered, that of the formal and the informal essay, is based upon structure. Another classification is based upon subject matter, which is the classification employed in this volume: the literary, the critical, the sociological, the scientific, and the biographical. In this type of essay, the essayist will give a synopsis of his subject and his personal opinion concerning that subject. If the essay is of the critical type, the synopsis will usually be placed solidly at or near the beginning of the discourse. This is the general practice. However, the synopsis may be hidden in the essay by the interweaving of the synopsis and the opinion from the beginning of the essay to the end. This is the method of Bernice Y. Mitchell in "Colonel Charles Young." She does not give the account of the life of Colonel Young and then her analysis or interpretation of his life, but carries the two on together.

For additional information on the essay or any other type of literature discussed here, the writer recommends the use of some high-school or college rhetoric of recent date.

William Edward Burghardt Du Bois

William Edward Burghardt Du Bois, the sociologist, historian, essayist, editor, poet, writer of the short story, dramatist, novelist, and biographer, was born at Great Barrington, Massachusetts, February 23, 1868. He

received his training at Fisk University, Harvard, and the University of Berlin.

Dr. Du Bois served as Director of Publicity and Research and as Editor of the *Crisis* for the National Association for the Advancement of Colored People. He is the founder of the Pan-African Congress and is Director of Research for the Negro Encyclopedia for the Phelps Stokes Fund.

Among his publications are the following: *The Suppression of the African Slave Trade, The Philadelphia Negro, The Souls of Black Folk, John Brown, Darkwater, The Gift of the Black Folk, Dark Princess* (novel), *The Quest of the Silver Fleece* (novel), *The Negro, The Negro Then and Now, Dusk of Dawn* (autobiography), and *Black Reconstruction*.

OF THE FAITH OF THE FATHERS [1]

Those who have not witnessed the frenzy of a Negro revival in the untouched backwoods of the South can but dimly realize the religious feeling of the slave; as described, such scenes appear grotesque and funny, but as seen they are awful. Three things characterized this religion of the slave—the Preacher, the Music, and the Frenzy. The Preacher is the most unique personality developed by the Negro on American soil. A leader, a politician, an orator, a "boss," an intriguer, an idealist—all these he is, and ever, too, the center of a group of men, now twenty, now a thousand in number. The combination of a certain adroitness with deep-seated earnestness, of tact with consummate ability, gives him his pre-eminence, and helps him maintain it. The type, of course, varies according to time and place, from the West Indies in the sixteenth century to New England in the nineteenth, and from the Mississippi bottoms to cities like New Orleans or New York.

The Music of Negro religion is that plaintive rhythmic melody, with its touching minor cadences, which, despite caricature and defilement, still remains the most original and beautiful expression of human life and longing yet born on American soil. Sprung from the African forests, where its counterpart can still be heard, it was adapted, changed, and intensified by the tragic soul-life of the slave, until, under the stress of law and whip, it became the one true expression of a people's sorrow, despair, and hope.

Finally the Frenzy or "Shouting," when the Spirit of the Lord passed by, and, seizing the devotee, made him mad with supernatural joy, was the last essential of Negro religion and the one more devoutly believed in than all the rest. It varied in expression from the silent rapt countenance or the low murmur and moan to the mad abandon of physical fervor—the stamping, shrieking, and shouting, the rushing to and fro and wild waving of arms, the weeping and laughing, the vision and the trance. All this is nothing new in the world, but old as religion, as Delphi and Endor. And so firm a hold did it have on the Negro, that many generations firmly believed that without this visible

[1] From *The Souls of Black Folk,* by William Edward Burghardt Du Bois. Copyright, 1938, by A. C. McClurg & Company, Chicago, Ill.

manifestation of the God there could be no true communion with the Invisible.

These were the characteristics of Negro religious life as developed up to the time of Emancipation. Since under the peculiar circumstances of the black man's environment they were the one expression of his higher life, they are of deep interest to the student of his development, both socially and psychologically. Numerous are the attractive lines of inquiry that here group themselves. What did slavery mean to the African savage? What was his attitude toward the World and Life? What seemed to him good and evil, God and Devil? Whither went his longings and strivings, and wherefore were his heart-burnings and disappointments? Answers to such questions can come only from a study of Negro religion as a development, through its gradual changes from the heathenism of the Gold Coast to the institutional Negro church of Chicago.

Moreover, the religious growth of millions of men, even though they be slaves, cannot be without potent influence upon their contemporaries. The Methodists and Baptists of America owe much of their condition to the silent but potent influence of their millions of Negro converts. Especially is this noticeable in the South, where theology and religious philosophy are on this account a long way behind the North, and where the religion of the poor whites is a plain copy of Negro thought and methods. The mass of "gospel" hymns which has swept through American churches and well-nigh ruined our sense of song consists largely of debased imitations of Negro melodies made by ears that caught the jingle but not the music, the body but not the soul, of the Jubilee songs. It is thus clear that the study of Negro religion is not only a vital part of the history of the Negro in America, but no uninteresting part of American history.

The Negro church of today is the social center of Negro life in the United States, and the most characteristic expression of African character. Take a typical church in a small Virginia town: It is the "First Baptist"—a roomy brick edifice seating five hundred or more persons, tastefully finished in Georgia pine, with a carpet, a small organ, and stained-glass windows. Underneath is a large assembly room with benches. This building is the central club-house of a community of a thousand or more Negroes. Various organizations meet here—the church proper, the Sunday School, two or three insurance societies, women's societies, secret societies, and mass meetings of various kinds. Entertainments, suppers, and lectures are held, besides the five or six regular weekly religious services. Considerable sums of money are collected and expended here, employment is found for the idle, strangers are introduced, news is disseminated and charity distributed. At the same time this social, intellectual, and economic center is a religious center of great power. Depravity, Sin, Redemption, Heaven, Hell, and Damnation are preached twice a Sunday with much fervor, and revivals take place every year after the crops are laid by; and few indeed of the community have the hardihood to withstand conversion. Back of this more formal religion, the Church often stands as a real conserver of morals, a strengthener of family life, and the final authority on what is Good and Right.

Thus one can see in the Negro church today, reproduced in microcosm, all that great world from which the Negro is cut off by color prejudice and social condition. In the great city churches the same tendency is noticeable and in many respects emphasized. A great church like the Bethel of Philadelphia has over eleven hundred members, an edifice seating fifteen hundred persons and valued at one hundred thousand dollars, an annual budget of $5000 [as of 1903], and a government consisting of a pastor with several assisting local preachers, an executive and legislative board, financial boards and tax collectors; general church meetings for making laws; sub-divided groups led by class leaders, a company of militia, and twenty-four auxiliary societies. The activity of a church like this is immense and far-reaching, and the bishops who preside over these organizations throughout the land are among the most powerful Negro rulers in the world.

Such churches are really governments of men, and consequently a little investigation reveals the curious fact that, in the South at least, practically every American Negro is a church member. . . .

Such, then, is the large development of the Negro church since Emancipation. The question now is, What have been the successive steps of this social history and what are the present tendencies? First, we must realize that no such institution as the Negro church could rear itself without definite historical foundations. These foundations we can find if we remember that the social history of the Negro did not start in America. He was brought from a definite social environment— the polygamous clan life under the headship of the chief and the potent influence of the priest. His religion was nature-worship, with profound belief in invisible surrounding influences, good and bad, and his worship was through incantation and sacrifice.

The first rude change in this life was the slave ship and the West Indian sugar-fields. The plantation organization replaced the clan and tribe, and the white master replaced the chief with far greater and more despotic powers. Forced and long-continued toil became the rule of life, the old ties of blood relationship and kinship disappeared, and instead of the family appeared a new polygamy and polyandry, which, in some cases, almost reached promiscuity.

It was a terrific social revolution, and yet some traces were retained of the former group life, and the chief remaining institution was the Priest or Medicine-man. He early appeared on the plantation and found his function as the healer of the sick, the interpreter of the Unknown, the comforter of the sorrowing, the supernatural avenger of wrong, and the one who rudely but picturesquely expressed the longing, disappointment, and resentment of a stolen and oppressed people. Thus, as bard, physician, judge, and priest, within the narrow limits allowed by the slave system, rose the Negro preacher, and under him the first Afro-American institution, the Negro church. This church was not at first by any means Christian nor definitely organized; rather it was an adaptation and mingling of heathen rites among the members of each plantation, and roughly designated as Voodooism. Association with the masters, missionary effort and motives of expediency gave these rites an early veneer of Christianity, and after the lapse of many generations the Negro church became Christian.

Two characteristic things must be noticed in regard to this church. First, it became almost entirely Baptist and Methodist in faith; secondly, as a social institution it antedated by many decades the monogamic Negro home. . . . Today the Baptist Church is still largest in membership among Negroes, and has a million and a half communicants.

Next in popularity came the churches organized in connection with the white neighboring churches, chiefly Baptist and Methodist, with a few Episcopalian and others. The Methodists still form the second greatest denomination, with nearly a million members. The faith of these two leading denominations was more suited to the slave church from the prominence they gave to religious feeling and fervor. The Negro membership in other denominations has always been small and relatively unimportant, although the Episcopalians and Presbyterians are gaining among the more intelligent classes today and the Catholic Church is making headway in certain sections. After Emancipation, and still earlier in the North, the Negro churches largely severed such affiliations as they had had with the white churches, either by choice or by compulsion. The Baptist churches became independent, but the Methodists were compelled early to unite for purposes of episcopal government. This gave rise to the great African Methodist Church, the greatest Negro organization in the world, to the Zion Church and the Colored Methodist, and to the black conferences and churches in this and other denominations.

The second fact noted, namely, that the Negro church antedates the Negro home, leads to an explanation of much that is paradoxical in this communistic institution and in the morals of its members. But especially it leads us to regard this institution as peculiarly the expression of the inner ethical life of a people in a sense seldom true elsewhere. . . .

By the middle of the eighteenth century the black slave had sunk, with hushed murmurs, to his place at the bottom of a new economic system, and was unconsciously ripe for a new philosophy of life. Nothing suited his condition then better than the doctrines of passive submission embodied in the newly learned Christianity. Slave masters early realized this and cheerfully aided religious propaganda within certain bounds. The long system of repression and degradation of the Negro tended to emphasize the elements in his character which made him a valuable chattel: courtesy became humility, moral strength degenerated into submission, and the exquisite native appreciation of the beautiful became an infinite capacity for dumb suffering.

The Negro, losing the joy of this world, eagerly seized upon the offered conceptions of the next; the avenging Spirit of the Lord enjoining patience in this world, under sorrow and tribulation until the Great Day when He should lead His dark children home—this became his comforting dream. His preacher repeated the prophecy, and his bards sang,

> Children, we all shall be free
> When the Lord shall appear!

This deep religious fatalism, painted so beautifully in "Uncle Tom," came soon to breed, as all fatalistic faiths will, the sensualist side by side with the martyr. Under the lax moral life of the plantation, where marriage was a farce, laziness a virtue, and property a theft, a religion of resignation and submission degenerated easily, in less strenuous minds, into a philosophy of indulgence and crime. Many of the worst characteristics of the Negro masses of today had their seed in this period of the slave's ethical growth. Here it was that the Home was ruined under the very shadow of the Church, white and black; here habits of shiftlessness took root, and sullen hopelessness replaced hopeful strife.

With the beginning of the abolition movement and the gradual growth of a class of free Negroes came a change. We often neglect the influence of the freedman before the war, because of the paucity of his numbers and the small weight he had in the history of the nation. But we must not forget that his chief influence was internal—was exerted on the black world; and that there he was the ethical and social leader. Huddled as he was in a few centers like Philadelphia, New York, and New Orleans, the masses of the freedmen sank into poverty and listlessness; but not all of them. The free Negro leader early arose, and his chief characteristic was intense earnestness and deep feeling on the slavery question. Freedom became to him a real thing and not a dream. His religion became darker and more intense, and into his ethics crept a note of revenge, into his songs a day of reckoning close at hand. The "Coming of the Lord" swept this side of Death, and came to be a thing to be hoped for in this day. Through fugitive slaves and irrepressible discussion this desire for freedom seized the black millions still in bondage, and became their one ideal of life. The black bards caught new notes, and sometimes even dared to sing,

> O Freedom, O Freedom, O Freedom over me!
> Before I'll be a slave
> I'll be buried in my grave,
> And go home to my Lord
> And be free.

For fifty years Negro religion thus transformed itself and identified itself with the dream of Abolition, until that which was a radical fad in the white North and an anarchistic plot in the white South had become a religion to the black world. Thus, when Emancipation finally came, it seemed to the freedman a literal Coming of the Lord. His fervid imagination was stirred as never before, by the tramp of armies, the blood and dust of battle, and the wail and whirl of social upheaval. He stood dumb and motionless before the whirlwind: What had he to do with it? Was it not the Lord's doing, and marvelous in his eyes? Joyed and bewildered with what came, he stood awaiting new wonders till the inevitable Age of Reaction swept over the nation and brought the crisis of today.

It is difficult to explain clearly the present critical stage of Negro religion. First, we must remember that living as the blacks do in close contact with a great modern nation, and sharing, although imperfectly, the soul-life of that nation, they must necessarily be affected more or less directly by all the religious and ethical forces that are today moving the United States. These questions and movements are, however, overshadowed and dwarfed by the (to them) all-important question of their civil, political, and economic status. They must perpetually discuss the "Negro Problem"—must live, move, and have their being in it, and interpret all else in its light or darkness. With this come, too, peculiar problems of their inner life—of the status of women, the maintenance of home, the training of children, the accumulation of wealth, and the prevention of crime. All this must mean a time of intense ethical ferment, of religious heart-searching and intellectual unrest. From the double life every American Negro must live, as a Negro and as an American, as swept on by the current of the nineteenth while yet struggling in the eddies of the fifteenth century

—from this must arise a painful self-consciousness, an almost morbid sense of personality and a moral hesitancy which is fatal to self-confidence. The worlds within and without the Veil of Color are changing, and changing rapidly, but not at the same rate, not in the same way; and this must produce a peculiar wrenching of the soul, a peculiar sense of doubt and bewilderment. Such a double life, with double thoughts, double duties, and double social classes, must give rise to double words and double ideals, and tempt the mind to pretense or to revolt, to hypocrisy or to radicalism.

·   ·   ·   ·

Today the two groups of Negroes, the one in the North, the other in the South, represent these divergent ethical tendencies, the first tending toward radicalism, the other toward hypocritical compromise. It is no idle regret with which the white South mourns the loss of the old-time Negro—the frank, honest, simple old servant who stood for the earlier religious age of submission and humility. With all his laziness and lack of many elements of true manhood, he was at least open-hearted, faithful, and sincere. Today he is gone, but who is to blame for his going? Is it not those very persons who mourn for him? Is it not the tendency, born of Reconstruction and Reaction, to found a society on lawlessness and deception, to tamper with the moral fiber of a naturally honest and straightforward people until the whites threaten to become ungovernable tyrants and the blacks criminals and hypocrites?

Deception is the natural defense of the weak against the strong, and the South used it for many years against its conquerors; today it must be prepared to see its black proletariat turn that same two-edged weapon against itself. And how natural this is! The death of Denmark Vesey and Nat Turner proved long since to the Negro the present hopelessness of physical defense. Political defense is becoming less and less available, and economic defense is still only partially effective. But there is a patent defense at hand—the defense of deception and flattery, of cajoling and lying. It is the same defense which the Jews of the Middle Ages used and which left its stamp on their character for centuries.

Today the young Negro of the South who would succeed cannot be frank and outspoken, honest and self-assertive, but rather he is daily tempted to be silent and wary, patient and sly; he must flatter and be pleasant, endure petty insults with a smile, shut his eyes to wrong; in too many cases he sees positive personal advantage in deception and lying. His real thoughts, his real aspirations, must be guarded in whispers; he must not criticize, he must not complain. Patience, humility, and adroitness must, in these growing black youth, replace impulse, manliness and courage. With this sacrifice there is an economic opening, and perhaps peace and some prosperity. Without this there is riot, migration, or crime. Nor is this situation peculiar to the Southern United States; is it not rather the only method by which undeveloped races have gained the right to share modern culture? The price of culture is a Lie.

On the other hand, in the North the tendency is to emphasize the radicalism of the Negro. Driven from his birthright in the South by a situation at which every fiber of his more outspoken and assertive nature revolts, he finds himself in a land where he can scarcely earn a decent living amid the harsh competition and the color discrimination. At the same time, through schools and periodicals, discussions and lectures, he is intellectually quickened and awakened. The soul, long pent up and dwarfed, suddenly expands in new-found freedom. What wonder that every tendency is to excess—radical complaint, radical remedies, bitter denunciation or angry silence. Some sink, some rise. The criminal and the sensualist leave the church for the gambling-hell and the brothel, and fill the slums of Chicago and Baltimore; the better classes segregate themselves from the group-life of both white and black, and form an aristocracy, cultured but pessimistic, whose bitter criticism stings while it points out no way of escape. They despise the submission and subserviency of the Southern Negroes, but offer no other means by which a poor and oppressed minority can exist side by side with its masters. Feeling deeply and keenly the tendencies and opportunities of the age in which they live, their souls are bitter at the fate which drops the Veil between; and the very fact that this bitterness is natural and justifiable only serves to intensify it and make it more maddening.

Between the two extreme types of ethical attitude which I have thus sought to make clear wavers the mass of the millions of Negroes, North and South; and their religious life and activity partake of this social conflict within their ranks. Their churches are differentiating —now into groups of cold, fashionable devotees, in no way distinguishable from similar white groups save in color of skin; now into large social and business institutions catering to the desire for information and amusement of their members, warily avoiding unpleasant questions both within and without the black world, and preaching in effect if not in word, *Dum vivimus, vivamus.*[1]

But back of this still broods silently the deep religious feeling of the real Negro heart, the stirring, unguided might of powerful human souls who have lost the guiding star of the past and are seeking in the great night a new religious ideal.

Lorenzo Johnston Greene

Lorenzo Johnston Greene, the historian, was born at Ansonia, Connecticut. His degree of Bachelor of Arts is from Howard University. He obtained the degrees of Master of Arts and Doctor of Philosophy from Columbia University. For three years he served as research assistant to Dr. Carter G. Woodson, Editor of the *Journal of Negro History*. Dr. Greene, who also served as a member of President Hoover's Committee on Negro Housing, is now Professor of History at Lincoln University, Jefferson City, Missouri.

Dr. Greene in 1949 became the editor of *The Midwest Journal,* a publication of the Lincoln University Press, Jefferson City, Mo. He is frequently sought as a speaker to address study groups, interracial groups, and college audiences on the history of the Negro not only in America but in other parts of the world.

Among his publications are the following: *The Negro Wage Earner,* with Dr. Carter G. Woodson as co-author; *Negro Employment in the District of Columbia,* with Myra Colson Callin as co-author; *The Negro in Colonial New England, 1620-1776.*

1 While we are alive, let us live.

SLAVE OCCUPATIONS [1]

The relatively small number of Negroes in New England during the colonial period raises the question of their economic importance. The answer is to be sought in the occupational development of this section and in the extent to which Negro slaves proved adequate to its labor demands. This was an important consideration, for New England's economy was necessarily diversified. A harsh climate, unfavorable topography, and, with few exceptions, thin, stony soil, prevented large-scale agriculture, and thus precluded the amassing of wealth from the land as in the middle and southern colonies. While Virginia and Carolina planters depended upon tobacco and rice as cash crops, New England settlers raised a variety of products, chiefly vegetables, forage crops, fruits, horses, cattle, and sheep. Farms, except in southern Rhode Island and eastern Connecticut, were relatively small. Even with hard labor most of the farmers eked out little more than a bare subsistence. Anything beyond this level had to come from sources other than agriculture. But these sources were not lacking. New England was blessed with abundant forests and numerous harbors, while off its coasts were the greatest fishing grounds in the world. Recognizing these opportunities, ambitious Yankees early turned to fishing, whaling, and commerce. Shipbuilding developed, and in time small manufactories, ranging from rum distilleries to iron forges, sprang up. The opulence that the plantation barons obtained from their extensive domains, the enterprising New Englanders secured largely from maritime pursuits and from the slave trade.

There was a great demand for workers in these industries, and laborers, skilled and unskilled, were needed for work on farms, in homes, shops, factories, shipyards, and on fishing and trading ships. Free labor was scarce and wages were high. Neither white indentured servants nor Indian slaves, both of whom were employed throughout the colonial period, could supply the much-needed workmen. It was primarily to furnish laborers that Negro slaves were brought into New England. They were introduced to satisfy not a specific but a general

---

[1] From *The Negro in Colonial New England, 1620-1776,* by Lorenzo Johnston Greene. Copyright, 1942, by Columbia University Press, New York.

need. To meet the demands of New England's diversified economy, the slave had to be more skilled and more versatile than the average plantation Negro accustomed to the routine cultivation of a single crop. The New England slave had to be equally at home in the cabbage patch and in the cornfield; he must be prepared (as will be demonstrated) not only to care for stock, to act as servant, repair a fence, serve on board ship, shoe a horse, print a newspaper, but even to manage his master's business.

The impression, nevertheless, has prevailed that because of adverse geographic and economic conditions slave labor was of little value to New England masters. This notion was expressed by several contemporary New Englanders. In 1708, for example, Governor Dudley of Massachusetts—in spite of the steady importation of Negroes into that colony—informed the British Board of Trade that the long winters kept the slaves idle during half the year. . . .

The facts, however, do not support these conclusions. Negroes were identified with every phase of New England's economy and, as a consequence, slave labor was highly diversified. The very character of New England's economic development rendered inevitable a variety of slave occupations. Naturally employment of the slaves depended upon the business of their masters, and Negroes accordingly were taught and followed whatever calling their owners pursued, whether farming, lumbering, trading, fishing, whaling, manufacturing or privateering.

Since colonial New England was fundamentally agricultural, a large proportion of the slaves worked on the farms. Instead of being employed extensively (as were the plantation blacks) in the cultivation of staples, like tobacco, rice, and indigo, New England Negroes were used in smaller numbers in the production of foodstuffs, forage crops, dairy products, and in the raising of livestock, although flax, hemp, and tobacco were also grown by slave labor in the New England colonies.

Contemporary newspapers offer abundant evidence regarding the agricultural employment of New England slaves. Advertisements described Negroes: "brought up in husbandry," "fit for town or country," "understanding the farming business exceedingly well," or as familiar "with all sorts of husbandry."

THE SLAVE FAMILY [1]

The personality of the New England slaves is also revealed by their marital relationships. As members of the Puritan family, they assimilated the manners and customs of their masters. This process was accelerated by the peculiar nature of the domestic institutions of colonial New England. Among the Puritans, the family was the fundamental unit, economically and socially, and preservation of its integrity was of paramount importance for it served as the chief means of perpetuating Puritan ideals and culture. Much of the responsibility for insuring the stability of the family fell upon the male head. The father, in accordance with Hebraic tradition, exercised considerable control over everyone who dwelt under his roof—whether wife, minor children, servants or slaves. Supplementing the paternal authority, as well as protecting the family from demoralizing influences, were the pronouncements of the Puritan legal code. Offenses against parental authority were capital crimes. Sons who rebelled against their fathers and children who cursed or struck their parents were to be put to death. . . .

Marriage was rigidly controlled. In an endeavor to rid themselves of Popish and Anglican influence the Puritans decreed that marriage was a civil contract. The Founding Fathers recognized no scriptural warrant for the performance of marriage by clergymen: marriage was concerned with business and property and was therefore the proper function of the magistrate and not the minister. For this reason up to 1686 clergymen were forbidden to perform the wedding ceremony in New England. Mutual consent of both parties was required before the marriage could take place. Furthermore, all the New England colonies required that wedding banns either be read at three public meetings or be posted in a public place at least fourteen days before

[1] From *The Negro in Colonial New England, 1620-1776,* by Lorenzo Johnston Greene. Copyright, 1942, by Columbia University Press, New York.

the wedding. These regulations applied to black as well as white persons, slaves as well as freemen. As a member of such a community the Negro was forced to revise the ideas, attitudes, and practices regarding marriage and sex relationship which he had brought from Africa, and to adopt those of the master class.

As a result, instead of the loose sexual relations generally characteristic of the plantation Negroes, New England slaves were compelled to marry in the manner prescribed for the general population. Once married, moreover, they were expected—as were free white persons —to observe the sanctity of the nuptial tie. The Puritans could not with consistency deny marriage to their slaves, for the Negroes were constant witnesses of the stringent efforts made by the master class to punish immorality. To withhold marriage from the slaves would have been demoralizing to the master's household; for the New England Negroes came into unusually close contact with the master's family and ordinarily lived in the same house with their owner. Furthermore, the general laws regulating marriage and sex relations could easily be applied to Negroes, because they not only constituted a small minority of the population but were largely concentrated in the towns.

Marriages amongst the blacks, accordingly, were duly solemnized and recorded in the same manner as those of white persons.

Kelly Miller

Kelly Miller, essayist and educator, was born at Winnsboro, South Carolina, July 3, 1863. He was educated at Howard and Johns Hopkins Universities, obtaining the degree of Master of Arts from Johns Hopkins in 1889. At Howard he taught mathematics, and served there also as Dean of the College of Liberal Arts.

Among his publications are the following: *Race Adjustment, Out of the House of Bondage, The Appeal To Conscience, The Everlasting Stain.* He contributed many articles to the *Atlantic Monthly* and other magazines.

THE FARM—THE NEGRO'S BEST CHANCE [1]

The vast majority of Negroes in the United States are engaged in agriculture and in domestic and personal service. Comparatively few of those listed in gainful pursuits are found outside of these lines. Broadly speaking, manufacture, mechanical pursuits, trade, and transportation are monopolized by white work folk. The few Negroes found in professional service depend vicariously upon the toiling masses below.

At the time the Negro was introduced into America, agriculture constituted practically 100 per cent of all gainful occupations. His chief function was to do the rough work of the field and relieve the white mistress of domestic drudgery. These have constituted his chief functions in the industrial scheme from the beginning until now. The bulk of the race was planted and has continued in the South for climatic and agricultural reasons. The farm did not flourish so well in the colder regions of the North, which early took to manufacture as its chief line of industry.

Slavery was not continued in the North because slave labor was too unprofitable in manufacturing pursuits. The rigorous climate made their maintenance too expensive and crowding too many together on one plantation tended to make their status insecure. The rise of abolitionism in the North did not grow out of humanitarian considerations; it was purely an economic by-product. When slavery began to be unprofitable it was soon looked upon as being immoral. But the conscience of the pocketbook was not limited to the North. When Thomas Jefferson, George Washington, George Mason, and their fellow Virginia planters found on their hands a large number of unprofitable slaves, they sought to get rid of them as an easement of conscience. Sir Harry Johnston tells us that the last three hundred years of human slavery would be reenacted today if man found it profitable to do so.

The abolition movement in the South was short-lived and quickly brought to an end by Eli Whitney's cotton gin, which enhanced the value of the culture of cotton. The looms of England called for an unlimited supply of the silver fleece. The virgin soil of the lower South-

[1] Copyright, 1935, by *Opportunity, Journal of Negro Life.*

ern states was requisitioned to meet this demand. The surplus slaves of Virginia were sent into this new territory. The Yankee ingenuity of New England built ships and captured African savages for Southern planters. Thus the Negro was settled in the rich cotton lands of the South, where the bulk of the race remains until this day. King Cotton cannot thrive without the Negro cotton picker. The function of the Negro in the industrial world rises and falls with the fate of cotton. He has never made much headway outside of this narrow agricultural field. In the border states of Missouri, Kentucky, Maryland, Delaware, and West Virginia, where cotton culture is of relatively small importance, the Negro is an industrial asset of diminishing value. Those found in these non-cotton states are for the most part centered in the large cities, where they function chiefly in domestic and personal service.

• • • •

Two fifths of the Negro population are now in the cities and subject to the necessitous conditions above described. I do not contend that these as a whole should return to the farm. The rural contingent have become accustomed to all lines of available work however humble; the city contingent has become so available only by the sternest compulsion. They are so effeminated in mind and body by urban influences that they do not possess the virility, the stubbornness of spirit, the hardihood of purpose to grapple with crude agricultural conditions. They would be of no service to the farm should they return. One half of the Negroes in the cities who are now on the relief rolls are being so weakened in initiative and enterprise that they are not calculated to be of any great service to city or country. The cities must grapple with this problem as best they can.

I plead mainly for those Negroes who are now on the farm and by force of circumstances are compelled to remain there. The cities already have as many Negroes as they can hold in solution without a dangerous precipitation.

The lot of the farmer is a hard one; for this reason the farm has been deserted during the past four or five decades to build up our great cities. Nearly sixty per cent of the American people are found in urban centers and the tendency is still city-ward. Negroes have followed in this movement out of sheer imitation, without understanding the underlying reason. White men and women abandon the farm in quest of better urban occupational opportunity. The essential function of the country is to produce raw material—food, fuel, and fiber. The chief function of the city is to manufacture and refine this raw material and make it available for ready use, and to redistribute it. The white race has all but monopolized the process of manufacture, trade, and transportation. The ascendancy of manufacture over agriculture is shown by the fact that the urban population has far outstripped the rural during the past half-century.

There are many more workers in manufacture than in agriculture. The white worker leaves the farm for the city in quest of more remunerative and attractive employment. On the other hand, when the Negro workman quits the farm he has no such assurance. The farm is still his best chance. On the farm the races are essentially on a parity; mother earth yields as readily and as abundantly to the persuasion of the black as of the white tiller. The markets are wholly without race prejudice; the black producer receives as much for his produce as his white competitor. But when the two leave the farm and go to the city, the white man gains a tremendous advantage by the change, while the Negro is more likely to lose. For example, of two farm hands, one white and the other black, the former might receive a few dollars a month more than his black co-worker; but when the two transfer to the city, the white worker can easily secure a position paying him two or three times as much as his former black fellow laborer. The Negro, therefore, need not be so much influenced by the example of the whites who are leaving the farm and going to the cities. The fact that the whites are abandoning the farms gives the Negro his chief opportunity.

N. B. Young

N. B. Young, lawyer, historian, and journalist, was born at Tuskegee, Alabama. He was educated at the Florida Agricultural and Mechanical College at Tallahassee, Florida, and Yale University. His law degree is from Yale.

For many years he served as editor of the *Saint Louis American*. He is the author of several short stories that appeared in the *Crisis*. He is also the author of a pictorial history of the Negro in Saint Louis, *Your St. Louis and Mine*.

THE GENEALOGY OF AN AMERICAN CHAMPION

It took four hundred years to make an American Champion.

The soil, the sun, the rain, the field rocks, the long-leaf pines and the scrub oaks, the winds blown up from the warm Gulf, all these, and the seasons, the equinoctial wet spells, the weeks of parched grasses, the dank swamp nights, the year of the New Madrid earthquakes, all these, and the rash men—the Aborigines, the Conquistadors,[1] the Tennesseeans and the African chiefs, all these, and the Declaration of Independence, the insurrection at Harpers Ferry, the fifth day after Antietam, the six years after Sarajevo, all these, and—the 13th day of May, 1914—all are in the direct lineage of the American Champion.

The Champion has a name, everybody now knows it, and still the name they all know is not his right name, his real name, his full name. His complete name goes like this: Mr. De Soto Tuscaloosa Nicholas Perkins Tecumseh Andrew Jackson Farragut Booker Washington Cudjoe. For short, call him plain Cudjoe or even just 'Joe. Yes, it took nearly four hundred years to get this Champion set upon his American pedestal and crowned. It was a masterful piece of creation, and could happen only in the United States. But the incredible thing is that it happened, of all places, in Alabama!

[1] Conquistador, any one of the leaders of the Spanish conquerors.

And only the God Almighty was capable of creating such a Champion. There are no archives, no genealogical records, no ancient tombstones, no gracious and patriotic ladies' society existent to base this pedigree upon——none except what those Alabama red hills and sandy loam bottoms offer in mute testimony; none but what the spray over Mobile Bay and the congress of crows on the bank of the Chattahoochee have passed down to their feathered generations. It requires some such divination as these wiser birds have suggested. For an American Champion to spring from the bounds of Alabama was perhaps meet but still is incredible.

So here is set down the pedigree of an American Champion, the ancestral tree from which the golden acorn was budded. If there is any heraldry, it is a shield in the shape of the State of Alabama, bounded on the north by the Tennessee River, on the west by the rivers Black Warrior and Tombigbee, to the south by the Mexican Gulf, and up the east side by the Chattahoochee River. Up in the vicinity of the "hills of Habersham" and the "Valleys of Hall," across on the Alabama side somewhere among the Buckalew Hills of Chambers County, is the birth site of the American Champion. Born as lowly as the Lincoln boy or the Edison lad, American Champions too. Of course! The country is too great, too big, to have just one kind of champion.

A little over four hundred years ago the making of the American Champion was officially begun. The moment the Spaniard Hernando De Soto and his Conquistadors crossed the Chattahoochee River into the land of the Alabamas, it started. De Soto was the first foreign champion to set sollerets [1] on American soil. In Spain he had been the champion horseback swordsman. And he later enhanced his title down in South America where he had saved the Pizarros, those master hijackers of the great Incas' gold. This De Soto was a tough hombre.[2] He came to North America, not just to conquer it, but to find and take away its gold. So the first test was arranged by the God Almighty soon after De Soto and his horde pitched camp on Alabama's soil.

De Soto was a challenger who wanted a million-dollar wager. He had been told by the Aborigines on the Georgia side of the Chattahoochee that there was gold in the red hills across the muddy river.

[1] A flexible steel shoe.   [2] Spanish for man.

So the Conquistador crossed over with his vainglorious caballeros [1] and mailed cross-bowmen and brave padres [2] and army of auxiliaries into what later was to be the vicinity of Chambers County, Alabama, where within four centuries the American Champion would eventually be born. Among this stouthearted Spaniard's host was a company of black men from Africa, brought along as hostlers. They were muscular and strong, for De Soto enlisted no punies.

The God Almighty quickly realized that it would take more than a series of mere births to make a champion in these parts, which eventually would be the great State of Alabama. He had had a hard enough experience with Adam in such a paradise as the Garden of Eden. And this was only the red-hill, scrubby oak country, one of the toughest spots on the whole continent to create a Champion. . . .

If one can comprehend the time-spread of four hundred years, this first of the championship preliminaries was the one the Spaniard De Soto rushed into here on Alabama soil. The defending North American champion was a towering Aborigine named Tuscaloosa, high chief of the powerful tribe of that name. What a physique, what a man, Tuscaloosa! He stood six-foot-seven in his moccasins and had a reach with one arm that would wrap around a fat buffalo and scratch its belly.

Hernando De Soto was really a light-heavyweight, but with strong legs and powerful arms from years of equestrianship [3] and heavy sword handling. But in sheer courage none ever excelled Hernando. Before the battle De Soto had presented Tuscaloosa with a horse, the first such animal the Aborigines had seen. It had to be the largest horse in the expedition, and when he was astride the animal Tuscaloosa's feet almost touched the earth. It was the only time that this early defender of American soil was known to smile—when he sat upon this gift-horse. Otherwise his expression was what would be called "dead-pan."

The site of this preliminary championship fight took place near the confluence of the Tombigbee and Alabama Rivers around the Abo-

---

[1] A Spanish knight or cavalryman
[2] Monk or priest
[3] Horsemanship

rigines' town of Mauville. It was a battle of assault and counter-assault, of powerful thrusts and sallies repelled by ferocious cudgellings and arrow stabs. The Spaniards had mailed fists, charging steeds, and even some gunpowder, against the Aborigines' tomahawks and flint-keen shafts plus the natural barricade around the town. The gallant De Soto charged again and again, and the rugged Tuscaloosa surged forward with counter blows until the smoke and dust and dark obliterated them in their sheer valor. The fight went on, round after round, into the night, when the weapon of fire was finally employed by each side; the Aborigines' citadel was set aflame and in turn the Spaniards' train of supplies was burned. . . . By early morning the God Almighty had declared it a draw. . . .

This important footnote of genealogy must be added: After that preliminary melée on Alabama soil, one of the African hostlers in De Soto's train took leave and started back trail in the search of the sea-coast where the expedition had landed, hoping to return across the big sea to his African fatherland. But he got no farther than the west bank of the Chattahoochee, where he settled among the friendly Alabamas. His name was Cudjoe, and from him a long succession of descendents have come, among whom always the strongest male was called Cudjoe.

The reason, according to the ancient rookery of crows in the Buckalew Hills, that this original Cudjoe halted at the river was because the God Almighty shouted down to him: "Cudjoe, stay right where you are. You were at that fight between the Spaniard De Soto and the Alabamas' chief Tuscaloosa, and it didn't quite please me. Some large morning in the bye-and-bye I'm going to produce a real Champion on this soil and, Cudjoe, I may need your help, so stay where you are." [1]

1 The next division of this essay mentions a Nicholas Perkins who prevented the escape of Aaron Burr by sea, which incident led to the arrest and trial of Burr for treason. Such courage as was exhibited by Perkins to the knowledge of Cudjoe became part of the heritage of the American Champion.

Another Indian chief, Tecumseh, a great warrior, an eloquent speaker, and an excellent organizer, came from Detroit to help organize the Alabamas against the conquerors. He entered also the line of the progenitors of the American Champion. The bravery of Andrew Jackson and of Admiral Farragut inspired a black woman, a slave, who happened to see these men in action. This tall, black woman was being smuggled as a slave into America.

Finally came the year for the American Champion to be born. It was 1914, another one of those tough years when the Mexican boll weevils were threatening Alabama cotton crops and the Prussian military leaders were threatening the peace of Europe.

This year of 1914 was a commemorative one: one hundred years before the Red Coats had burned the public buildings in Washington, and a month later, while Fort McHenry was under British bombardment, a young American had written a living epic of the American star-spangled flag.

•   •   •   •

So the American Champion had been born but no one of the hundred million Americans other than the humble neighbors of the Cudjoes suspected it. Besides, across the Atlantic down in the Balkans, which was to Europe what Alabama was to the United States, Old Scratch had instigated a serious crisis: a Serbian student had assassinated the Austrian Archduke, and that caused the God Almighty to spend the next five years away from the North American continent.

Those five bellicose years the God Almighty was abroad nearly caused the forfeiture of the American Champion. The babe had grown into a strong barefoot boy, but there was a growing belief that Old Scratch had finally gotten the secret into his Congressman's head. . . . The Cudjoe family became afraid. . . . Mamma Cudjoe prayed each night for the God Almighty to return and complete the making of the Champion. . . .

So the God Almighty returned to the vicinity of Chambers County down in Alabama none too soon. From the chinaberry tree in the cabin yard under which Mamma Cudjoe was toiling at the wash tub, the God Almighty spoke:

"How's my little American Champion?"

"Is that you, God Almighty?" she looked up and asked, wringing her strong brown hands in her apron. "We thought you had forsaken us 'way down here in Alabama——thought you'd turned us over to old Tom Tom's crowd for keeps before li'l Cudjoe got a chance to prove he was the Champion you expected him to be."

"I understand. Those old men at Versailles [1] kept me longer than I should have let them. But what about little 'Joe?"

She up and told all about the new kind of law that was threatening to keep them on the cotton plantation. It was then that the God Almighty remembered Tecumseh and how his parents had moved with him from Alabama up to Detroit so he could grow up to be a real Champion. That was where the genealogy of Tecumseh came to good use.

"Don't worry," said the God Almighty as the breeze suddenly began leaving the chinaberry tree and all was still. "Get your things together and tomorrow go over to Opelika and get on board the Central passenger train and keep riding North until you get to Detroit. After you have been up there awhile, little 'Joe will do the rest. He'll start patting his feet and swinging his arms so that it will be felt way down here in Chambers County. Take all that money you hid away and start tomorrow." . . .

So the American Champion and his folks got aboard the long vestibule train and in another day arrived at Detroit. The rest of the genealogical record everybody knows: how the young 'Joe became the great American Champion of the boxing world and how the blows from his two fists reverberated down through the red hills of Alabama clear to the shores of the Mexican Gulf; and how he kept on defending his title until he got down to that old promise the God Almighty had made to his great-great-grandma down on Mobile Bay about showing reverence for Admiral Farragut and the American fighting forces.

It came to pass when he defended his championship for the twenty-first time and donated all of his share of the money to the American Navy Relief Fund.

.   .   .   .

Then as good as Andy Jackson's example, the young Champion hung up his boxing gloves and went out to Camp Upton on Long Island, where they fitted him in a khaki uniform of the United States Army and a pair of number twelve shoes. . . . There was a band

1 Versailles, France, the seat of the Peace Conference that followed the First World War.

playing the "Stars and Stripes Forever," but not on account of the arrival and induction of the Champion. It was a cold day in January and some leather-lunged recruit holloed: "Well, Joe, I see you made it."

"Yeah, I made it."

And that was considered a whole speech of celebration on the part of the American Champion making good the promise of the God Almighty. . . .

Alain Locke

One of the greatest scholars of his age and the only Rhodes Scholar the American Negro has had is Alain Locke, diminutive in stature but profound in intellect. He was born in Philadelphia September 13, 1886. Harvard, the University of Pennsylvania, the University of Berlin, and Oxford University, which he attended from 1907 to 1910—all have conferred honors upon him. For many years he was professor of philosophy at Howard University; today he is professor of philosophy at the University of Wisconsin.

Among his publications are *The New Negro* (1925), *Plays of Negro Life* (1927), the Harlem number of *Survey Graphic* (1925), and *When Peoples Meet* (1942), in which he is co-author with Bernhard J. Stern.

THE NEW NEGRO [1]

With this renewed self-respect and self-dependence, the life of the Negro community is bound to enter a new dynamic phase, the buoyancy from within compensating for whatever pressure there may be of conditions from without. The migrant masses, shifting from countryside to city, hurdle several generations of experience at a leap, but, more important, the same thing happens spiritually in the life-attitudes and self-expression of the young Negro, in his poetry, his art, his education, and his new outlook, with the additional advantage, of course, of the poise and greater certainty of knowing what it is all about.

[1] From *The New Negro*, by Alain Locke. Copyright, 1925, by Albert and Charles Boni, New York.

From this comes the promise and warrant of a new leadership. As one of them has discerningly put it:

> We have tomorrow
> Bright before us
> Like a flame.
>
> Yesterday, a night-gone thing
> A sun-down name.
>
> And dawn today
> Broad arch above the road we came.
> We march!

This is what, even more than any "most creditable record of fifty years of freedom," requires that the Negro of today be seen through other than the dusty spectacles of past controversy. The day of "aunties," "uncles," and "mammies" is equally gone. Uncle Tom and Sambo have passed on, and even the "Colonel" and "George" play barnstorm rôles from which they escape with relief when the public spotlight is off. The popular melodrama has about played itself out, and it is time to scrap the fictions, garret the bogeys, and settle down to a realistic facing of facts.

First, we must observe some of the changes which since the traditional lines of opinion were drawn have rendered these quite obsolete. A main change has been, of course, that shifting of the Negro population which has made the Negro problem no longer exclusively or even predominantly Southern. Why should our minds remain sectionalized, when the problem itself no longer is? Then the trend of migration has not only been toward the North and the Central Midwest, but city-ward and to the great centers of industry——the problems of adjustment are new, practical, local, and not peculiarly racial. Rather they are an integral part of the large industrial and social problems of our present-day democracy. And finally, with the Negro rapidly in process of class differentiation, if it ever was warrantable to regard and treat the Negro en masse it is becoming with every day less possible, more unjust and more ridiculous.

In the very process of being transplanted, the Negro is becoming transformed.

The tide of Negro migration, northward and city-ward, is not to be fully explained as a blind flood started by the demands of war industry coupled with the shutting off of foreign migration, or by the pressure of poor crops coupled with increased social terrorism in certain sections of the South and Southwest. Neither labor demand, the boll weevil, nor the Ku Klux Klan is a basic factor, however contributory any or all of them may have been. The wash and rush of this human tide on the beach line of the northern city centers is to be explained primarily in terms of a new vision of opportunity, of social and economic freedom, of a spirit to seize, even in the face of an extortionate and heavy toll, a chance for the improvement of conditions. With each successive wave of it, the movement of the Negro becomes more and more a mass movement toward the larger and the more democratic chance—in the Negro's case a deliberate flight not only from countryside to city, but from medieval America to modern.

Take Harlem as an instance of this. Here in Manhattan is not merely the largest Negro community in the world, but the first concentration in history of so many diverse elements of Negro life. It has attracted the African, the West Indian, the Negro American; has brought together the Negro of the North and the Negro of the South; the man from the city and the man from the town and village; the peasant, the student, the businessman, the professional man, artist, poet, musician, adventurer and worker, preacher and criminal, exploiter and social outcast. Each group has come with its own separate motives and for its own special ends, but their greatest experience has been the finding of one another. Proscription and prejudice have thrown these dissimilar elements into a common area of contact and interaction. Within this area, race sympathy and unity have determined a further fusing of sentiment and experience. So what began in terms of segregation becomes more and more, as its elements mix and react, the laboratory of a great race-welding. Hitherto, it must be admitted that American Negroes have been a race more in name than in fact, or, to be exact, more in sentiment than in experience. The chief bond between them has been that of a common condition rather than a common consciousness; a problem in common rather than a life in common. In Harlem, Negro life is seizing upon its first chances for group expression and self-determination. Harlem is—or promises, at

least, to be—a race capital. That is why our comparison is taken
with those nascent centers of folk-expression and self-determination
which are playing a creative part in the world today. Without pretense to their political significance, Harlem has the same rôle to play
for the New Negro as Dublin has had for the New Ireland or Prague
for the New Czechoslovakia.

Harlem, I grant you, isn't typical—but it is significant, it is
prophetic. No sane observer, however sympathetic to the new trend,
would contend that the great masses are articulate as yet, but they
stir, they move, they are more than physically restless. The challenge
of the new intellectuals among them is clear enough—the "race
radicals" and realists who have broken with the old epoch of philanthropic guidance, sentimental appeal, and protest. But are we after all
only reading into the stirring of a sleeping giant the dreams of an
agitator? The answer is in the migrating peasant. It is the "man farthest down" who is more active in getting up. One of the most characteristic symptoms of this is the professional man, himself migrating to
recapture his constituency after a vain effort to maintain in some
Southern corner what for years back seemed an established living and
clientele. The clergyman following his errant flock, the physician or
lawyer trailing his clients, supply the true clues. In a real sense it is
the rank and file who are leading, and the leaders who are following.
A transformed and transforming psychology permeates the masses.

When the racial leaders of twenty years ago spoke of developing
race pride and stimulating race consciousness, and of the desirability
of race solidarity, they could not in any accurate degree have antici-
pated the abrupt feeling that has surged up and now pervades the
awakened centers. Some of the recognized Negro leaders and a powerful section of white opinion identified with "race work" of the older
order have indeed attempted to discount this feeling as a "passing
phase," an attack of "race nerves," so to speak, an "aftermath of the
war," and the like. It has not abated, however, if we are to gauge by
the present tone and temper of the Negro press, or by the shift in
popular support from the officially recognized and orthodox spokes-
men to those of the independent, popular, and often radical type who
are unmistakable symptoms of a new order. It is a social disservice to

blunt the fact that the Negro of the Northern centers has reached a stage where tutelage, even of the most interested and well-intentioned sort, must give place to new relationships, where positive self-direction must be reckoned with in ever-increasing measure. The American mind must reckon with a fundamentally changed Negro.

The Negro too, for his part, has idols of the tribe to smash. If on the one hand the white man has erred in making the Negro appear to be that which would excuse or extenuate his treatment of him, the Negro, in turn, has too often unnecessarily excused himself because of the way he has been treated. The intelligent Negro of today is resolved not to make discrimination an extenuation for his shortcomings in performance, individual or collective; he is trying to hold himself at par, neither inflated by sentimental allowances nor depreciated by current social discounts. For this he must know himself and be known for precisely what he is, and for that reason he welcomes the new scientific rather than the old sentimental interest. Sentimental interest in the Negro has ebbed. We used to lament this as the falling off of our friends; now we rejoice and pray to be delivered both from self-pity and from condescension. The mind of each racial group has had a bitter weaning, apathy or hatred on one side matching disillusionment or resentment on the other; but they face each other today with the possibility at least of entirely new mutual attitudes.

It does not follow that if the Negro were better known, he would be better liked or better treated. But mutual understanding is basic for any subsequent cooperation and adjustment. The effort toward this will at least have the effect of remedying in large part what has been the most unsatisfactory feature of our present stage of race relationships in America, namely the fact that the more intelligent and representative elements of the two race groups have at so many points got quite out of vital touch with one another.

The fiction is that the life of the race is separate, and increasingly so. The fact is that they have touched too closely at the unfavorable and too lightly at the favorable levels.

While interracial councils have sprung up in the South, drawing on forward elements of both races, in the Northern cities manual laborers may brush elbows in their everyday work, but the community and business leaders have experienced no such interplay or far too little of it. These segments must achieve contact or the race situation in America becomes desperate. Fortunately this is happening. There is a growing realization that in social effort the cooperative basis must supplant long-distance philanthropy, and that the only safeguard for mass relations in the future must be provided in the carefully maintained contacts of the enlightened minorities of both race groups. In the intellectual realm a renewed and keen curiosity is replacing the recent apathy; the Negro is being carefully studied, not just talked about and discussed. In art and letters, instead of being wholly caricatured, he is being seriously portrayed and painted.

James Weldon Johnson
(See page 36.)

MARCUS GARVEY [1]

Marcus Garvey is a full-blooded black man, born, and born poor, in Jamaica, British West Indies, in 1887. He grew up under the triple race scheme that prevails in many of the West Indian islands— white, mulatto, and black. The conditions of this system aroused in him, even as a boy, a deep resentment, which increased as he grew older. His resentment against the mulattoes was, perhaps, deeper than his resentment against the whites. At about the time he became of age, he left Jamaica and travelled in South America. He next went to England, where he stayed for several years. All the while he was seeking some escape from the terrible pressure of the color bar. In England he met one or two African agitators. He became intimate with Duse Muhamed Effendi, an African political writer, who was running a small revolutionary newspaper in London, and from him learned something about world politics, especially with relation to Africa. It

[1] From *Black Manhattan,* by James Weldon Johnson. Copyright, 1930, by Alfred A. Knopf, New York.

was probably then that he began to dream of a land where black men ruled. England was a disappointment. In 1914 he returned to Jamaica, determined to do something to raise the status of the black masses of the island. He began his public career by organizing the Universal Negro Improvement Association. He was discouraged by the fact that he aroused more interest and gained more support among the whites than among the blacks. He wrote Booker T. Washington about his plans—plans probably for establishing industrial training for the natives of Jamaica—and received a reply encouraging him to come to the United States. Before he could perfect arrangements to come, Booker T. Washington had died. But on March 23, 1916, Garvey landed in Harlem.

In some way or other he got about the country, visiting, as he says, thirty-eight states, studying the condition of the Negro in America, and then returned to New York. On June 12, 1917, a large mass meeting, called by Hubert Harrison, was held in Bethel A.M.E. Church in Harlem for the purpose of organizing the Liberty League. Some two thousand people were present, and among them was Marcus Garvey. Mr. Harrison introduced him to the audience and asked him to say a few words. This was Harlem's first real sight of Garvey, and his first real chance at Harlem. The man spoke, and his magnetic personality, torrential eloquence, and intuitive knowledge of mob psychology were all brought into play. He swept the audience along with him. He made his speech an endorsement of the new movement and a pledge of his hearty support of it; but Garvey was not of the kind to support anybody's movement. He had seen the United States and he had seen Harlem. He had doubtless been the keenest observer at the Liberty League organization meeting; and it may be that it was then he decided upon New York as the center for his activities.

He soon organized and incorporated the Universal Negro Improvement Association in the United States, with New York as headquarters. He made his first appeal to the West Indian elements, not only to British, but to Spanish and French, and they flocked to him. He established the *Negro World* as his organ and included in it Spanish and French sections. He built Liberty Hall, a great basement that held five or six thousand people. There the association held its first convention in 1919, during the whole month of August, with delegates from the various States and the West Indies. By this time the scheme of the organization had expanded from the idea of economic solution of the race problem through the establishment of "Universal" shops and factories and financial institutions to that of its solution through the redemption of Africa and the establishment of a Negro merchant marine. At the mass meeting held in Carnegie Hall during this convention, Garvey in his address said:

> We are striking homeward toward Africa to make her the big black republic. And in the making of Africa the big black republic, what is the barrier? The barrier is the white man; and we say to the white man who dominates Africa that it is to his interest to clear out now, because we are coming, not as in the time of Father Abraham, 200,000 strong, but we are coming 400,000,000 strong and we mean to retake every square inch of the 12,000,000 square miles of African territory belonging to us by right Divine.

Money poured in; wartime prosperity made it possible. Three ships were bought and placed in commission. Garvey had grown to be High Potentate of the association and "Provisional President of Africa." Around him he established a court of nobles and ladies. There were dukes and duchesses, knight commanders of the Distinguished Order of Ethiopia, and knight commanders of the Sublime Order of the Nile. There were gorgeous uniforms, regalia, decorations, and insignia. There was a strict court etiquette, and the constitution provided that "No lady below the age of eighteen shall be presented at the 'Court Reception' and no gentleman below the age of twenty-one." There was established the African Legion, with a full line of commissioned officers and a quartermaster staff and commissariat for each brigade. The Black Cross nurses were organized. In fact, an embryo army was set up with Marcus Garvey as commander-in-chief. A mission was sent to Liberia to negotiate an agreement whereby the Universal Negro Improvement Association would establish a colony there and aid in the development of the country.

Garvey became a world figure, and his movements and utterances were watched by the great governmental powers. (Even today from his exile in Jamaica his actions and words are considered international news.) The U.N.I.A. grew in the United States and spread through the region of the Caribbean. The movement became more than a movement, it became a religion, its members became zealots. Meetings at Liberty Hall were conducted with an elaborate liturgy. The moment for the entry of the "Provisional President" into the auditorium was solemn; a hushed and expectant silence on the throng, the African Legion and Black Cross nurses flanking the long aisle and coming to attention, the band and audience joining in the hymn: "Long Live Our President," and Garvey, surrounded by his guard of honor from the Legion, marching majestically through the double line and mounting the rostrum; it was impressive if for no other reason than the way in which it impressed the throng. Garvey made a four months' tour of the West Indies in a Black Star liner, gathering in many converts to the movement, but no freight for the vessel. Of course, the bubble burst. Neither Garvey nor anyone with him knew how to operate ships. And if they had known, they could not have succeeded at the very time when ships were the greatest drug on the market. So the Black Star Line, after swallowing up hundreds of thousands of dollars, collapsed in December 1921. The Federal Government investigated Garvey's share-selling scheme and he was indicted and convicted on a charge of using the mails to defraud. While out of the Tombs on bail, he made an unsuccessful attempt to revive his shipping venture as the Black Cross Line.

Within ten years after reaching New York Marcus Garvey had risen and fallen, been made a prisoner in the Atlanta Federal Penitentiary, and finally been deported to his native island. Within that brief period a black West Indian, here in the United States, in the twentieth century, had actually played an imperial role such as Eugene O'Neill never imagined in his *Emperor Jones*.

Garvey failed; yet he might have succeeded with more than moderate success. He had energy and daring and the Napoleonic personality, the personality that draws masses of followers. He stirred the imagination of the Negro masses as no Negro ever had. He raised more money in a few years than any other Negro organization had ever dreamed of. He had great power and great possibilities within his grasp. But his deficiencies as a leader outweighed his abilities. He is a supreme egotist, his egotism amounting to megalomania; and so the men surrounding him had to be for the most part cringing sycophants; and among them there were also cunning knaves. Upon them he now lays the entire blame for failure, taking no part of it to himself. As he grew in power, he fought every other Negro rights organization in the country, especially the National Association for the Advancement of Colored People, centering his attacks upon Dr. Du Bois.

Garvey made several vital blunders, which, with any intelligent advice, he might have avoided. He proceeded upon the assumption of a triple race scheme in the United States; whereas the facts are that the whites in the United States, unlike the whites of the West Indies, make no distinction between people of color and blacks, nor do the Negroes. There may be places where a very flexible social line exists, but Negroes in the United States of every complexion have always maintained a solid front on the rights of the race. This policy of Garvey's, going to the logical limit of calling upon his followers to conceive of God as black, did arouse a latent pride of the Negro in his blackness, but it wrought an overbalancing damage by the effort to drive a wedge between the blacks and the mixed bloods, an effort that might have brought on disaster had it been more successful.

He made the mistake of ignoring or looking with disdain upon the technique of the American Negro in dealing with his problems of race, a technique acquired through three hundred years of such experience as the West Indian has not had and never can have. If he had availed himself of the counsel and advice of an able and honest American Negro, he would have avoided many of the barbed wires against which he ran and many of the pits into which he fell.

But the main reason for Garvey's failure with thoughtful American Negroes was his African scheme. It was recognized at once by them to be impracticable and fantastic. Indeed, it is difficult to give the man credit for either honesty or sanity in these imperialistic designs, unless, as there are some reasons to suppose, his designs involved the purpose of going into Liberia as an agent of development and then by gradual steps or a coup taking over the government and making the country the center of the activities and efforts for an Africa Redeemed. But thoughtful colored Americans knew that, under existing political conditions in Africa, even that plan could ultimately meet with nothing but failure. Had there been every prospect of success, however, the scheme would not have appealed to them. It was simply a restatement of the Colonization Society scheme advanced just one hundred years before, which had occasioned the assembling of the first national convention of Negroes in America, called to oppose "the operations and misrepresentations of the American Colonization Society in these United States." The central idea of Garvey's scheme was absolute abdication and the recognition as facts of the assertions that this is a white man's country, a country in which the Negro has no place, no right, no chance, no future. To that idea the overwhelming majority of thoughtful American Negroes will not subscribe. And behind this attitude is the common-sense realization that as the world is at present, the United States, with all of its limitations, offers the millions of Negroes within its borders greater opportunities than any other land.

Garvey's last great mistake came about through his transcending egotism. He had as leading counsel for his trial Henry Lincoln Johnson, one of the shrewdest and ablest Negro lawyers in the country. But the temptation to strut and pose before a crowded court and on the front pages of the New York newspapers was too great for Garvey to resist; so he brushed his lawyers aside and handled his own case. He himself examined and cross-examined the witnesses; he himself harangued the judge and jury; and he was convicted.

Garvey, practically exiled on an island in the Caribbean, becomes a somewhat tragic figure. There arises a slight analogy between him and that former and greater dreamer in empires, exiled on another island. But the heart of the tragedy is that to this man came an opportunity such as comes to few men, and he clutched greedily at the glitter and let the substance slip from his fingers.

Bernice Young Mitchell Wells

Bernice Young Mitchell Wells was born at Zanesville, Ohio. She was edu-
cated at the public school there, Wilberforce University, and Ohio State
University. From Ohio State she obtained the degree of Master of Arts.
Her uncle, Colonel Charles Young, was a schoolmate at West Point of
General John J. Pershing.

"A Versatile Relative of Mine" was originally a talk delivered at a Sunday Vesper Service of Douglass University. It is an excellent example of the
biographical essay. As it is also of the personal type, it approaches the style
of Charles Lamb, the English essayist.

A VERSATILE RELATIVE OF MINE: COLONEL CHARLES YOUNG [1]

A twelve-room house surrounded by acres and acres of land on
both sides of the Columbus Pike in Ohio proved to be too small to
accommodate the many welcome guests who came, bidden and un-
bidden, but still welcome to its doors, front, back, and side. Another
wing of four rooms was added, and still very often the sixteen rooms
were crowded beyond capacity. The enlarging of the home and the
principles of "The more the merrier" and "There's always room for
one more" were applicable likewise to the immense heart of the host,
Colonel Charles Young. That is all the name he had, incidentally. I
have seen his name written with various middle initials, but he had no
middle name.

He loved this huge farm on which virtually every type of domestic
plant and animal was raised and was loved. One day, my aunt was
sitting in the yard and a flock of what I thought were geese came
trooping by, and she said, "There are my beauties!"

I said, "Are you talking about those geese?"

She said, "Please don't let your Uncle Charlie hear you call those
beautiful guineas geese. I think it would certainly make him feel bad.
He loves them."

[1] Reprinted with the permission of the author.

Later, I learned that he did love them—too much to kill them to eat, and I considered that love. Cows, hogs, horses, poultry, bees, cats (whole families of them), dogs, all were part of this hustling farm. The latch-string hung outside for all of the homeless of God's creatures, whether human or otherwise. Important personages of both races came and went, but many obscure persons, even the flotsam and jetsam of society, were made welcome, too.

The genial lord of the manor loved the soil and the life of the country. Someone referred to him once, upon seeing him in a wide straw hat and overalls, as a gentleman farmer. His characteristic reply was, "I'm not a gentleman farmer. I'm a dirt farmer. Look at my 'britches'."

There was a welcome for all strangers, and peace, harmony, love, and goodwill within the home. My most pleasant early recollection of being taken to Wilberforce to visit is of gathering around the piano in the huge old-fashioned music room after supper; and the family, the farm hands, the servants, children's nurse and the guests who happened to be there, would sing for an hour or two. I should say that all sang but the family, because there never was anyone named Young in our family lines whom I have ever known who could carry a tune; but the occasions were pleasant and were always looked forward to.

My earliest recollection of my uncle was hearing him spoken of during his first trip to Africa. He passed through the home town en route to Fort Huachucha, Arizona, when I was about five years old. At that time, I got the impression of a man who was quite tall. Later, it was a surprise to discover that he was only of average height.

I have said that I was going to tell you about a versatile person, and versatile he was, without being enigmatic or a Dr. Jekyll and Mr. Hyde. He was a *scholar*. His facility in handling many languages is shown in the nicknames he gave his two children. Marie, the younger, he called Kiki, which is French for "Tomboy," and Charles, the elder, he called "Ton Ton," which is African for "Big Boy." He knew German, Italian, Spanish, Latin, and Greek. The possessor of a priceless library of literature of many nations, he was a voracious reader and could quote from scores of sources. It was through him that I began my study of French. I had studied German and Latin, and had had a year of Greek, and considered myself a linguist of parts. But he showed me the vast realms of famous literature which would be closed to me without a knowledge of modern languages. So I immediately sought to have my program rearranged to permit me to take French.

A sense of humor never deserted him. On one occasion, a Southern white private met him and failed to salute him. The private was embarrassed not to salute a colonel, who, he knew, outranked him and was entitled to the salute. Yet to salute this particular Colonel was to acknowledge the superiority of at least one Negro to at least one white man. Colonel Young at once sensed the embarrassment. Seeing a stick, he stuck it in the ground and placed his cap upon it. Then he walked to one side and said, "Salute the cap, young man." The private did so promptly. Colonel Young then replaced his cap upon his head and went to his headquarters.

The idea of a soldier being interested in the fine arts always impressed most people as being quite incongruous. However, he played both the piano and the violin, and composed for these instruments several short selections—one of them, a sweet, tuneful, little cradle song at the time of the birth of his daughter; also an African suite, and a Caribbean suite. On one occasion, when Paul Laurence Dunbar, our great poet, Dr. William E. B. Du Bois, and my uncle were at Wilberforce University, Dunbar wrote a song for Dr. John W. Evans, now principal of the Lincoln School of St. Louis, Missouri, but then a student at Wilberforce. My uncle wrote the music for this song and Dr. Evans with great pride sang the song at a chapel service.

He also wrote a pageant depicting the development of Negro culture, and several poems on subjects not often used as poetical themes. They were short, crisp, terse, and ironical.

He lived and made friends in many parts of the world. One man who was Minister of Finance in Haiti at the time he was stationed there remained his life-long friend. They found in each other kindred spirits. A Frenchwoman, a Mme. Chapteau, visited the home many times. When his children were ten and eight respectively, they were sent to Paris to Mme. Chapteau, who placed them in a convent boarding school. Both children were pupils at the school in 1914 at the outbreak of the World War. The convent was bombed by the Germans and the nuns fled to Belgium with eight children. Among them were my two young cousins, who were at that time sixteen and fourteen years old respectively. My uncle and aunt were in Africa at the time and it was nearly six months before they were able to locate their children. Immediately upon locating them, my aunt brought them back to America and kept them here for the duration of the War.

During the War, my uncle was recalled from Africa. He came jubilantly, expecting to be given an assignment at some place where he might serve his country with the same daring and courage with which he and his fighting Tenth Cavalry had charged up San Juan Hill in Cuba with President Theodore Roosevelt's Rough Riders.

Most of you recall what did happen, when he reached Washington. He was asked to accept retirement "because he was physically unfit for active service." He returned to his home in Wilberforce, where he behaved like a combination of caged lion and antagonized schoolboy. Finally, the indomitable will that could not be checked drove him to put one of his favorite horses on a Baltimore and Ohio freight train and ship it to Cumberland, Maryland, mount his other favorite, a huge black mare, whom he called Blacksmith, and ride horseback from Wilberforce to Cumberland, change horses, and gallop to Washington on the only 500 mile non-stop horseback ride on record. On arriving there, he presented himself at the White House in all his dust and grime and waited five hours for an interview with the President.

When finally he was received, he remarked, "Mr. President, I have ridden here on horseback from Wilberforce, Ohio. Do I look like a man ready for your military scrap-heap?" After several more months, he was given a post at Camp Grant, in Illinois, from where, at the end of the War, he was returned to Africa, to his death. The circumstances surrounding his death are shrouded in secrecy. What the family knows concerning the way in which he met his death was told us verbally by his two good friends, who were in Africa at the time, Lendell Ridley and Allan Bean.

It is difficult to believe that any vital, animated person has died, and it was not until I visited his grave in Arlington Cemetery that I could at all realize that fact. His physical presence has been for seventeen years removed from this earth, but this program this afternoon is proof positive of the fact that his memory has not died. It could not, for at his passing he left behind a trail of grateful hearts. His benefactions knew no limits.

On one of his leaves during the time he was stationed in Africa, he brought home with him a little black boy whom he called Alfie. Alfie remained in the home at Wilberforce, was educated, opened a bake shop in a small nearby town, married, and became a substantial citizen. A Haitian boy accompanied the family to America as a nurse for the children. He was likewise schooled and given a start in life. Indigent students who were brought to Colonel Young's notice were given aid, advice, comfort, and counsel. I recall on coming in from school one day hearing a sound in the house which I was unable to identify. Upon going to ascertain its source, I found my uncle at his desk in the library, sobbing with horrible, tearing sobs. I started to back out of the room because I was frightened; but he raised up and said, "Come in. You're old enough to learn to suffer with humanity, too. Look at this." He held up a sheaf of letters. "There are too many of them. I can't do what they ask and I can't tell them no."

I sat down and read about twenty-five letters from people, most of them unknown to him, asking for money—money for operations for small children, care for blind persons, for youngsters who wished to attend college, but who, for lack of funds, were unable to. "I can't," went on the desperate voice filled with soul-sickness. "I can't—they ask too much. I haven't enough money, but I can't say, 'No.' The poor devils!"

When young college students leave home, many of them are fledglings with wings, both mentally and physically untried. Certain principles have been taught in the home, and when the youngster gets to college he does practically the first independent thinking of his life. He hears discussed frequently things that are diametrically opposed to his parents' teachings and he finds himself sometimes at a loss to know what to believe. This was my case so far as my religious teachings were concerned. I had been taught that Biblical facts were literally true and were to be accepted without question. Hence when I began to hear, early in my college life, the miracles of the Bible scoffed at, and even the existence of God questioned, I wondered if I had been deluded again as I had been concerning Santa Claus and the Easter Bunny. So, one day, I decided to go to the fount of all knowledge, my uncle, who, I thought, knew everything.

The interview was an unforgettable one. I mounted the stairs to his attic den and interrupted his reading to say that I wanted to ask him something. "How much do you want?" he asked, and ran his hand into his pocket. I said that I did not want any money that time, and I explained the things I had been hearing concerning the Bible and religion. Finally, I asked him to tell me his conception of God. His face lit up like a sudden burst of sunlight in a darkened room, and he said with no hesitation, "I conceive of God as a great sea of soul, from which we mortals have bubbled away to form little rivulets, ponds, streams, and the like, but the Mother Sea has her grip on us and in time will attract us back to Her. Then, She will hold us close on her bosom, give us back those atoms that have evaporated away, and will keep us there on and on through eternity. Don't worry about what you hear. Faith can be shaken, but not destroyed, and you will believe all the stronger from now on."

I know from the life he lived that he also believed strongly, just as he admonished me to do.

PART VI

Addresses

Introduction   Speech, address, and oration are terms used to refer
to that literary form in prose which is intended to
be delivered orally. If it is informal, it is generally called a speech. If
it is formal, it will be called an address, an oration, or a sermon in accordance with the occasion. As the only type of this literary form
included in this volume is of the formal type, it is not necessary to discuss it to any great extent.

You probably have read Abraham Lincoln's "Gettysburg Address."
It would be helpful for you to read it again, as well as Lincoln's "Second Inaugural." Both are brief.

It would be well for you to re-read the introduction to the Essay as
background for the material now about to be presented. Just as the
peculiar style of the essayist is determined by the fact that the essay
is intended for silent reading, so is the style of the address or oration
determined by the fact that the aim of the orator is to arouse the emotions and move to action.

The paragraphs best suited to arousing the feelings are those developed by Comparison and Contrast, by Negation or Obverse Statements, and by the many types of Repetition. The essayist may use all
types of paragraphs and so may the orator; but the essayist relies
chiefly upon paragraphs developed by Definition of Terms, Particulars, Examples, and Cause and Effect. Especially effective for the
speaker is a paragraph developed by Comparison and Contrast, when

it is composed of balanced sentences, with the two ideas compared and contrasted appearing in every sentence. If the speaker discusses one idea in the first half of the paragraph and then the other idea in the remaining half of the paragraph, the emotional appeal is less effective than it would be if the two ideas are kept together from the beginning to the end of the paragraph.

Negation, or the method of Obverse Statements, has produced some of the greatest climaxes or oratorical flights for the public speaker. In using this method, the orator uses a topic sentence that is in the affirmative. After stating the thought in his topic sentence, the speaker will use three or more sentences, generally five or six, stating what his idea is not or what it is not like. Then he will use an equal number of sentences in which he will state what his idea is or is like. To make his thought unusually effective, he will often end with a long periodic sentence. This type of paragraph arouses curiosity by causing the audience to wonder what is this idea or what it is like. The answer is generally begun with a short sentence, and then follow other answers in sentences of increasing length, with each sentence varied in structure.

Variety is the fundamental principle to be observed by the orator. He must vary his sentences. He must vary their length. He will use the declarative sentence, as does the essayist, to convey information; but he will intersperse his oration with the imperative, the exclamatory, and the interrogative sentences, to arouse the emotions of his hearers. Especially will he use the periodic sentence, because he must hold his audience in suspense. Other effects he will gain by use of parallel construction.

From the earliest times, the chief orator of the American Negro has been his preacher. Du Bois discusses him in "Of the Faith of the Fathers." The most distinguished orators the Negro had before the Civil War were Charles Lenox Remond and Frederick Douglass.

Most Negro churches still appreciate most the florid type of oratory, not the intellectual. The Catholic, the Episcopalian, and the Presbyterian congregations desire intellectual preaching; but the great masses of the Negro, who are in the Baptist and Methodist churches, require of their pastors emotional preaching. The sermon is not to exhibit the style of an essay but the style of the oration as discussed in this introduction. The Negro wants oratorical flights, descriptive metaphors, and elaborate periodic sentences. He will accept some of the intellectual; but he wants the sermon eventually to rise to an emotional climax. Among the ministers of recent times who had this technique of the effective intellectual and emotional appeal were Dr. L. K. Williams, pastor of the Olivet Baptist Church of Chicago; Dr. M. C. B. Mason of the Methodist Episcopal Church; Dr. W. T. Vernon of the African Methodist Episcopal Church; and Bishop Alexander Walters of the African Methodist Episcopal Zion Church.

Among the living ministers who are similarly effective pulpit orators are Dr. Junius C. Austin, pastor of Pilgrim Baptist Church, and Dr. J. H. Jackson, pastor of Olivet Baptist Church, both of Chicago; Bishops Noah H. Williams and Frank Madison Reid of the A. M. E. Church; Bishop W. J. Walls of the A. M. E. Zion Church; and Bishop W. Yancy Bell of the C. M. E. Church. Along with these might be mentioned the one professional orator among Negroes, Colonel Roscoe Conkling Simmons of Chicago, who makes his living entirely by public speaking. Should you have the opportunity of hearing him, you will observe that he is a master of every technique of the orator. If one were to read in its entirety "The Fourth of July Oration" of Frederick Douglass, he would similarly discover that Frederick Douglass, who did not attend school a day in his life, was just such a master. His mastery of English was remarkable.

Frederick Douglass

Frederick Douglass, abolitionist, orator, journalist, statesman, and humanitarian, was born February 14(?), 1817 at Tuckahoe, Maryland, as a slave. His master's wife, Mrs. Auld, gave him a few lessons in reading until she was stopped by her husband. However, Douglass by clandestine methods eventually learned to read and write, practically teaching himself. His genius put him so far ahead of most men of his day that many began to doubt that he had ever been a slave. To prove that he was no impostor, he wrote *Frederick Douglass' Narrative,* after the publication of which he had to flee from America.

In England his eloquence and his personality, as well as his cause, gained for him his purchase price and money with which to start a news-

paper, *The North Star,* at Rochester, New York. He spoke not only for the freedom of the slave, but also for temperance and woman suffrage. On February 20, 1895, when about to deliver a speech in behalf of woman suffrage, he died.

Among his publications were *My Bondage and My Freedom, Life and Times of Frederick Douglass,* and *Speeches of Frederick Douglass.*

Douglass, when thirty-five years of age, because of his eminence as a citizen of Rochester, New York, was asked to be the orator of the day on July 4, 1852, when the citizens of that city held their Independence Day Celebration. It was the seventy-sixth anniversary of the signing of the Declaration of Independence. The following excerpt from his oration is reprinted here with the permission of Haley Douglass, his grandson.

FOURTH OF JULY ORATION

Fellow-citizens, pardon me, allow me to ask, why am I called upon to speak here today? What have I, or those I represent, to do with your national independence? Are the great principles of political freedom and of natural justice, embodied in that Declaration of Independence, extended to us? And am I, therefore, called upon to bring our humble offering to the national altar, and to confess the benefits and express devout gratitude for the blessings resulting from your independence to us?

Would to God, both for your sakes and ours, that an affirmative answer could be truthfully returned to these questions! Then would my task be light, and my burden easy and delightful. For who is there so cold, that a nation's sympathy could not warm him? Who so obdurate and dead to the claims of gratitude, that would not thankfully acknowledge such priceless benefits? Who so stolid and selfish, that would not give his voice to swell the hallelujahs of a nation's jubilee, when the chains of servitude had been torn from his limbs? I am not that man. In a case like that, the dumb might eloquently speak, and the "lame man leap as an hart."

But such is not the state of the case. I say it with a sad sense of the disparity between us. I am not included within the pale of this glorious anniversary! Your high independence only reveals the immeasurable distance between us. The blessings in which you, this day, rejoice, are not enjoyed in common. The rich inheritance of justice, liberty, prosperity, and independence, bequeathed by your fathers, is shared by you, not by me. The sunlight that brought light and healing to you has brought stripes and death to me. This Fourth of July is *yours,* not *mine. You* may rejoice, I must mourn. To drag a man in fetters into the grand illuminated temple of liberty, and call upon him to join you in joyous anthems, were inhuman mockery and sacrilegious irony. Do you mean, citizens, to mock me, by asking me to speak today? If so, there is a parallel to your conduct. And let me warn you that it is dangerous to copy the example of a nation whose crimes, towering up to heaven, were thrown down by the breath of the Almighty, burying that nation in irrevocable ruin! I can today take up the plaintive lament of a peeled and woe-smitten people!

"By the rivers of Babylon, there we sat down. Yea! we wept when we remembered Zion. We hanged our harps upon the willows in the midst thereof. For there, they that carried us away captive, required of us a song; and they who wasted us required of us mirth, saying, Sing us one of the songs of Zion. How can we sing the Lord's song in a strange land? If I forget thee, O Jerusalem, let my right hand forget her cunning. If I do not remember thee, let my tongue cleave to the roof of my mouth."

Fellow-citizens, above your national, tumultuous joy, I hear the mournful wail of millions, whose chains, heavy and grievous yesterday, are today rendered more intolerable by the jubilee shouts that reach them. If I do forget, if I do not faithfully remember those bleeding children of sorrow this day, "may my right hand forget her cunning, and may my tongue cleave to the roof of my mouth!" To forget them, to pass lightly over their wrongs, and to chime in with the popular theme, would be treason most scandalous and shocking, and would make me a reproach before God and the world.

My subject, then, fellow-citizens, is *American Slavery*. I shall see this day and its popular characteristics from the slave's point of view.

Standing here identified with the American bondman, making his wrongs mine, I do not hesitate to declare, with all my soul, that the character and conduct of this nation never looked blacker to me than on this Fourth of July! Whether we turn to the declarations of the past, or to the professions of the present, the conduct of the nation seems equally hideous and revolting. America is false to the past, false to the present, and solemnly binds herself to be false to the future. Standing with God and the crushed and bleeding slave on this occasion, I will, in the name of humanity which is outraged, in the name of liberty which is fettered, in the name of the Constitution and the Bible which are disregarded and trampled upon, dare to call in question and to denounce, with all the emphasis I can command, everything that serves to perpetuate slavery—the great sin and shame of America! "I will not equivocate; I will not excuse"; I will use the severest language I can command; and yet not one word shall escape me that any man, whose judgment is not blinded by prejudice, or who is not at heart a slaveholder, shall not confess to be right and just.

But I fancy I hear some one of my audience say, "It is just in this circumstance that you and your brother abolitionists fail to make a favorable impression on the public mind. Would you argue more, and denounce less; would you persuade more, and rebuke less; your cause would be much more likely to succeed." But, I submit, where all is plain there is nothing to be argued. What point in the anti-slavery creed would you have me argue? On what branch of the subject do the people of this country need light? Must I undertake to prove that the slave is a man? That point is conceded already. Nobody doubts it. The slaveholders themselves acknowledge it in the enactment of laws for their government. They acknowledge it when they punish disobedience on the part of the slave. There are seventy-two crimes in the State of Virginia which, if committed by a black man (no matter how ignorant he be), subject him to the punishment of death; while only two of the same crimes will subject a white man to the like punishment. What is this but the acknowledgment that the slave is a moral, intellectual, and responsible being?

The manhood of the slave is conceded. It is admitted in the fact that Southern statute books are covered with enactments forbidding, under severe fines and penalties, the teaching of the slave to read or to write. When you can point to any such laws in reference to the beasts of the field, then I may consent to argue the manhood of the slave. When the dogs in your streets, when the fowls of the air, when the cattle on your hills, when the fish of the sea, and the reptiles that crawl, shall be unable to distinguish the slave from a brute, *then* will I argue with you that the slave is a man!

For the present, it is enough to affirm the equal manhood of the Negro race. Is it not astonishing that, while we are ploughing, planting, and reaping, using all kinds of mechanical tools, erecting houses, constructing bridges, building ships, working in metals of brass, iron, copper, silver, and gold; that, while we are reading, writing, and ciphering, acting as clerks, merchants, and secretaries, having among us lawyers, doctors, ministers, poets, authors, editors, orators, and teachers; that, while we are engaged in all manner of enterprises common to other men, digging gold in California, capturing the whale in the Pacific, feeding sheep and cattle on the hillside, living, moving, acting, thinking, planning, living in families as husbands, wives, and children, and, above all, confessing and worshipping the Christian's God, and looking hopefully for life and immortality beyond the grave, we are called upon to prove that we are men?

Would you have me argue that man is entitled to liberty? That he is the rightful owner of his own body? You have already declared it. Must I argue the wrongfulness of slavery? Is that a question for Republicans? Is it to be settled by the rules of logic and argumentation, as a matter beset with great difficulty, involving a doubtful application of the principle of justice, hard to be understood? How should I look today, in the presence of Americans, dividing and subdividing a discourse, to show that men have a natural right to freedom, speaking of it relatively and positively, negatively and affirmatively? To do so would be to make myself ridiculous, and to offer an insult to your understanding. There is not a man beneath the canopy of heaven that does not know that slavery is wrong *for him.*

What, am I to argue that it is wrong to make men brutes, to rob them of their liberty, to work them without wages, to keep them ignorant of their relations to their fellow men, to beat them with sticks, to flay their flesh with the lash, to load their limbs with irons, to hunt them with dogs, to sell them at auction, to sunder their families, to knock out their teeth, to burn their flesh, to starve them into obedience and submission to their masters? Must I argue that a system thus marked with blood, and stained with pollution, is *wrong?* No! I will not. I have better employment for my time and strength than such arguments would imply.

What, then, remains to be argued? Is it that slavery is not divine; that God did not establish it; that our doctors of divinity are mistaken? There is blasphemy in the thought. That which is inhuman cannot be divine! *Who* can reason on such a proposition? They that can, may; I cannot. The time for such argument has passed.

At a time like this, scorching irony, not convincing argument, is needed. O! had I the ability, and could I reach the nation's ear, I would, today, pour out a fiery stream of biting ridicule, blasting reproach, withering sarcasm, and stern rebuke. For it is not light that is needed, but fire; it is not the gentle shower, but thunder. We need the storm, the whirlwind, and the earthquake. The feeling of the nation must be quickened; the conscience of the nation must be roused; the propriety of the nation must be startled; the hypocrisy of the nation must be exposed; and its crimes against God and man must be proclaimed and denounced.

What, to the American slave, is your Fourth of July? I answer: a day that reveals to him, more than all other days in the year, the gross injustice and cruelty of which he is the constant victim. To him, your celebration is a sham; your boasted liberty, an unholy license; your national greatness, swelling vanity. Your sounds of rejoicing are empty and heartless; your denunciation of tyrants, brass-fronted impudence; your shouts of liberty and equality, hollow mockery; your prayers and hymns, your sermons and thanksgivings, with all your religious parade and solemnity, are, to him, mere bombast, fraud, deception, impiety, and hypocrisy——a thin veil to cover up crimes which would disgrace a nation of savages. There is not a nation on the earth guilty of practices more shocking and bloody than are the people of the United States, at this very hour.

Go where you may, search where you will, roam through all the monarchies and despotisms of the Old World, travel through South America, search out every abuse, and when you have found the last, lay your facts by the side of the everyday practices of this nation, and you will say with me that, for revolting barbarity and shameless hypocrisy, America reigns without a rival.

Booker T. Washington

(See page 121.)

THE ATLANTA EXPOSITION ADDRESS [1]

MR. PRESIDENT AND GENTLEMEN OF THE
BOARD OF DIRECTORS AND CITIZENS:

One third of the population of the South is of the Negro race. No enterprise seeking the material, civil, or moral welfare of this section can disregard this element of our population and reach the highest success. I but convey to you, Mr. President and Directors, the sentiment of the masses of my race when I say that in no way have the value and manhood of the American Negro been more fittingly and generously recognized than by the managers of this magnificent Exposition at every stage of its progress. It is a recognition that will do more to cement the friendship of the two races than any occurrence since the dawn of our freedom.

Not only this, but the opportunity here afforded will awaken among us a new era of industrial progress. Ignorant and inexperienced, it is not strange that in the first years of our new life we began at the top instead of at the bottom; that a seat in Congress or the state legislature was more sought than real estate or industrial skill; that the political convention of stump speaking had more attractions than starting a dairy farm or truck garden.

A ship lost at sea for many days suddenly sighted a friendly vessel.

---

[1] Delivered in 1895. Reprinted from *Up from Slavery*. Copyright, 1900, 1901, by Booker T. Washington. Reprinted by permission of Doubleday & Company, Inc., New York.

From the mast of the unfortunate vessel was seen a signal, "Water, water; we die of thirst!" The answer from the friendly vessel at once came back, "Cast down your bucket where you are." A second time the signal, "Water, water; send us water!" ran up from the distressed vessel, and was answered, "Cast down your bucket where you are." And a third and fourth signal for water was answered, "Cast down your bucket where you are." The captain of the distressed vessel, at last heeding the injunction, cast down his bucket, and it came up full of fresh, sparkling water from the mouth of the Amazon River. To those of my race who depend on bettering their condition in a foreign land or who underestimate the importance of cultivating friendly relations with the Southern white man, who is their next-door neighbor, I would say: "Cast down your bucket where you are"——cast it down in making friends in every manly way of the people of all races by whom we are surrounded.

Cast it down in agriculture, mechanics, in commerce, in domestic service, and in the professions. And in this connection it is well to bear in mind that whatever other sins the South may be called to bear, when it comes to business, pure and simple, it is in the South that the Negro is given a man's chance in the commercial world, and in nothing is this Exposition more eloquent than in emphasizing this chance. Our greatest danger is that in the great leap from slavery to freedom we may overlook the fact that the masses of us are to live by the productions of our hands, and fail to keep in mind that we shall prosper in proportion as we learn to dignify and glorify common labor and put brains and skill into the common occupations of life; shall prosper in proportion as we learn to draw the line between the superficial and the substantial, the ornamental gewgaws of life and the useful. No race can prosper till it learns that there is as much dignity in tilling a field as in writing a poem. It is at the bottom of life we must begin, and not at the top. Nor should we permit our grievances to overshadow our opportunities.

To those of the white race who look to the incoming of those of foreign birth and strange tongue and habits for the prosperity of the South, were I permitted I would repeat what I say to my own race, "Cast down your bucket where you are." Cast it down among the eight millions of Negroes whose habits you know, whose fidelity and love you have tested in days when to have proved treacherous meant the ruin of your firesides. Cast down your bucket among these people who have, without strikes and labor war, tilled your fields, cleared your forests, builded your railroads and cities, and brought forth treasures from the bowels of the earth, and helped make possible this magnificent representation of the progress of the South.

Casting down your bucket among my people, helping and encouraging them as you are doing on these grounds, and to education of head, hand, and heart, you will find that they will buy your surplus land, make blossom the waste places in your fields, and run your factories. While doing this, you can be sure in the future, as in the past, that you and your families will be surrounded by the most patient, faithful, law-abiding, and unresentful people that the world has seen. As we have proved our loyalty to you in the past, in nursing your children, watching by the sick-bed of your mothers and fathers, and often following them with tear-dimmed eyes to their graves, so in the future, in our humble way, we shall stand by you with a devotion that no foreigner can approach, ready to lay down our lives, if need be, in defense of yours, interlacing our industrial, commercial, civil, and religious life with yours in a way that shall make the interests of both races one. In all things that are purely social we can be as separate as the fingers, yet one as the hand in all things essential to mutual progress.

There is no defense or security for any of us except in the highest intelligence and development of all. If anywhere there are efforts tending to curtail the fullest growth of the Negro, let these efforts be turned into stimulating, encouraging, and making him the most useful and intelligent citizen. Effort or means so invested will pay a thousand per cent interest. These efforts will be twice blessed——"blessing him that gives and him that takes."

There is no escape through law of man or God from the inevitable:

> The laws of changeless justice bind
> Oppressor with oppressed;
> And close as sin and suffering joined
> We march to fate abreast.

Nearly sixteen millions of hands will aid you in pulling the load upward, or they will pull against you the load downward. We shall constitute one third and more of the ignorance and crime of the South, or one third its intelligence and progress; we shall contribute one third to the business and industrial prosperity of the South, or we shall prove a veritable body of death, stagnating, depressing, retarding every effort to advance the body politic.

Gentlemen of the Exposition, as we present to you our humble effort at an exhibition of our progress, you must not expect overmuch. Starting thirty years ago with ownership here and there in a few quilts and pumpkins and chickens (gathered from miscellaneous sources), remember the path that has led from these to the inventions and production of agricultural implements, buggies, steam engines, newspapers, books, statuary, carving, paintings, the management of drugstores and banks, has not been trodden without contact with thorns and thistles. While we take pride in what we exhibit as a result of our independent efforts, we do not for a moment forget that our part in this exhibition would fall far short of your expectations but for the constant help that has come to our educational life, not only from the Southern states but especially from Northern philanthropists, who have made their gifts a constant stream of blessing and encouragement.

The wisest among my race understand that the agitation of questions of social equality is the extremest folly, and that progress in the enjoyment of all the privileges that will come to us must be the result of severe and constant struggle rather than of artificial forcing. No race that has anything to contribute to the markets of the world is long in any degree ostracized. It is important and right that all privileges of the law be ours, but it is vastly more important that we be prepared for the exercise of these privileges. The opportunity to earn a dollar in a factory just now is worth infinitely more than the opportunity to spend a dollar in an opera house.

In conclusion, may I repeat that nothing in thirty years has given us more hope and encouragement, and drawn us so near to you of the white race, as this opportunity offered by the Exposition; and here bending, as it were, over the altar that represents the results of the struggles of your race and mine, both starting practically empty-handed three decades ago, I pledge that in your effort to work out the great and intricate problem which God has laid at the doors of the South, you shall have at all times the patient, sympathetic help of my race; only let this be constantly in mind, that, from representations in these buildings of the product of field, of forest, of mine, of factory, letters, and art, much good will come in a blotting out of sectional differences and racial animosities and suspicions, in a determination to administer absolute justice, in a willing obedience among all classes to the mandates of law. This, then, coupled with our material prosperity, will bring into our beloved South a new heaven and a new earth.

Ulysses S. Donaldson

Ulysses S. Donaldson, educator, journalist, minister, and essayist, was born at Baton Rouge, Louisiana. He was educated at the Crispus Attucks Public School of Carbondale, Illinois, the Lovejoy High School of Mound City, Illinois; Hillsdale College of Michigan; the University of London; and Indiana State Teachers College. Among his publications are *The Humanity of Jesus* and "The Life of Frederick C. Alston." He has served as Editor of the *Journal of Education* for the Missouri State Association of Negro Teachers.

GEORGE WASHINGTON AND THE NEGRO [1]

George Washington, representative of the finest Cavalier stock in Virginia, generalissimo of the Continental Army and father of his country, was none the less a *Virginia slaveholder*. Mazyck [2] takes the position that, had he "been other than a slaveholder in Virginia in the eighteenth century, he would not have risen high in the affairs of the nation. Strange anomaly, that the morals [and the economic and social traditions] of his time should have decreed that he must be one who deprived his fellowmen of liberty if he would also be father of the land of the free."

[1] A radio address. Reprinted with the permission of the author.
[2] Mazyck, Walter H., *George Washington and the Negro*, p. v.

It was only in some such paradox as this that he could develop the powers and the principles that would guarantee his rise in the affairs of this nation. Only as a master of slaves could he acquire unbiased, reliable, first-hand knowledge of the benefits, if any, and the evils of slavery. The inhumanity of the institution of slavery clashed with his humanity and his insistence on the rights of man, evinced by the 17th resolution of the "Fairfax Resolves." He early deplored the slave trade, and eventually manifested his opposition to the system by his oft-expressed willingness to draft plans for gradual emancipation, provided only that suitable legislation could be enacted so that detriment would come neither to the freedmen nor to their former masters. This position represented a revolt against the system in vogue when he arrived on the scene.

As a master of slaves, Washington took exceeding care of their health; saw to it that they were comfortably sheltered and clothed, that they were taught useful arts and crafts by employed artisans, white and black. His discipline was strict, his regulations rigidly enforced, and tasks had to be efficiently performed. All of this, and much more, was accomplished without the obvious, customary brutality, characteristic of the slave system. It obtained as much because of the master's consciousness of good results in the development of the slave as it was a matter of acknowledged good business in the management of his estates.

Without doubt, Washington was actuated by a fine motive when, in his will, he made provisions for the care of the aged and the totally disabled, and the emancipation of the rest of "my people"—as he called his slaves—after the death of himself and his wife. He knew that, while he lived, he would not sell any of them, since he was "principled" against selling slaves, and that he would see to it that they worked and had proper food, shelter, and clothing.

In the management of his estates, he sought to effect every possible economy. He recognized the advantages of skilled slave labor over free labor. It was in keeping with this knowledge that he employed both white and black journeymen artisans to teach talented slaves on his estates the trades. A remarkable instance was that of Benjamin Buckler, foreman of carpenters.

When and wherever he had "merit in black" brought to his attention, he took notice of it. Note his acknowledgement of an ode dedicated to him by Phillis Wheatley, Negro poetess of the eighteenth century, and in addition thereunto, his invitation to "Miss Phillis" to visit his headquarters at Cambridge. A short time thereafter, she made the visit. Another example: On the recommendation of Thomas Jefferson, he appointed Benjamin Banneker, Negro mathematician, surveyor, and astronomer, one of the six commissioners to lay out the city of Washington in the District of Columbia.

Although prudence demanded the reversal of his policy to exclude the Negro from participation in the Revolutionary War, Washington demands some credit for his acceptance of the lesser of two evils: the possibility of losing the war with the Negro fighting against him; on the other hand, the possibility of losing the contest with the Negro fighting with him. His original exclusion policy was compatible with the conventional status of the Negro. The Negro's admission into the ranks of the Continental Army was on the side of human rights. It was, therefore, a triumph for him. Thereby, the Negro contributed Peter Salem and Salem Poor at Bunker Hill, and Pompey at Stony Point.

For any merit set forth in this talk and for the much more unenumerated for the lack of time, we believe Washington to be still, "first in war, first in peace, and first in the hearts of his countrymen."

George L. Vaughn

George L. Vaughn, lawyer, essayist, historian, and fraternal and civic leader, was born in Kentucky. In St. Louis, Missouri, in the practice of his profession, he attained national fame. He was a graduate of the Law School of Walden University of Nashville, Tennessee. As a municipal judge, as the first president of the Mound City Bar Association, and as a member of several leading national organizations, he brought honor to each organization with which he was identified. As a leader, he was responsible for initiating many movements that have resulted in reforms in St. Louis for the Negro. In his death in August, 1949, the country lost a great citizen.

Among his writings are *The Negro Origin of Free Masonry, Sumerian Civilization, Antar, Arabian Negro Poet and General,* and *The Negro's Armageddon.*

THE NEGRO'S ARMAGEDDON [1]

"They go forth unto the kings of the earth and of the whole world to gather them to the battle of the Great Day of God Almighty. . . . And He gathered them together unto a place called in the Hebrew tongue Har Mageddon."

Between the great Arabian Desert and the eastern shore of the Mediterranean Sea there lies a narrow strip of land known in ancient times as Syria. It was the highway between the continents of Africa and Asia. The armies of the Egyptians, Ethiopians, and Hittites passed thither on their war-like missions into Assyria, Babylonia and Persia; and the armies of these, in turn, traversed the same route on their expeditions into Africa. Commercial caravans, as well as travelers on other missions, also used this route as being more direct and less hazardous than either the desert sands or the raging sea.

Through this territory several mountain ranges run in a general north-and-south direction, with the valleys between paralleling the length of the country and furnishing natural highways between these two continents. In this territory were to be found the well-known cities of Sidon and Tyre, Samaria and Jerusalem, Gaza and Damascus, and the village called by the Greeks, Armageddon. Almost at right angles with these mountains and valleys, lofty Mount Carmel reared its head and formed a natural barrier against these invading hordes. At the eastern side lay the broad plain of Armageddon—the battleground of the ancient world. The western edge of this mountain was too close to the coast to be of service to an invading army, and the narrow Aruna road, leading through its defiles, furnished too many chances for successful ambush, while robber kings levied tribute on victor and vanquished; so that the main route lay around the eastern end of the mountain and through the Armageddon plain.

[1] An excerpt from an address delivered at a public forum of the Pine Street (St. Louis) Y.M.C.A. in 1916. Copyright, 1916, by St. Louis Argus Publishing Company, St. Louis, Mo.

Thither hurried the contending armies, each intent upon taking possession of this coveted plain ahead of its adversary. Failing in this design, the only alternative was to win by force and skill of arms what
speed and strategy had not been able to accomplish. So important was
the possession of this plain considered, that the great Thutmose of
Egypt celebrated its surrender with the exultant shout:

"Behold, it is the capture of a thousand cities, the capture of
Meggedo."

Here then were fought out the issues of civilization for thousands of
years; here the destinies of nations and continents were determined,
and the deeds of their heroes were heralded to the utmost parts of the
civilized world. It was this city and plain to which the writer of the
lines quoted at the beginning of this address referred; and, to the nations of the earth, the term "Armageddon" has come to signify the
struggle of contending ideas and forces for their right to a place in the
sun.

In my opinion, such a struggle, such a crisis, confronts the Negro
group in America today.

A Big World Question

The question uppermost in the mind of the world today is the race
question. From every quarter of the globe there are tidings of racial
conflicts, clashings, and strivings which drive home the realization of
the truth that the world is undergoing a social revolution which has
been largely precipitated by the race question. This factor is inter-
twined with each and all of the other great questions now agitating the
nations of the world. At every turn in the road it is met; in trade, politics, social relations, religion, art, science, and the momentous questions of peace and war. Egypt and the Sudan, the South African question, the Riffians in Morocco, the Chinese riots, the Turks and Mosul,
the Jews and Russia, the situation in India, the Japanese question, the
Haitian occupation, and the so-called Negro problem in America,——
all show that the world is in a great dilemma with respect to the race
question. . . .

It is with the American Negro phase of this question that I wish
to deal.

The Color Line

Here in America, we have erected as a means of distinction between the races what is known as the "color line." Not that the physical phenomenon of difference in color is applicable to all, or nearly all, of the persons designated as Negroes; but, embracing as it does the large majority of them, it is a convenient means of group identification. But the color line, in America, embraces every individual in the Negro group, from the blackest man of purest African blood to the whitest individual in whose veins courses any of that blood. Biologically speaking there is no Negro group in America, for fully eighty-five percent of the race here is of mixed white and Negro, or Indian and Negro, blood. . . .

The Heritage of Slavery

Out of American slavery both slaveholder and slave received a terrible heritage. Whose was the worse, it is difficult to tell. Perhaps only time will solve the riddle. But any consideration of the race question in America, to be even worth the name, must take the fact of slavery and its heritage into account. Thus we see that the color line in America is a tradition, and that tradition is the heritage of slavery.

The Color Line Is the Battle Line

How does this color line, this tradition, affect the Negro American in his every-day living? What handicaps does it place about him? And how are these to be interpreted in relation to his physical, spiritual, and social advancement? Methinks the answer to these questions will show the Negro his battleground—his Armageddon.

Given his freedom as a war measure imperatively necessary to the success of Union arms, the Negro was thrust into a new economic environment without preparation to meet it. To most of these former slaves even the task of providing food and clothing was a new and untried experience. Ignorant, penniless, well-nigh helpless, the Negro found himself face to face with responsibilities little dreamed of before. Add to these circumstances the hostile feelings of his former masters, who believed themselves to be grossly injured by the forcible taking of their human property, and you have a fairly accurate picture of the Negro's condition at emancipation. But he did not falter under these almost superhuman burdens. Accustomed to work, he soon set himself at the task of rebuilding the fortunes of the South and creating his own. . . . How well he has succeeded is shown by the splendid advancement which he has made. The story reads almost like a tale from the *Arabian Nights*. From paupers to taxpayers on millions of property holdings, from 98 per cent illiterate to 80 per cent literate, from a fence corner in which to live to a mansion, the owner of a million homes, big and little, with standards of living grading with the rest of the community,—these tell the story in such eloquent terms that mere words of praise are idle.

Be it said to the eternal credit of the Negro that the story of his reaction to freedom and the living of a new life thereunder records fewer excesses on his part than can be found in the experience of any other people on earth. . . .

The Negro's leaving the South is but one phase of his battle against the color line. . . . Its burdens are almost beyond the powers of human beings to endure. . . .

In the North the color line is evidenced by riots for economic reasons, such as the East St. Louis riot a few years ago; by the bombing of churches and homes, as in Chicago, Kansas City, and Detroit; by restrictive clauses in deeds prohibiting the sale of property to Negroes as is being done in St. Louis, and even at the nation's capital.[1] . . .

From a national standpoint the color line is evidenced by segregation in the departments at Washington, by closing the doors of West Point and Annapolis [2] to Negro youths, and by gross discrimination against colored men in the army and navy.

A few years ago, in the City of St. Louis, one of the large commercial houses received a big order for goods from a South American country. The order was written in Spanish, and a search of the clerical

[1] Judge Vaughn in 1948 won from the Supreme Court of the United States a unanimous decision outlawing residential restrictive covenants.
[2] With the liberal sentiment of the world on the increase, Negroes in 1949 are going to West Point and Annapolis in increasing numbers. In May 1948 the first Negro graduated from Annapolis.

force disclosed the fact that not a single white man in all that big establishment understood the idiom of the Spanish tongue sufficiently well to do anything with that order. In the middle of this dilemma, someone remembered that there was a Negro boy on the elevator who understood the Spanish language. He had acquired it at night after toiling all day as an elevator operator. He was called in and, to the joy of the management, read and interpreted the order, which proved to be much larger than had at first been suspected. A force of seven white clerks was put under his charge, and for three days they worked incessantly filling this huge order for the goods dealt in by this house. Here, then, was the opportunity which this lad had sought. By diligent study and honest conduct he had fitted himself for this very moment. The firm by which he was employed was anxious to win South American trade, and had not been able to do so theretofore largely because it could not interpret the Latin American mind as expressed in the Spanish tongue. Here was the man to supply that need. He was a ready-prepared agency with which to win that trade and bring millions to his employers and gain a competence for himself. He had won the place by every rule of the game, and surely justice, decency and self interest, all, demanded that it be given to him. But it was not to be so. He was a Negro; and, when the order was filled, he was sent back to the elevator, where he could not earn enough even to think of establishing a family. Disillusioned, humiliated, and with an exceedingly clear idea of the meaning of the color line in America, he did the only decent thing left for him to do. He quit, and went out into the world jobless instead of reaping the just rewards of being honest, industrious, and intelligent. Should he become a criminal, it must be charged to the brutal unfairness of the color line.

I would have the Negro know that his is the most patient race on earth; and that patience is the bedrock of fortitude. That patience he learned through the vicissitudes of ten thousand years of civilization. It possesses his soul. It enabled him "to discover the arts and sciences, while other people were yet barbarians, and to found, on the study of the laws of nature, those civil and religious systems which still govern the universe." It was that patience which enabled him to survive the terrible middle passage and endure the hardships of American slavery; and now it lends him the fortitude to carry on and to thrive under the hard conditions which American life has imposed on him.

> That is why he can sing where others are silent,
> Why he laughs where others might sigh,
> Why he smiles where others curse,
> Why he lives while others die.

I would have him know that he possesses a brave and kindly heart; that, upon a thousand fields of honor, whether mastering the raging lion in his native jungle with a single spear or facing the armies of the world on the field of battle, he taught that heart to know no fear. . . .

Charles Harris Wesley

Charles Harris Wesley, historian, essayist, minister, and educator, was born at Louisville, Kentucky. He was educated in the public schools of Louisville and at Fisk University, and studied also at Yale, Harvard, and the Guilde Internationale, Paris. For some time he was pastor of the Ebenezer A. M. E. Church of Washington, D. C. Later he served as Head of the Department of History and Dean of the Graduate School of Howard University. He is now President of the Academic Division of Wilberforce University.

Among his publications are the following: *Negro Labor in the United States, The Collapse of the Confederacy, Richard Allen,* "Problems of Sources and Methods in History Teaching," "The Struggle of Haiti and Liberia for Recognition," "Lincoln's Plan for Colonizing Emancipated Negroes," "The Employment of Negroes as Soldiers in the Confederate Army," "Henry O. Tanner."

THE PURSUIT OF THINGS [1]

I want to direct your attention to the subject, "The Pursuit of Things," and I shall use as a basis for our thought the twelfth chapter of Luke, the fifteenth verse: "For a man's life consisteth not in the abundance of things which he possesseth."

[1] From the Baccalaureate Address delivered to the Class of 1943 at Wilberforce University. Reprinted with the permission of the author.

We have been and are facing the twentieth century, an age dominated not only by the mass production of things but also by "the
pursuit of things." This entire century has so far been characterized
by the development of machines used for the production of things——
things for individual comforts; things for group comfort; things which
give ease and satisfaction and cessation from manual labor; and things
which satisfy the desires, numerous as they are, of the individual
person. . . .

Jesus did not underestimate the value of things. On one occasion
he said to his disciples, "Your Father knoweth ye have need of these
things," and again, "Seek ye first the Kingdom of God and all these
things shall be added unto you." He thus made a place for things in
life, but this place was always a secondary one. His ideal was neither
wealth nor poverty. The Middle Age Church and some churchmen
of the present day have made an error in idealizing poverty. There
has been and there is no virtue in poverty. We admire St. Francis, who
would give away his inheritance and accept a life of poverty; but what
is admired is not his poverty, but his devotion to the high ideal of
service, of which his acceptance of poverty was only a symbol. We
need this Jesus view of life in our lives to prevent warped thinking on
life's objectives.

Contrary to this philosophy, American life and thought have followed the increasing possession of an abundance of things as a supreme objective. We have made the machines which made the things
and remade them to make larger numbers of things. Our inventive
genius has continued to make things faster and in more abundance.
Machine processes, intricate mass production, and horsepower in
larger amounts have been symbols of our national success. But when
1929 came on, we were stirred from our security and satisfied circumstances. We then rode in 1929 automobiles and airplanes, but we clung
to the ox-cart ideas of the contemporaries of Jesus. We wanted modern
things for our homes and ourselves, but we forgot the things which
really made the home great and ourselves worthy. Things then took
to the saddle and they rode mankind almost to his doom.

There are three phases of life in which this principle of life oper-
ates to man's detriment. The first of these is the sphere of warfare.

This has been the scourge of humanity. The war-god has harnessed us to his chariot and dragged us while he pursued his search for things. Wars have been caused by the clash of economic and political forces in competition for things. The rivalry among nations for the control of the economic resources of the earth has been a basic factor in the creation of modern wars. Other causes have been alleged, but if the seeker searches carefully, he will find ultimately some such basis in fact. The competition has become keener in the atmosphere of hostility which has been created by modern nationalism. The industrially backward regions have been parcelled out among the nations as sources for needed things and as markets for things. National propaganda has been able to conceal the barren facts under such concepts as "the balance of power" and "the white man's burden."

Nations continue to seek things for themselves to protect and increase their abundances even to the detriment of other nations and peoples. The expansion of industrialism has increased competition between the nations for raw materials, food, markets, and investment areas. The United States has been no exception to this rule. . . .

Our present economic order is another sphere in which things rule, and greed for more is dominant. Self-interest and competition for profits are basic factors in our present economic life. These are fundamental concepts. The result is that in this competitive life, the few strong individuals possess in increasing fashion the things, the comforts of life, while the many do not have even the necessities of life. The privileged few have more luxuries than they need, while many live in extreme poverty and need. Malnutrition, wretched housing, disease, poverty, sickness, crime, are the lot of the many. Vast disparities have developed between the successful few and the unfortunate many in our present economic order. In many communities, there are those who live with the opportunity of gratifying every physical desire for things of the earth, while their neighbors live in severe privation. We ought to know that the nation's life, just as the individual's, does not have its happiness rest in the abundance of things for a small percentage of its people. The wealth of these few gives them power over their fellows. . . . The press has been dominated by the rich. Education has been controlled. Poor men are able to rise to power in politics at times, mainly because they are backed by men of wealth. . . .

As a special population group, which experiences some isolation, it is desirable that we interest ourselves more fully in economic endeavors and that business, technical, and industrial pursuits, particularly on the cooperative basis, should have greater consideration from our schools and colleges and our leadership. In a technical age we cannot continue to sing the song, "You can have all the world but give me Jesus." There is need for emphasis upon participation in the American program of economic abundance, but this should not be one of selfish possession but rather one of cooperative endeavor with the abundant life equally enjoyed by all the people. . . .

A third aspect of this concept of the pursuit of things is apparent in the group antagonisms within nations based upon the idea of race. These antagonisms arise more often from the desire to possess things and the concepts which grow out of it. Opposition to the Jews was based partly upon this idea, as well as upon religious hatreds. Slavery was basically economic, and was founded upon the production of things by the many for the few. Discriminations against Negroes, so widespread in this country, have been outgrowths of economic causes arising from false pride. Violence between white and Negro workers is based in part upon the desire to keep things or get things in the form of work and wages. Lynching and mob violence have their economic foundations. Oriental peoples, though born in the United States, are subjected to similar treatments, growing out of their competition with American workers. Immigrants to our country have experienced the same reactions. The prevailing hatred and cruelties towards groups of people in our Christian era, rising out of competition among the peoples for things, almost belie the designation of "Christian," and in no case can they be reconciled with the idea of the Kingdom of God. If, then, life in these aspects and in many others does not consist in the abundance of things which a man possesses, of what does it consist? It consists, in accordance with this fundamental concept of Jesus, of two factors; one is personal character and the other is social responsibility.

Character includes the reaction tendencies towards life situations which involve moral, ethical, and religious codes, and socially approved standards of conduct. . . .

Henry N. Wieman tells of a college classmate who decided that he needed the things of college life in order to be a good student. Being a young man of a wealthy family he could purchase some of the greater comforts of life. He got an easy chair, soft slippers, a lounging jacket, an adjustable lamp, a comfortable desk, and a revolving bookcase. Then with these things about him, Wieman describes how often he repeatedly fell asleep over his books. On the contrary, *Pilgrim's Progress* came out of a prison, as did Raleigh's *History of the World*. Cervantes' *Don Quixote* came out of a life which had been enslaved, which suffered from torture and had been distressed from misfortune, and "Paradise Lost" came from eyes which were blind. . . .

Members of the Graduating Class, we frequently have to lose our lives in order to find them. We lose them in great adventures, great causes, great purposes; and real accomplishments are the result. We forget ourselves in music, and we find the truest enjoyment. We lose ourselves in the playing of a game, and the thrill is surprising. We sink ourselves in a friend, and we learn to know the value of true friendship. But to seek directly the happiness which comes from these and other spheres of life is to miss it. Happiness is more frequently a by-product. It comes to us while we labor with forgetfulness in other areas.

Let us rescue the part of our age with which we are associated from the dominance of things, from the imperialism which seeks things and makes wars, and from the exploitation which produces things and brings physical exhaustion and spiritual impoverishment to our nation. Our democracy, born in the travail of revolution, continues to give devotion to the tenets of life, liberty, and the pursuit of happiness. The developments of our era would seem to change these to life, liberty, and property. This was not the objective of our national beginnings, neither should we adopt its pursuit now. We must realize that the fatherhood of God, the brotherhood of man, love, truth, peace are also the most real things.

Vernon S. Johns

Vernon S. Johns, minister and educator, was born at Farmville, Virginia. After graduating from the Virginia Theological Seminary and College, he became the pastor of the Court Street Baptist Church at Lynchburg, Virginia. After he obtained the degree of Bachelor of Divinity from Oberlin College, he became pastor of the First Baptist Church of Charleston, West Virginia. While serving as Dean and later President of Virginia Theological Seminary, he organized and directed the Farm and City Club and an Institute for Rural Preachers of Virginia, which he conducted for almost ten years. Recently he accepted the pastorate of the Dexter Avenue Baptist Church of Montgomery, Alabama.

"Transfigured Moments," one of his sermons, was published by the Right Reverend Joseph Forte Newton in *The Best Sermons of 1926*.

CIVILIZED INTERIORS [1]

"The Kingdom of God is Within"—Jesus.
"Some perversity in us has conkered twenty-one civilizations."
George E. Buttrick.

At some time in the remote past, man made the great appeal from nature to civilization. Arising in the physical order of which he is a part, man turned with transforming impact upon his environment and undertook to reshape it after his liking. In this undertaking he has had the most astounding success.

He found his world, for instance, adequately lighted only on clear days between sunrise and sunset, and, revolting against the limitations imposed by excessive darkness, he went from one degree of illumination to another until, finally, "night shines as the day." There was something he wanted to say and he invented speech. Annoyed further by the inconvenience of limiting the transfer of ideas to the carrying power of his voice, he grappled with his problem of communication until now, over the radio, he belts the globe with an undertone. He started his pilgrimage on foot and stepped up transportation until

1 Reprinted with the permission of the author.

today he is not more than three days from anywhere. "Nor rain nor hail nor wintry wind stay his faithful couriers from the swift accomplishment of their appointed tasks."

At times the animals disputed his passage, but he picked up the challenge laid down by mammoth, mastodon, and microbe. He made his animal enemy a chief bearer of his burdens and a main source of his fats and proteins; and then he added delicacies to his diet until today he eats ice cream in the tropics and strawberries at the poles. He lives in luxurious lodgings and rides on rubber to absorb the shock of his on-going and says to himself, "What a piece of work is Man!"

Twenty-one different times since the record was kept, men have reared up civilizations at great pains and cost, and twenty-one times they have gone to pieces, carrying down in ruins the creation of centuries and millenniums and occasioning untold misery for the multitudes on whom they fell. For all the sorrows of a society are summed up in its decline: failure and disillusionment, blood and tears, cursing and hate, murder and rapine; starvation and despair; the groans of the dying; the stench of the dead; the broken hopes of men; the broken hearts of women; the unutterable sadness of little children; decaying palaces and deserted temples.

For half a lifetime now, prophets of gloom have been pointing us toward the twilight of our Western culture. One writes of the passing of the Great Race; another shows us the Decline of the West. Henry George writes, "The forces which will either revivify American Civilization or convulse it in ruins will soon set in—if they be not already begun." Lord Macaulay pictures the savage New Zealander leaning on the broken rails of London Bridge. In his farewell to America, Lloyd George said, "We are by no means sure of the future of civilization." H. G. Wells, who was called by Anatole France "the greatest intellectual Force in the English-speaking Race," defined civilization as a "Race between Education and Catastrophe." And one of the scientists who let loose the first atomic bomb in the desert said, "They were afraid its chain reaction might let loose its destruction in unending relays, until the whole face of the planet was seared with ruin."

Thirty years ago a great Negro said to a white American audience, "We know that your civilization is falling, because it is falling on us."

In the last five years we have actually seen the heart of our Western civilization miss a dangerous number of beats; its pulse became fitful and feverish, and its circulatory system disrupted. Our tea stopped coming from China and spices stopped coming from Arabia. Babies lost their cod liver oil and some of them lost their very diapers. Highly developed nations were deprived of elemental necessities, like wholesome bread and pure water. The amenities of civilization vanished. Instead of a cordial greeting when strangers appeared, men sat around the world nervous and jittery, watching for a glimpse of a fellow being, and at the shaking of a bush their machines spat out violent death. Our youth turned from the pursuit of culture to the murderous pursuit of other youths. The continent of Europe, which had been a great light in darkness, became the burial ground of decency and the cornerstone of a new world of tyranny, in which such concepts as Liberty, Fraternity, Equality threatened to be submerged like some fabled Atlantis, leaving generations to become confused as to whether they were myths or memories. Everywhere, the dignity and security of man were menaced. His honor turned to craftiness and his honesty became stealth. For wars are won by lies no less than by logistics and armaments. And now that we have achieved in international affairs the interlude of exhaustion, which we mistake for peace, our civilization is missing as many heartbeats from selfishness within as it missed afore time from selfishness without.

No one appreciated more than Jesus the external beauty of the face of things. "Consider the lilies of the field, how they grow. They toil not, neither do they spin. Yet I say unto you that even Solomon in all his splendor was not arrayed like one of these." And no zealot of his day could elicit from Jesus any support for overthrowing the framework of the Roman state. He knew that no state could, by its governmental form, save itself, its subjects, or its rivals. It was not a new form the world needed, it was a new essence; not new laws but new lives. The same citizens who adorned their homes within as beautifully as they adorned them without, had failed to see that any culture in which men alter their environment without adorning their inner lives was a civilization dressed but unwashed. To preserve the externals of their culture men must bring its interior up to date. This they have never done. James Harvey Robinson reminds us that Aristotle's treatise on Mechanics would be a joke to modern man, but Aristotle's treatises on Ethics and Politics are up to date. The trouble with modern man is that his Interior lags a thousand years behind his Exterior.

PART VII

The Short Story

Introduction   Though short stories are almost as old as man, the short story as a type was first defined by Edgar Allan Poe, the American essayist and father of the short story. This literary form can boast of some great masters: for instance, Rudyard Kipling of England, who wrote "The Jungle Book" and "Soldiers Three"; Robert Louis Stevenson, author of "Dr. Jekyll and Mr. Hyde," "Will o' the Mill," and "Sire de Maletroit's Door"; Guy de Maupassant, author of "The Necklace" and "A Piece of String"; Edgar Allan Poe, author of "The Fall of the House of Usher," "The Purloined Letter," and "The Murders of the Rue Morgue"; and Nathaniel Hawthorne, author of "The Great Stone Face," "Dr. Heidegger's Experiment," and "Dr. Rappoccini's Daughter."

The Negro author has mastered this literary form as evidenced by the collections of Paul Laurence Dunbar, *Folks from Dixie* and *The Strength of Gideon,* and Charles W. Chesnutt's "The Wife of His Youth" and "The Conjure Woman," as well as the stories of more recent writers.

In writing fiction, the author may write as a realist showing the good and the bad side of life, as a pessimist portraying only the worst side, or as an idealist portraying life as he hopes it will be. Both Dunbar and Chesnutt are realists without the obscenity and vulgarity of modern realists.

The student should understand that the short story is not just a narrative that is short, so far as length is concerned, but that it is a definite literary form. It is a prose narrative with only one major climax; that is, with one important incident, which decides the fate of the chief character or chief characters for better or for worse. There may be any number of characters in the short story; but the short story is at its best when it contains only a few outstanding characters and all the others are shadowy in the background. For instance, in Dunbar's "The Strength of Gideon" there are only two outstanding characters: Gideon and the girl he loved. In Chesnutt's "The Wife of His Youth" there are only three outstanding characters: Mr. Ryder and two women.

There are several ways in which the short story may effectively begin. It may start with description or exposition applied to the setting or to an important character. It may begin with an incident or with dialogue. Early in the narrative the chief character or characters should be introduced. For the short story, a character is not introduced unless he speaks or acts. After the chief character is introduced, another character should be introduced by an incident to complicate the action of the early incident that introduced a problem to be solved. The story should then proceed to a major incident, the climax, which is the turning point of the story and decides the fate of the chief character or characters. To be effective, shortly after the climax, with a paragraph or a few sentences, the story must come to an end.

This technique is well observed by each story included in this volume. In "There Will Always Be Hope," by Colleen Williams, this technique is closely followed. There are only two important characters, Judith Trent and Dr. John Paul. Judith opens the story and Dr. Paul appears early in a big incident that complicates the plot. Then follow several other incidents of importance, each more important than the previous one. A big incident closes the story, deciding the fates of the two chief characters. Immediately thereafter the story comes to an end.

As to the length of the story in words or time, there is no set rule, provided there is unity of impression. "The Strength of Gideon" covers a number of years, but the story is well knit together by the integrity of Gideon. This is the one great impression that gives unity to the story.

Aristotle in his *Poetics* mentions three principles observed by the ancient Greeks in the composition of their dramas that can effectively be used to give unity to a short story or to a one-act play. They are called the three classic unities: the unity of time, the unity of place, the unity of mood. According to the unity of time, all the incidents allowed to occur on the stage in the case of a Greek drama should occur within twenty-four hours. According to the unity of place, the scene should not change. Finally, the unity of mood requires the play to be all comedy or all tragedy; that is, there should be no intermingling of comedy and tragedy.

Any one of these classic unities, if observed by a writer of the short story, will produce compression and help give unity of impression. If he can observe two of the classic unities or all three, he will be even more likely to attain the desired unity of impression.

The events of a short story should proceed rapidly once the main action is started. Description and exposition can retard the progress of a story; therefore, if a paragraph of either is to be introduced into the story, it should come well before the main action starts. Otherwise, it should be blended with the narrative by scattered phrases in sentences carrying the action. Robert Louis Stevenson so handles his description and exposition in "Sire de Maletroit's Door."

The speed or momentum of a story may be accelerated by the use of dialogue. The greatest possible speed for a story is obtained by direct narration; that is, by the author's relating the story without the use of description or exposition, or by the use of what some critics call pure narration.

There are several ways in which an author may handle his plot. For the most part, only two methods are used. According to one method, the chief character may begin with a problem to be solved, as is true of "The Wife of His Youth" and "There Will Always Be Hope," with the author devoting the story to a solution of that problem. On the other hand, the story may begin with no problem. In such a case, the problem is created early in the story for the chief character, and the author devotes the rest of his story to an effort to solve that problem. This is the technique of Dunbar in "The Strength of Gideon."

As to types of the short story, "The Strength of Gideon" is a combination of the love story and the character sketch, with the character sketch predominating. Chesnutt's "The Wife of His Youth" is a character sketch blended with romantic adventure. Colleen Williams' "There Will Always Be Hope" is a love story. "The Wife of His Youth" also has the technique of a story within a story, as is characteristic of the detective stories of Poe ("The Purloined Letter," "The Murders of the Rue Morgue") and Kipling's "The Courting of Dinah Shadd." The stories in this volume are sufficient to give a general idea of the technique of the Negro author of the short story.

Paul Laurence Dunbar
(See page 26.)

THE STRENGTH OF GIDEON [1]

Old Mam' Henry, and her word may be taken, said that it was "De powerfulles' sehmont she ever had hyeahd in all huh bo'n days." That was saying a good deal, for the old woman had lived many years on the Stone place and had heard many sermons from preachers, white and black. She was a judge, too.

It really must have been a powerful sermon that Brother Lucius preached, for Aunt Doshy Scott had fallen in a trance in the middle of the aisle, while "Merlatter Mag," who was famed all over the place for having white folks' religion and never "waking up," had broken through her reserve and shouted all over the camp ground.

Several times Cassie had shown signs of giving way, but because she was frail some of the solicitous sisters held her with self-congratulatory care, relieving each other now and then, that each might have a turn in the rejoicings. But as the preacher waded out deeper and deeper in the spiritual stream, Cassie's efforts to make her feelings known became more and more decided. He told them how the spears of the Midianites had "clashed upon de shields of de Gideonites, an' aftah while, wid de powah of de Lawd behin' him, de man Gideon triumphed

[1] From The Strength of Gideon, by Paul Laurence Dunbar. Copyright, 1900, 1928, by Mathilde Dunbar.

mightily," and swaying then and wailing in the dark woods, with grim branches waving in the breath of their own excitement, they could hear above the tumult the clamor of the fight, the clashing of the spears, and the ringing of the shields. They could see the conqueror coming home in triumph. Then when he cried, "A-who, I say, a-who is in Gideon's ahmy today?" and the wailing chorus took up the note, "A-who!" it was too much even for frail Cassie, and, deserted by the solicitous sisters, in the words of Mam' Henry, "she broke a-loose, and faihly tuk de place."

Gideon had certainly triumphed, and when a little boy baby came to Cassie two or three days later, she named him Gideon in honor of the great Hebrew warrior whose story had so wrought upon her. All the plantation knew the spiritual significance of the name, and from the day of his birth the child was as one set apart to a holy mission on earth.

Say what you will of the influences which the circumstances surrounding birth have upon a child, upon this one at least the effect was unmistakable. Even as a baby he seemed to realize the weight of responsibility which had been laid upon his little black shoulders, and there was a complacent dignity in the very way in which he drew upon the sweets of his dirty sugar-teat when the maternal breast was too far away, bending over the sheaves of the field.

He was a child early destined to sacrifice and self-effacement, and as he grew older and other youngsters came to fill Cassie's cabin he took up his lot with the meekness of an infantile Moses. Like Moses he was, too, leading his little flock to the promised land, when he grew to the age at which, bare-footed and one-shifted, he led or carried his little brothers and sisters about the quarters. But the "promised land" never took him in the direction of the stables, where the other pickaninnies worried the horses, or into the region of the hen-coops, where eggsucking was a common crime.

No boy ever rolled or tumbled in the dirt with a heartier glee than did Gideon, but no warrior, not even his illustrious prototype himself, ever kept sterner discipline in his ranks when his followers seemed prone to overstep the bounds of right. At a very early age his shrill voice could be heard calling in admonitory tones, caught from his mother's very lips, "You 'Nelius, don' you let me ketch you th'owin' at ol' mis' guinea-hens no mo'; you hyeah me?" or "Hi'am, you come offen de top er dat shed 'fo' you fall an' brek you' naik all to pieces."

It was a common sight in the evening to see him sitting upon the low rail fence which ran before the quarters, his shift blowing in the wind, and his black legs lean and bony against the white-washed rails, as he swayed to and fro, rocking and singing one of his numerous brothers to sleep, and always his song was of war and victory, albeit crooned in a low, soothing voice. Sometimes it was "Turn Back Pharaoh's Army," at others "Jinin' Gideon's Band." The latter was a favorite, for he seemed to have a proprietary interest in it, although, despite the martial inspiration of his name, "Gideon's Band" to him meant an aggregation of people with horns and fiddles.

Steve, who was Cassie's man, declared that he had never seen such a child, and, being quite as religious as Cassie herself, early began to talk Scripture and religion to the boy. He was aided in this when his master, Dudley Stone, a man of the faith, began a little Sunday class for the religiously inclined of the quarters, where the old familiar stories were told in simple language to the slaves and explained. At these meetings Gideon became a shining light. No one listened more eagerly to the teacher's words, or more readily answered his questions at review. No one was wider-mouthed or whiter-eyed. His admonitions to his family now took on a different complexion, and he could be heard calling across a lot to a mischievous sister, "Bettah tek keer daih, Lucy Jane, Gawd's a-watchin' you; bettah tek keer."

The appointed man is always marked, and so Gideon was by always receiving his full name. No one ever shortened his scriptural appellation into Gid. He was always Gideon from the time he bore the name out of the heat of camp-meeting fervor until his master discovered his worthiness and filled Cassie's breast with pride by taking him into the house to learn "mannahs and 'po'tment."

As a house servant he was beyond reproach, and next to his religion his Mas' Dudley and Miss Ellen claimed his devotion and fidelity. The young mistress and young master learned to depend fearlessly upon his faithfulness.

It was good to hear old Dudley Stone going through the house in a mock fury, crying, "Well, I never saw such a house; it seems as if there isn't a soul in it that can do without Gideon. Here I've got him up here to wait on me, and it's Gideon here and Gideon there, and every time I turn around some of you have sneaked him off. Gideon, come here!" And the black boy smiled and came.

But all his days were not days devoted to men's service, for there came a time when love claimed him for her own, when the clouds took on a new color, when the sound of the wind was music in his ears, and he saw heaven in Martha's eyes. It all came about in this way.

Gideon was young when he got religion and joined the church, and he grew up strong in the faith. Almost by the time he had become a valuable house servant he had grown to be an invaluable servant of the Lord. He had a good, clear voice that could raise a hymn out of all the labyrinthian wanderings of an ignorant congregation, even when he had to improvise words and music; and he was a mighty man of prayer. It was thus he met Martha. Martha was brown and buxom and comely, and her rich contralto voice was loud and high on the sisters' side in meeting time. It was the voices that did it at first. There was no hymn or "spiritual" that Gideon could start to which Martha could not sing an easy blending second, and never did she open a tune that Gideon did not swing into it with a wonderfully sweet, flowing, natural bass. Often he did not know the piece, but that did not matter, he sang anyway. Perhaps when they were out he would go to her and ask, "Sis Martha, what was that hymn you stahrted today?" and she would probably answer, "Oh, dat was jes' one o' my mammy's ol' songs."

"Well, it sholy was mighty pretty. Indeed it was."

"Oh, thanky, Brothah Gidjon, thanky."

Then a little later they began to walk back to the master's house together, for Martha, too, was one of the favored ones, and served, not in the field, but in the big house.

The old women looked on and conversed in whispers about the pair, for they were wise, and what their old eyes saw, they saw.

"Oomph," said Mam' Henry, for she commented on everything, "dem too is jes' natchelly singin' demse'ves togeddah."

"Dey's lak de mo'nin' stahs," interjected Aunt Sophy.

"How 'bout dat?" sniffed the older woman, for she objected to any one's alluding to subjects she did not understand.

"Why, Mam' Henry, ain' you nevah hyeahd tell o' de mo'nin' stahs whut sung deyse'ves togeddah?"

"No, I ain't, an' I been livin' a mighty sight longah'n you, too. I knows all 'bout when de stahs fell, but dey ain' nevah done no singin' dat I knows 'bout."

"Do heish, Mam' Henry, you sho' su'prises me. W'y, dat ain' happenin's, dat's Scripter."

"Look hyeah, gal, don't you tell me dat's Scripter, an' me been a-settin' undah de Scripter fu' nigh onto sixty yeah."

"Well, Mam' Henry, I may 'a' been mistook, but sho' I took hit fu' Scripter. Mebbe de preachah I hyeahd was jes' inlinin'."

"Well, wheddah hit's Scripter er not, dey's one t'ing su'tain, I tell you,—dem two is singin' deyse'ves togeddah."

"Hit's a fac', an' I believe it."

"An' it's a mighty good thing, too. Brothah Gidjon is de nicest house dahky dat I ever hyeahd tell on. Dey jes' de same diffunce 'twixt him an' de othah house-boys as dey is 'tween real quality an' strainers —he got mannahs, but he ain't got aihs."

"Heish, ain't you right!"

"An' while de res' of dem ain't thinkin' 'bout nothin' but dancin' an' ca'in' on, he's makin' his peace, callin', an' 'lection sho'."

"I tell you, Mam' Henry, dey ain' nothin' like a spichul named chile."

"Humph! g'long, gal; 'tain't in de name; de biggest devil I evah knowed was named Moses Aaron. 'Tain't in de name, hit's all in de man hisse'f."

But notwithstanding what the gossips said of him, Gideon went on his way, and knew not that the one great power of earth had taken hold of him until they gave the great party down in the quarters, and he saw Martha in all her glory. Then love spoke to him with no uncertain sound.

It was a dancing-party, and because neither he nor Martha dared countenance dancing, they had strolled away together under the pines that lined the white road, whiter now in the soft moonlight. He had never known the pine-cones to smell so sweet before in all his life. She had never known just how the moonlight flecked the road before. This was lovers' lane to them. He didn't understand why his heart kept throbbing so furiously, for they were walking slowly, and when a shadow thrown across the road from a bystanding bush frightened her into pressing close up to him, he could not have told why his arm stole round her waist and drew her slim form up to him, or why his lips found hers, as eye looked into eye. For their simple hearts love's mystery was too deep, as it is for wiser ones.

Some few stammering words came to his lips and she answered the best she could. Then why did the moonlight flood them so, and why were the heavens so full of stars? Out yonder in the black hedge a mocking-bird was singing, and he was translating—oh, so poorly—the song of their hearts. They forgot the dance, they forgot all but their love.

"An' you won't ma'y nobody else but me, Martha?"

"You know I won't, Gidjon."

"But I mus' wait de yeah out?"

"Yes, an' den don't you think Mas' Stone'll let us have a little cabin of ouah own jest outside de quahtahs?"

"Won't it be blessid? Won't it be blessid?" he cried, and then the kindly moon went under a cloud for a moment and came out smiling, for he had peeped through and seen what passed. Then they walked back hand in hand to the dance along the transfigured road, and they found that the first part of the festivities was over, and all the people had sat down to supper. Everyone laughed when they went in. Martha held back and perspired with embarrassment. But even though he saw some of the older heads whispering in a corner, Gideon was not ashamed. A new light was in his eyes, and a new boldness had come to him. He led Martha up to the grinning group, and said in his best singing voice, "Whut you laughin' at? Yes, I's popped de question, an' she says 'Yes,' an long 'bout a yeah f'om now you kin all 'spec' a' invitation." This was a formal announcement. A shout arose from the happy-go-lucky people, who sorrowed alike in each other's sorrows and joyed in each other's joys. They sat down at a table, and their health was drunk in cups of cider and persimmon beer.

Over in the corner Mam' Henry mumbled over her pipe, "Wha'd I tell you? Wha'd I tell you?" and Aunt Sophy replied, "Hit's de pa'able of de mo'nin' stahs."

"Don't talk to me 'bout no mo'nin' stahs," the mammy snorted; "Gawd jes' fitted dey voices togeddah, an' den j'ined dey hea's. De mo'nin' stahs ain't got nothin' to do wid it."

"Mam' Henry," said Aunt Sophy, impressively, "you's a' oldah ooman den I is, an' I ain' 'sputin' hit; but I say dey done 'filled Scripter 'bout de mo'nin' stahs; dey's done sung deyse'ves togeddah."

The old woman sniffed.

The next Sunday at meeting some one got the start of Gideon, and began a new hymn. It ran:

> At de ma'ige of de Lamb, oh Lawd,
> God done gin His 'sent.
> Dey dressed de Lamb all up in white,
> God done gin His 'sent.
> Oh, wasn't dat a happy day
> Oh, wasn't dat a happy day, Good Lawd,
> Oh, wasn't dat a happy day
> De ma'ige of de Lamb!

The wailing minor of the beginning broke into a joyous chorus at the end, and Gideon wept and laughed in turn, for it was his wedding-song.

The young man had a confidential chat with his master the next morning, and the happy secret was revealed.

"What, you scamp!" said Dudley Stone. "Why, you've got even more sense than I gave you credit for; you've picked out the finest girl on the plantation, and the one best suited to you. You couldn't have done better if the match had been made for you. I reckon this must've been one of the marriages that are made in heaven. Marry her, yes, and with a preacher. I don't see why you want to wait a year."

Gideon told him his hopes of a near cabin.

"Better still," his master went on; "with you two joined and up near the big house, I'll feel as safe for the folks as if an army was camped around, and, Gideon, my boy"—he put his arms on the black man's shoulders—"if I should slip away some day——"

The slave looked up, startled.

"I mean if I should die—I'm not going to run off, don't be alarmed —I want you to help your young Mas' Dud look after his mother and Miss Ellen; you hear? Now that's the one promise I ask of you—come what may, look after the women-folks." And the man promised and went away smiling.

His year of engagement, the happiest time of a young man's life, began on golden wings. There came rumors of war, and the wings of the glad-hued year drooped sadly. Sadly they drooped, and seemed to fold, when one day, between the rumors and predictions of strife, Dudley Stone, the old master, slipped quietly away out into the unknown.

There were wife, daughter, son, and faithful slaves about his bed, and they wept for him sincere tears, for he had been a good husband and father and a kind master. But he smiled, and, conscious to the last, whispered to them a cheery good-bye. Then turning to Gideon, who stood there bowed with grief, he raised one weak finger, and his lips made the word, "Remember!"

They laid him where they had laid one generation after another of the Stones and it seemed as if a pall of sorrow had fallen upon the whole place. Then, still grieving, they turned their long-distracted attention to the things that had been going on around, and lo! the ominous mutterings were loud, and the cloud of war was black above them.

It was on an April morning when the storm broke, and the plantation, master and man, stood dumb with consternation, for they had hoped, they had believed, it would pass. And now there was the buzz of men who talked in secret corners. There were hurried saddlings and feverish rides to town. Somewhere in the quarters was whispered the forbidden word "freedom," and it was taken up and dropped breathlessly from the ends of a hundred tongues. Some of the older ones scouted it, but from some who held young children to their breasts there were deep-souled prayers in the dead of the night. Over the meetings in the woods or in the log church a strange reserve brooded, and even the prayers took on a guarded tone. Even from the fullness of their hearts, which longed for liberty, no open word that could offend the mistress or the young master went up to the Almighty.

He might know their hearts, but no tongue in meeting gave vent to what was in them, and even Gideon sang no more of the gospel army. He was sad because of this new trouble coming hard upon the heels of the old, and Martha was grieved because he was.

Finally the trips into town budded into something, and on a memorable evening when the sun looked peacefully through the pines, young Dudley Stone rode into the yard dressed in a suit of gray, and on his shoulders were the straps of office. The servants gathered around him with a sort of awe and followed him until he alighted at the porch. Only Mam' Henry, who had been nurse to both him and his sister, dared follow him in. It was a sad scene within, but such a one as any Southern home where there were sons might have shown that awful year. The mother tried to be brave, but her old hands shook, and her tears fell upon her son's brown head, tears of grief at parting, but through which shone the fire of a noble pride. The young Ellen hung about his neck with sobs and caresses.

"Would you have me stay?" he asked her.

"No! no! I know where your place is, but oh, my brother!"

"Ellen," said the mother in a trembling voice, "you are the sister of a soldier now."

The girl dried her tears and drew herself up.

"We won't burden your heart, Dudley, with our tears, but we will weight you down with our love and prayers."

It was not so easy with Mam' Henry. Without protest, she took him to her bosom and rocked to and fro, wailing "My baby! my baby!" and the tears that fell from the young man's eyes upon her grey old head cost his manhood nothing.

Gideon was behind the door when his master called him. His sleeve was traveling down from his eyes as he emerged.

"Gideon," said his master, pointing to his uniform, "you know what this means?"

"Yes, suh."

"I wish I could take you along with me. But——"

"Mas' Dud," Gideon threw out his arms in supplication.

"You remember father's charge to you, take care of the women-folks." He took the servant's hand, and, black man and white, they looked into each other's eyes, and the compact was made. Then Gideon gulped and said "Yes, suh," again.

Another boy held the master's horse and rode away behind him when he vaulted into the saddle, and the man of battle-song and warrior-name went back to mind the women-folks.

Then began the disintegration of the plantation's population. First Yellow Bob slipped away, and no one pursued him. A few blamed him, but they soon followed as the year rolled away. More were missing every time a Union camp lay near, and great tales were told of the chances for young Negroes who would go as body-servants to the Yankee officers. Gideon heard all and was silent.

Then as the day of his marriage drew near he felt a greater strength, for there was one who would be with him to help him keep his promise and his faith.

The spirit of freedom had grown strong in Martha as the days passed, and when her lover went to see her she had strange things to say. Was he going to stay? Was he going to be a slave when freedom and a livelihood lay right within his grasp? Would he keep her a slave? Yes, he would do it all—all.

She asked him to wait.

Another year began, and one day they brought Dudley Stone to lie beside his father. Then most of the remaining Negroes went. There was no master now. The two bereaved women wept, and Gideon forgot that he wore the garb of manhood and wept with them.

Martha came to him.

"Gidjon," she said, "I's waited a long while now. Mos' eve'ybody else is gone. Ain't you goin'?"

"No."

"But, Gidjon, I wants to be free. I know how good dey've been to us; but, oh, I wants to own myse'f. They're talkin' 'bout settin' us free every hour."

"I can wait."

"They's a camp right near here."

"I promised."

"The of'cers wants body-servants, Gidjon——"

"Go, Martha, if you want to, but I stay."

She went away from him, but she or someone else got word to young Captain Jack Griswold of the near-by camp that there was an excellent servant on the plantation who only needed a little persuading, and he came up to see him.

"Look here," he said, "I want a body-servant. I'll give you ten dollars a month."

"I've got to stay here."

"But, you fool, what have you to gain by staying here?"

"I'm goin' to stay."

"Why, you'll be free in a little while, anyway."

"All right."

"Of all fools," said the Captain. "I'll give you fifteen dollars."

"I do' want it."

"Well, your girl's going, anyway. I don't blame her for leaving such a fool as you are."

Gideon turned and looked at him.

"The camp is going to be moved up on this plantation, and there will be a requisition for this house for officers' quarters, so I'll see you again," and Captain Griswold went his way.

Martha going! Martha! Gideon could not believe it. He would not. He saw her, and she confirmed it. She was going as an aid to the nurses. He gasped, and went back to mind the women-folks.

They did move the camp up nearer, and Captain Griswold came to see Gideon again, but he could get no word from him, save "I'm goin' to stay," and he went away in disgust, entirely unable to understand such obstinacy, as he called it.

But the slave had his moments alone, when the agony tore at his breast and rended him. Should he stay? The others were going. He would soon be free. Everyone had said so, even his mistress one day. Then Martha was going. "Martha! Martha!" his heart called.

The day came when the soldiers were to leave, and he went out sadly to watch them go. All the plantation, that had been white with tents, was dark again, and everywhere were moving blue-coated figures.

Once more his tempter came to him. "I'll make it twenty dollars," he said, but Gideon shook his head. Then they started. The drums tapped. Away they went, the flag kissing the breeze. Martha stole up to say good-bye to him. Her eyes were overflowing, and she clung to him.

"Come, Gidjon," she plead, "fu' my sake. Oh, my God, won't you come with us—it's freedom." He kissed her, but shook his head.

"Hunt me up when you do come," she said, crying bitterly, "fu' I do love you, Gidjon, but I must go. Out yonder is freedom," and she was gone with them.

He drew out a pace after the troops, and then, turning, looked back at the house. He went a step farther, and then a woman's gentle voice called him, "Gideon!" He stopped. He crushed his cap in his hands, and the tears came into his eyes. Then he answered, "Yes, Mis' Ellen, I's a-comin'."

He stood and watched the dusty column until the last blue leg swung out of sight and over the grey hills the last drum-tap died away, and then turned and retraced his steps toward the house.

Gideon had triumphed mightily.

Charles Waddell Chesnutt

The first Negro to write the short story and the novel, aware of the techniques of these literary forms as genuine art, was Charles Waddell Chesnutt, who was born in Cleveland, Ohio in 1858 and educated there largely during the Reconstruction that followed the Civil War. Having been brought up in an atmosphere of culture, he could appreciate the great distance between his intellectual attainment and that of the large numbers of Negroes who came immediately out of the South to Cleveland as a city of refuge or a sort of heavenly Promised Land. There also came to Cleveland some mulattoes, who regarded themselves as superior to the blacks who had worked in the fields.

These contrasts in attitudes and expectations interested Chesnutt and caused him to study the different types of Negroes carefully. His interpretation of the unsophisticated Negro appears in "The Goophered Grapevine," which was published by the Atlantic Monthly Magazine in 1887, and in "The Conjure Woman," which first appeared in 1899. His treatment of the Negro who had had some intellectual training appears in his short story, "The Wife of His Youth," and in his first novel, *The House Behind the Cedars*.

For nine years he taught in the public schools of North Carolina, culminating his career as a teacher as the Principal of the State Normal School at Fayetteville, North Carolina. While in that state, he had the opportunity of studying the primitive American Negro at close range in large numbers and to observe some of the conflicts and dilemmas of the color line that he portrayed in his novels. In 1887 he gave up teaching, as he was licensed to practice law in Ohio. He continued in this field until his death in 1932.

In 1900 there appeared the novel, *The House Behind the Cedars,* the story of a mulatto girl faced with the dilemma of deciding when to pass for white and when to acknowledge her colored origin. *The Marrow of Tradition,* his next novel, appeared in 1901. It deals with the problems of the color line in the same family and uses as its setting the year 1898, the time of thè race riots at Wilmington, North Carolina. His last novel, *The Colonel's Dream,* which was published in 1905, deals with the efforts of a colonel of the Confederate Army to improve the relations between white and colored in the South.

His other important work is *The Life of Frederick Douglass.*

As a literary artist producing short stories and novels comparable to the works of other writers of American fiction, Chesnutt deserves a high place. In 1928, the National Association for the Advancement of Colored People awarded him the Spingarn Medal for his eminence as a literary artist depicting the life, struggles, and aspirations of the American Negro to rise unto great place.

THE WIFE OF HIS YOUTH [1]

Mr. Ryder was going to give a ball. There were several reasons why this was an opportune time for such an event.

Mr. Ryder might aptly be called the dean of the Blue Veins. The original Blue Veins were a little society of colored persons organized in a certain Northern city shortly after the war. Its purpose was to establish and maintain correct social standards among a people whose social condition presented almost unlimited room for improvement. By accident, combined perhaps with some natural affinity, the society consisted of individuals who were, generally speaking, more white

[1] From *The Wife of His Youth and Other Stories*. Reprinted by permission of Helen M. Chesnutt.

than black. Some envious outsider made the suggestion that no one was eligible for membership who was not white enough to show blue veins. The suggestion was readily adopted by those who were not of the favored few, and since that time the society, though possessing a longer and more pretentious name, had been known far and wide as the "Blue Vein Society," and its members as the "Blue Veins."

The Blue Veins did not allow that any such requirement existed for admission to their circle, but, on the contrary, declared that character and culture were the only things considered; and that if most of their members were light-colored, it was because such persons, as a rule, had had better opportunities to qualify themselves for membership. Opinions differed, too, as to the usefulness of the society. There were those who had been known to assail it violently as a glaring example of the very prejudice from which the colored race had suffered most; and later, when such critics had succeeded in getting on the inside, they had been heard to maintain with zeal and earnestness that the society was a life-boat, an anchor, a bulwark and a shield—— a pillar of cloud by day and of fire by night, to guide their people through the social wilderness. Another alleged prerequisite for Blue Vein membership was that of free birth; and while there was really no such requirement, it is doubtless true that very few of the members would have been unable to meet it if there had been. If there were one or two of the older members who had come up from the South and from slavery, their history presented enough romantic circumstances to rob their servile origin of its grosser aspects.

While there were no such tests of eligibility, it is true that the Blue Veins had their notions on these subjects, and that not all of them were equally liberal in regard to the things they collectively disclaimed. Mr. Ryder was one of the most conservative. Though he had not been among the founders of the society, but had come in later, his genius for social leadership was such that he had speedily become its recognized adviser and head, the custodian of its standards, and the preserver of its traditions. He shaped its social policy, was active in providing for its entertainment, and when the interest fell off, as it sometimes did, he fanned the embers until they burst again into a cheerful flame.

There were still other reasons for his popularity. While he was not as white as some of the Blue Veins, his appearance was such as to confer distinction upon them. His features were of a refined type, his hair was almost straight; he was always neatly dressed; his manners were irreproachable, and his morals above suspicion. He had come to Groveland a young man, and obtaining employment in the office of a railroad company as messenger had in time worked himself up to the position of stationery clerk, having charge of the distribution of the office supplies for the whole company. Although the lack of early training had hindered the orderly development of a naturally fine mind, it had not prevented him from doing a great deal of reading or from forming decidedly literary tastes. Poetry was his passion. He could repeat whole pages of the great English poets; and if his pronunciation was sometimes faulty, his eye, his voice, his gestures, would respond to the changing sentiment with a precision that revealed a poetic soul and disarmed criticism. He was economical, and had saved money; he owned and occupied a very comfortable house on a respectable street. His residence was handsomely furnished, containing among other things a good library, especially rich in poetry, a piano, and some choice engravings. He generally shared his house with some young couple, who looked after his wants and were company for him; for Mr. Ryder was a single man. In the early days of his connection with the Blue Veins he had been regarded as quite a catch, and young ladies and their mothers had manoeuvred with much ingenuity to capture him. Not, however, until Mrs. Molly Dixon visited Groveland had any woman ever made him wish to change his condition to that of a married man.

Mrs. Dixon had come to Groveland from Washington in the spring, and before the summer was over she had won Mr. Ryder's heart. She possessed many attractive qualities. She was much younger than he; in fact, he was old enough to have been her father, though no one knew exactly how old he was. She was whiter than he, and better educated. She had moved in the best colored society of the country, at Washington, and had taught in the schools of that city. Such a superior person had been eagerly welcomed to the Blue Vein Society, and had taken a leading part in its activities. Mr. Ryder had at first been attracted by her charms of person, for she was very good-looking and not over twenty-five; then by her refined manners and the vivacity of her wit. Her husband had been a government clerk, and at his death had left a considerable life insurance. She was visiting friends in Groveland, and, finding the town and the people to her liking, had prolonged her stay indefinitely. She had not seemed displeased at Mr. Ryder's attentions, but on the contrary had given him every proper encouragement; and indeed, a younger and less cautious man would long since have spoken. But he had made up his mind, and had only to determine the time when he would ask her to be his wife. He decided to give a ball in her honor, and at some time during the evening of the ball to offer her his heart and hand. He had no special fears about the outcome, but, with a little touch of romance, he wanted the surroundings to be in harmony with his own feelings when he should have received the answer he expected.

Mr. Ryder resolved that this ball should mark an epoch in the social history of Groveland. He knew, of course—no one could know better—the entertainments that had taken place in past years, and what must be done to surpass them. His ball must be worthy of the lady in whose honor it was to be given, and must, by the quality of its guests, set an example for the future. He had observed of late a growing liberality, almost a laxity, in social matters, even among members of his own set, and had several times been forced to meet in a social way persons whose complexions and callings in life were hardly up to the standard which he considered proper for the society to maintain. He had a theory of his own.

"I have no race prejudice," he would say, "but we people of mixed blood are ground between the upper and the nether millstone. Our fate lies between absorption by the white race and extinction in the black. The one doesn't want us yet, but may take us in time. The other would welcome us, but it would be for us a backward step. 'With malice towards none, with charity for all,' we must do the best we can for ourselves and those who are to follow us. Self-preservation is the first law of nature."

His ball would serve by its exclusiveness to counteract leveling

tendencies, and his marriage with Mrs. Dixon would help to further
the upward process of absorption he had been wishing and waiting for.

II

The ball was to take place on Friday night. The house had been put
in order, the carpets covered with canvas, the halls and stairs deco-
rated with palms and potted plants; and in the afternoon Mr. Ryder
sat on his front porch, which the shade of a vine running up over
a wire netting made a cool and pleasant lounging place. He expected
to respond to the toast "The Ladies" at the supper, and from a volume
of Tennyson—his favorite poet—was fortifying himself with apt quota-
tions. The volume was open at "A Dream of Fair Women." His eyes
fell on these lines, and he read them aloud to judge better of their
effect:

> At length I saw a lady within call,
>   Stiller than chisell'd marble, standing there;
> A daughter of the gods, divinely tall,
>   And most divinely fair.

He remarked the verse, and turning the page read the stanza beginning

> O sweet pale Margaret,
> O rare pale Margaret.

He weighed the passage a moment, and decided that it would not do.
Mrs. Dixon was the palest lady he expected at the ball, and she was of
a rather ruddy complexion, and of lively disposition and buxom build.
So he ran over the leaves until his eye rested on the description of
Queen Guinevere:

> She seem'd a part of joyous Spring:
> A gown of grass-green silk she wore,
> Buckled with golden clasps before;
> A light-green tuft of plumes she bore
> Closed in a golden ring.
>
> .   .   .   .   .
>
> She look'd so lovely, as she sway'd
> The rein with dainty finger-tips,
> A man had given all other bliss,
> And all his worldly worth for this,
> To waste his whole heart in one kiss
> Upon her perfect lips.

As Mr. Ryder murmured these words audibly, with an appreciative thrill, he heard the latch of his gate click, and a light footfall sounding on the steps. He turned his head, and saw a woman standing before his door.

She was a little woman, not five feet tall, and proportioned to her height. Although she stood erect, and looked around her with very bright and restless eyes, she seemed quite old; for her face was crossed and recrossed with a hundred wrinkles, and around the edges of her bonnet could be seen protruding here and there a tuft of short gray wool. She wore a blue calico gown of ancient cut, a little red shawl fastened around her shoulders with an old-fashioned brass brooch, and a large bonnet profusely ornamented with faded red and yellow artificial flowers. And she was very black, so that her toothless gums, revealed when she opened her mouth to speak, were not red, but blue. She looked like a bit of the old plantation life, summoned up from the past by the wave of a magician's wand, as the poet's fancy had called into being the gracious shapes of which Mr. Ryder had just been reading.

He rose from his chair and came over to where she stood. "Good afternoon, madam," he said.

"Good evenin', suh," she answered, ducking suddenly with a quaint curtsy. Her voice was shrill and piping, but softened somewhat by age. "Is dis yere whar Mistuh Ryduh lib, suh?" she asked, looking around her doubtfully, and glancing into the open windows, through which some of the preparations for the evening were visible.

"Yes," he replied, with an air of kingly patronage, unconsciously flattered by her manner, "I am Mr. Ryder. Did you want to see me?"

"Yas, suh, ef I ain't 'sturbin' of you too much."

"Not at all. Have a seat over here behind the vine, where it is cool. What can I do for you?"

" 'Scuse me, suh," she continued, when she had sat down on the edge of a chair, " 'scuse me, suh, I's lookin' for my husban'. I heerd you wuz a big man an' had libbed heah a long time, an' I 'lowed you would n't min' ef I'd come roun' an' ax you ef a man by de name er Sam Taylor been 'quirin' roun' in de chu'ches ermongs' de people fer his wife 'Liza Jane?"

Mr. Ryder seemed to think for a moment.

"There used to be many such cases right after the war," he said, "but it has been so long that I have forgotten them. There are very few now. But tell me your story, and it may refresh my memory."

She sat back farther in her chair so as to be more comfortable, and folded her withered hands in her lap.

"My name's 'Liza," she began, " 'Liza Jane. W'en I wuz young I us'ter b'long ter Marse Bob Smif, down in ole Missoura. I wuz bawn down dere. W'en I wuz a gal I wuz married ter a man named Jim. But Jim died, an' after dat I married a merlatter man named Sam Taylor. Sam wuz frebawn, but his mammy and daddy died, an' de w'ite folks 'prenticed him ter my marster fer ter work fer 'im 'tel he wuz growed up. Sam worked in de fiel', an' I wuz de cook. One day Ma'y Ann, ole miss's maid, came rushin' out ter de kitchen, an' says she, ' 'Liza Jane, old marse gwine sell yo' Sam down de ribber.' "

" 'Go way f'm yere,' says I; 'my husban's free!' "

" 'Don' make no diff'ence. I heerd ole marse tell ole miss he wuz gwine take yo' Sam 'way wid 'im ter-morrow, fer he needed money, an' he knowd whar he could git a t'ousan' dollars fer Sam an' no questions axed.' "

"W'en Sam come home f'm de fiel' dat night, I tole him 'bout ole marse gwine steal 'im, an' Sam run erway. His time wuz mos' up, an' he swo' dat w'en he wuz twenty-one he would come back an' he'p me run erway, er else save up de money ter buy my freedom. An' I know he'd 'a' done it, fer he thought a heap er me, Sam did. But w'en he come back he did n' fin' me, fer I wuzn' dere. Ole marse had heerd dat I warned Sam, so he had me whip' an' sol' down de ribber.

"Den de wah broke out, an' w'en it wuz ober de cullud folks wuz scattered. I went back ter de ole home; but Sam wuzn' dere, an' I could n' l'arn nuffin' 'bout 'im. But I knowed he'd be'n dere to look fer me an' had n' foun' me, an' had gone erway ter hunt fer me.

"I's be'n lookin' fer 'im eber sence," she added simply, as though twenty-five years were but a couple of weeks, "an' I knows he's be'n lookin' fer me. Fer he sot a heap sto' by me, Sam did, an' I know he's be'n huntin' fer me all dese years—'les'n he's be'n sick er sump'n, so he could n' work, er out'n his head, so he could n' 'member his promise. I went back down de ribber, fer I 'lowed he'd gone down dere lookin' fer me. I's be'n ter Noo Orleens, an' Atlanty, an' Charleston, an' Richmon'; an' w'en I'd be'n all ober de Souf I come ter de Norf. Fer I knows I'll fin' 'im some er dese days," she said softly, "er he'll fin' me, an' den we'll bofe be as happy in freedom as we wuz in de ole days befo' de wah." A smile stole over her withered countenance as she paused a moment, and her bright eyes softened into a far-away look.

This was the substance of the old woman's story. She had wandered a little here and there. Mr. Ryder was looking at her curiously when she finished.

"How have you lived all these years?" he asked.

"Cookin', suh. I's a good cook. Does you know anybody w'at needs a good cook, suh? I's stoppin' wid a cullud fam'ly roun' de corner yonder 'tel I kin git a place."

"Do you really expect to find your husband? He may be dead long ago."

She shook her head emphatically. "Oh, no, he ain' dead. De signs an' de tokens tells me. I dremp three nights runnin' on'y dis las' week dat I foun' him."

"He may have married another woman. Your slave marriage would not have prevented him, for you never lived with him after the war, and without that your marriage doesn't count."

"Wouldn' make no diff'ence wid Sam. He would n' marry no yuther 'ooman 'tel he foun' out 'bout me. I knows it," she added. "Sump'n's be'n tellin' me all dese years dat I's gwine fin' Sam 'fo' I dies."

"Perhaps he's outgrown you, and climbed up in the world where he wouldn't care to have you find him."

"No, indeed, suh," she replied, "Sam ain' dat kin' er man. He wuz good ter me, Sam wuz, but he wuzn' much good ter nobody e'se, fer he wuz one er de triflin'es' han's on de plantation. I 'spec's ter haf ter suppo't 'im w'en I fin' 'im, fer he nebber would work 'less'n he had ter. But den he wuz free, an' he did n' git no pay fer his work, an' I don' blame 'im much."

"You may have passed him on the street a hundred times during the twenty-five years, and not have known him; time works great changes."

She smiled incredulously. "I'd know 'im 'mongs' a hund'ed men. Fer dey wuzn' no yuther merlatter man like my man Sam, an' I could n' be mistook. I's toted his picture roun' wid me twenty-five years."

"May I see it?" asked Mr. Ryder. "It might help me to remember whether I have seen the original."

As she drew a small parcel from her bosom he saw that it was fastened to a string that went around her neck. Removing several wrappers, she brought to light an old-fashioned daguerreotype in a black case. He looked long and intently at the portrait. It was faded with time, but the features were still distinct, and it was easy to see what manner of man it had represented.

He closed the case, and with a slow movement handed it back to her.

"I don't know of any man in town who goes by that name," he said, "nor have I heard of any one making such inquiries. But if you will leave me your address, I will give the matter some attention, and if I find out anything I will let you know."

She gave him the number of a house in the neighborhood, and went away, after thanking him warmly.

He wrote the address on the fly-leaf of the volume of Tennyson, and, when she had gone, rose to his feet and stood looking after her curiously. As she walked down the street with mincing step, he saw several persons whom she passed turn and look back at her with a smile of kindly amusement. When she had turned the corner, he went upstairs to his bedroom, and stood for a long time before the mirror of his dressing-case, gazing thoughtfully at the reflection of his own face.

III

At eight o'clock the ballroom was a blaze of light and the guests had begun to assemble; for there was a literary programme and some routine business of the society to be gone through with before the dancing. A black servant in evening dress waited at the door and directed the guests to the dressing-rooms.

The occasion was long memorable among the colored people of the city; not alone for the dress and display, but for the high average of intelligence and culture that distinguished the gathering as a whole. There were a number of school teachers, several young doctors, three or four lawyers, some professional singers, an editor, a lieutenant in the United States Army spending his furlough in the city, and others in various polite callings; these were colored, though most of them would not have attracted even a casual glance because of any marked difference from white people. Most of the ladies were in evening costume, and dress coats and dancing pumps were the rule among the men. A band of string music, stationed in an alcove behind a row of palms, played popular airs while the guests were gathering.

The dancing began at half past nine. At eleven o'clock supper was served. Mr. Ryder had left the ballroom some little time before the intermission, but reappeared at the supper table. The spread was worthy of the occasion, and the guests did full justice to it. When the coffee had been served, the toastmaster, Mr. Solomon Sadler, rapped for order. He made a brief introductory speech, complimenting host and guests, and then presented in their order the toasts of the evening. They were responded to with a very fair display of after-dinner wit.

"The last toast," said the toastmaster, when he reached the end of the list, "is one which must appeal to us all. There is no one of us of the sterner sex who is not at some time dependent upon woman— in infancy for protection, in manhood for companionship, in old age for care and comforting. Our good host has been trying to live alone, but the fair faces I see around me tonight prove that he is too largely dependent upon the gentler sex for most that makes life worth living —the society and love of friends—and rumor is at fault if he does not soon yield entire subjection to one of them. Mr. Ryder will now respond to the toast—The Ladies."

There was a pensive look in Mr. Ryder's eyes as he took the floor and adjusted his eye-glasses. He began by speaking of woman as the gift of Heaven to man, and after some general observations on the relations of the sexes he said: "But perhaps the quality which most distinguishes woman is her fidelity and devotion to those she loves.

History is full of examples, but has recorded none more striking than one which only today came under my notice."

He then related, simply but effectively, the story told by his visitor of the afternoon. He gave it in the same soft dialect, which came readily to his lips, while the company listened attentively and sympathetically. For the story had awakened a responsive thrill in many hearts. There were some present who had seen, and others who had heard their fathers and grandfathers tell, the wrongs and sufferings of this past generation, and all of them still felt, in their darker moments, the shadow hanging over them. Mr. Ryder went on:

"Such devotion and confidence are rare even among women. There are many who would have searched a year, some who would have waited five years, a few who might have hoped ten years; but for twenty-five years this woman has retained her affection for and her faith in a man she has not seen or heard of in all that time.

"She came to me today in the hope that I might be able to help her find this long-lost husband. And when she was gone I gave my fancy rein, and imagined a case I will put to you.

"Suppose that this husband, soon after his escape, had learned that his wife had been sold away, and that such inquiries as he could make brought no information of her whereabouts. Suppose that he was young, and she much older than he; that he was light, and she was black; that their marriage was a slave marriage, and legally binding only if they chose to make it so after the war. Suppose, too, that he made his way to the North, as some of us have done, and there, where he had larger opportunities, had improved them, and had in the course of all these years grown to be as different from the ignorant boy who ran away from fear of slavery as the day is from the night. Suppose, even, that he had qualified himself, by industry, by thrift, and by study, to win the friendship and be considered worthy of the society of such people as these I see around me to-night, gracing my board and filling my heart with gladness; for I am old enough to remember the day when such a gathering would not have been possible in this land. Suppose, too, that, as the years went by, this man's memory of the past grew more and more indistinct, until at last it was rarely, except in his dreams, that any image of this bygone period rose before his mind. And then suppose that accident should bring to his knowledge the fact that the wife of his youth, the wife he had left behind him—not one who had walked by his side and kept pace with him in his upward struggle, but one upon whom advancing years and a laborious life had set their mark—was alive and seeking him, but that he was absolutely safe from recognition or discovery, unless he chose to reveal himself. My friends, what would the man do? I will presume that he was one who loved honor, and tried to deal justly with all men. I will even carry the case further, and suppose that perhaps he had set his heart upon another, whom he had hoped to call his own. What would he do, or rather what ought he to do, in such a crisis of a lifetime?

"It seemed to me that he might hesitate, and I imagined that I was an old friend, a near friend, and that he had come to me for advice; and I argued the case with him. I tried to discuss it impartially. After we had looked upon the matter from every point of view, I said to him, in words that we all know——

> This above all: to thine own self be true,
> And it must follow, as the night the day,
> Thou canst not then be false to any man.

Then, finally, I put the question to him, 'Shall you acknowledge her?'

"And now, ladies and gentlemen, friends and companions, I ask you, what should he have done?"

There was something in Mr. Ryder's voice that stirred the hearts of those who sat around him. It suggested more than mere sympathy with an imaginary situation; it seemed rather in the nature of a personal appeal. It was observed, too, that his look rested more especially upon Mrs. Dixon, with a mingled expression of renunciation and inquiry.

She had listened, with parted lips and streaming eyes. She was the first to speak: "He should have acknowledged her."

"Yes," they all echoed, "he should have acknowledged her."

"My friends and companions," responded Mr. Ryder, "I thank you, one and all. It is the answer I expected, for I knew your hearts."

He turned and walked toward the closed door of an adjoining room, while every eye followed him in wondering curiosity. He came back in a moment, leading by the hand his visitor of the afternoon, who stood startled and trembling at the sudden plunge into this scene of brilliant gayety. She was neatly dressed in gray, and wore the white cap of an elderly woman.

"Ladies and gentlemen," he said, "this is the woman, and I am the man, whose story I have told you. Permit me to introduce to you the wife of my youth."

Colleen Williams

Out of the South from a little village in Arkansas between six and seven miles from a railroad came little Colleen Williams, following the North Star. Her parents, being impressed with St. Louis because of the World's Fair there in 1904, believed paths to prosperity led to this metropolitan city. They placed their little girl in the public schools of St. Louis. From the Sumner High School she went to Stowe Teachers College. She is now a teacher at the Lincoln School in St. Louis.

THERE WILL ALWAYS BE HOPE [1]

Judith Trent sat in her modern New York office, a ray of sunshine falling across her desk. This had been the office of her father, Leroy Trent, known all over the world for his famous dress-designing. Her father had suddenly been taken away from her in that dreadful automobile accident, and her dear mother along with him. Judith had been left alone, feeling that life was no longer worth living after her whole world, her parents, had been taken from her. It had been in this office that she had found strength to go on, doing the work in which her father had excelled and in which her talent was said to be surpassingly good. At that, she had been interested and had worked so hard, that she had not had time to think. In fact her work had been so endless that lately she always felt tired, never rested.

1 Reprinted with the permission of the author.

That explains how she had happened to go to see Doctor Howard this morning for a general check up and that accounts for the doctor's discovery that she had a heart which would function only two years longer at the most.

She had not expected her condition to be this serious and at first was stunned by this news; but as she walked out of the office and drove to her own, as she sat now thinking, she was almost glad. Yes, glad —two more years and this loneliness would be over; two more years and she would be happy again with Mom and Dad; two more years and they would be together again forever.

There was a knock at the door. Judith jumped to her feet and shook her head as if coming out of a daze. Presently she said, "Come in" in her usual musical, yet serious voice.

"Good morning, Judy; here's your mail and those two off-the-shoulder evening designs which you asked for last night."

"Oh, thank you, Charlotta, you are such an able assistant. Really you are my nurse, my mother, my father, and my all around handy 'man'. I don't know what I would do without you."

"And just what may I attribute this burst of praise to, my pretty little one? Are you in love or something?" Charlotte retorted as she arranged her black and silver curls piled high upon her head, while glancing at the mirrored wall of the office, which reflected a perfectly groomed woman of about forty-five years of age.

"Oh, no, Charlie, it's just that I'm beginning to realize how much I've depended upon you for the past four years since Mom and Dad . . ."

"Listen, young lady, we have no time for chatter. You haven't forgotten that this is the last week before our spring fashion show? And you know what that means: getting models, fitting them and rehearsing, rehearsing, rehearsing. You know we've got to make the Trent fashions the best of this year, the same as they've been the best for the past twenty years."

"All right, Charlie, you win. On your way out will you see that Number Fourteen has her hair reset for that dinner picture which she poses for this afternoon?"

"Sure, Judy. Don't work too hard now." Charlie wrinkled her

pretty nose mischievously. "After all, we need you here." And she was gone.

Judith worked hard that day and every day thereafter until the fashion show was over. Again the Trent Fashions had been voted the best of the year.

That night, Madame Vanderberg, one of her best customers, was having a party at her Fifth Avenue penthouse. It was absolutely necessary that Judith go and wear one of her creations. There could be no better model than Judith herself. She was a "bronze" model. Debonair, she went to the Vanderberg party, looking as if she had just stepped out of *Vogue*.

Madame Vanderberg, a middle-aged hunk of woman with diamonds dripping from her fingers, greeted her. "Judith, darling, you look simply astounding. My dear, you must design something for me on that order. I'm sure it would do things for me."

"Oh, yes, Madame Vanderberg, if you really like it."

"If I like it? I love it. Oh, but come now and join us. You know most of the people. Over half of the gowns here must be Trent Creations."

Judith moved about through the crowd of over-dressed women and tuxedoed men, chatting here and there. She never talked too much. She was a serious-minded young woman of thirty, who kept her thoughts generally to herself.

Near midnight she found it unbearably stuffy inside; so she slipped out to the terrace, and stood at the far end looking over Fifth Avenue. There was a full moon above, and a brisk breeze passed over the terrace. It chilled Judith through and through and she "loved" it. She had always liked the feel of being chilled. It made her feel so fresh and free.

"Do you find it boring too?" asked a clear, low voice from behind.

Judith turned and there stood before her a tall, dark, handsome man with a boyish grin, a wide kind mouth, and a dark mass of hair that lay restlessly in place.

"Yes," she replied quite frankly. "I don't suppose it's really fair to run out on them like this. They are my customers."

"I know," he said, "you're Miss Trent, aren't you? They are my customers too. I'm the family doctor to many of them."

"Oh, well," replied Judith, "you are all apologies too. Maybe we'd better get back to them. Shall we go?"

About a week later Judith opened her eyes to stare up into a familiar face. Where had she seen it before? Where? Before she had answered the question in her mind——

"On the terrace at Madame Vanderberg's party. Remember?" That low clear voice. She remembered, he was a doctor.

"Oh, yes, and where am I and why are you here, Doctor-er-er?"

"Paul, John Paul is my name and you just fainted. I was the nearest doctor at hand, so here I am. Listen, you should take a rest. Take it easy for a while. You've been working too hard, not getting the proper rest."

"Yes, I suppose that is true," Judith said as she turned her head to the back of the office studio couch on which she lay. Then she turned her head back and smiled at Doctor Paul. "Thank you, Doctor, for coming to my rescue. Will it be all right for me to rest at my home?"

"Oh, yes, Miss Trent," said the doctor, smiling broadly down at her. To his surprise, she smiled back. What was there about that pretty, mysterious face, those big, warm, searching, brown eyes that had stayed with him since that night on the terrace at Madame Vanderberg's party? Why did he find himself wanting to go out of his way to assist this strange girl in any way that she might need him; for he felt that she needed someone.

"My car is outside," John heard himself saying, "and I could drive you home. You shouldn't drive, you know."

"Thank you, Doctor Paul, but Charlie, my assistant, can drive me home." Judith then said coldly, "You will send me the bill. Good day, Doctor."

The doctor turned abruptly and strode through the office door. Judith's eyes followed him. "Why was he putting himself out of the way?" she thought. She had seen a look of disappointment come into his eyes, she thought, as she spoke coldly to him. She had been rude.

Charlie was thinking along the same lines, "My dear, you must be ill. I've never seen you so rude before. Come, and I'll drive you home."

The next night at eight o'clock Judith sat in her spacious bedroom with two huge satin pillows at her back, with designs and sketches strewn all over the bed. The wide luxurious mirror of her dressing table across the room reflected a pale young woman with black hair falling in waves loosely about her pink bedjacketed shoulders, critically eyeing designs of the latest fall fashions.

Presently there was a knock at the door and her maid entered. "Miss Trent, the doctor's here to see you."

"Doctor? Why, Doctor is out of town."

"This is a Doctor Paul, Miss Trent, shall I show him in?"

"Oh, Doctor Paul? Of course, Dionne, show him in."

Judith glanced across at herself in the mirror. She was quite pale. "Should have used a little make-up. Oh, well," she thought, "this was only a doctor."

There was his knock. "Come in," Judith invited.

"Good evening, Miss Trent, how are you feeling this evening?"

"Oh, fine. This day in bed has done wonders for me. I feel as if I'm fit for years and years more of hard work." Judith smiled, yet there was an unconvincing tone to her voice.

Doctor Paul half smiled, picking up one of the designs from the bed. "I see you've already begun working again."

"No, I was just looking over some new fall styles."

"Oh, I see," he said, "then I apologize for my accusation."

"Really, Doctor Paul, I'm the one who should apologize for my rudeness to you last evening. I'm afraid I acted like a spoiled child. You see I'm really not. There's no one to spoil me."

"I understand. It's all right," and his clear black eyes looked into hers with a great seriousness as he said, "Miss Trent, I really came here this evening to ask your permission to re-examine you. You see, last evening I thought I detected some irregularity when I took your pulse. No doctor is satisfied until he is certain of the condition of his patient. Would you mind too much? I realize, though, I must be taking a great deal of authority since I'm not your physician."

"Doctor Paul, I think you're acting as any good doctor would. Besides, my doctor is out of the city. It will be quite all right for you to re-examine me." Judith answered, and all the time through her mind ran the questions: "Has he discovered what Dr. Howard discovered? Is it really true? Maybe Doctor Howard was wrong. He's only one doctor. He had to be right, though. Just had to."

"Thank you, Miss Trent," Doctor Paul said as he proceeded to take his instruments from their case.

He examined Judith thoroughly. Some phases of the examination were repeated several times. Throughout the examination she watched his face, but it told nothing. After completing the diagnosis he carefully placed his instruments back in their case without saying a word. Having no reason for keeping silent any longer he said finally, "Miss Trent, I'm only one doctor and not too experienced at that. Thirty-five! So you see what I think could be all wrong. Have you seen your physician lately?"

"Yes, a week ago."

"Did he discuss with you any disorder of any kind?"

"Yes," Judith said softly, yet clearly, "he told me that I have but two years to live."

"I'd make the same prediction," he said slowly. Then he hastily added, "But we both could be wrong, you know."

"Oh, you can't be," she retorted quite calmly, "that is, I hope you aren't."

Dr. Paul rose to his feet as if he wasn't sure of what he had heard.

"Yes, Doctor Paul," Judith was saying, "I want to die."

"But I can't understand it. A successful young woman like you wanting to die. You're beautiful. You have everything a girl could want."

"Yes, Doctor, I have everything a girl could want, wealth, success, everything but love, everything but my parents whom I loved more than myself. You see, they were all I had. Now I'm alone in the world. I find myself wandering through this big house, alone. I see ghosts of my father and mother everywhere, yet they cannot speak to me nor I to them."

As she spoke, Doctor Paul looked at a miserably lonely girl hungering for love, for someone to care for. And wasn't it that way with him too? Wasn't he lonely? An orphan, adopted by a rich bachelor who knew nothing of showering affection upon a child. Dr. Paul had gone through medical school, in fact through life, all alone. But somehow he had never wanted to die. He wanted to live because he felt that some day he would find someone who would end his loneliness, who could make up for the love which he had never had, who could make his life worth living forever.

Now Judith spoke, "I'm sure you must think I'm a fool," and then she turned her head toward the window away from him and he thought he saw a tear, but she came back with "Doctor, when may I go back to the office?"

"At the end of a week," said the doctor. "Well, I'll say good night, Miss Trent. Thank you for your kindness."

"Good night, Doctor, I hope I'm not the biggest fool of a patient you've ever met."

"Oh no, Miss Trent! Good night."

The next night Miss Trent had a caller and every night that week thereafter. It was Doctor Paul.

About a month later Judith and Doctor Paul drove from the swank Eastbough Country Club. They had spent the whole day there, swimming, picnicking, and dancing. It was a May night but the weather was deceiving. It became cloudy and looked like rain. Doctor Paul had the top of his convertible Cadillac turned back. He was about to put it up when Judith protested. "Oh, please don't. I like the feel of the wind and the rain beating down upon me. It sounds so crazy, but do you mind?"

"No, my lady," John said bowing mischievously, "anything that pleases you pleases me."

So they rolled slowly along and presently it began to rain. At first a few drops fell and then there came a slow drizzle, the wind blew moderately and it was very dark. Judith sat with her head resting back, face up as the rain fell upon her. Finally she said, "John, isn't this fun?"

"Say that again," he said.

"What?" she replied.

"What you just said."

She raised her head and again she said "John, isn't this fun?"

His hand reached in the dark to find hers and he said "Yes, Judy, just to think of you for me is fun."

Four months later John stood in Judy's living room. She had been too busy lately for "dates." He hadn't seen her for two weeks. She was always out when he called. Today he had called her at the office and pleaded with her to see him this evening. He wanted to tell her something. And now he stood in the huge living room with its big fireplace, elaborate furniture, and beautiful drapes. He was looking at the picture of Judith's mother on the piano. Judith had her big brown eyes, and her beautiful oval-shaped face. "She must have been a wonderful mother, just as Judy would be," he thought.

"Hello, John." He turned to Judith as she entered. She looked lovely, like a little girl. Her hair fell loosely about her shoulders, a small rose was tucked near her temples. She wore a powder blue dress with a string of roses about its white yoke.

"Hello, Judy," he said and then, "Judy, why did you stop seeing me? What did I do? We did have fun, didn't we? I've missed you terribly. I didn't come here to tell you that; but it's too late now. I've said it. I really came to tell you that I'm leaving New York. I'm tired of being a society doctor. Those people don't need me. I feel like a cheat accepting a high salary for nothing. It makes me feel so cheap. I'm going to Glen Falls. They need a doctor there. I think I can help. I'm leaving next week."

At this Judy lowered her head and said, "You're leaving next week?"

"Yes, I meant to tell you before now, but you wouldn't let me see you. You've been working too hard. I can tell."

"John, I just realized that I was taking up quite a bit of your time. You had no time for yourself. Why should you waste your time on someone like me? I have nothing to offer you, not even time. Why should someone like you even think of someone like me, whose days are limited? I know it was selfish of me to accept, but for a while I did forget I was Judith Trent, who had forgotten how to laugh, how to have fun, to be gay and carefree. John, you made me forget. And now you've done your part, so——"

"Stop it, Judy," John spoke in a voice of agony. "You must know that I learned to be gay, to forget too. I was as lonely as you were, it was you that brightened up my life, not I, yours—oh, Judy, can't you see, couldn't you see that first night on the terrace at Madame Vanderberg's that I had found the someone I had been waiting for all my life? Judy, I love you with all the power that is within me to love."

The next moment she was in his arms and he met her lips with his own in a kiss that ended the loneliness of both of them and opened to them a new road to a new world of happiness.

Judith was crying, "John, it's so unfair to you—I——"

"Darling, for you to love but a day would not be unfair. You are my love and will be forever. It would have been unfair for me not to have found you; but now that I have, I'm satisfied," John spoke softly into her ear as he pressed her trembling hands to his heart.

"John, I do love you. Why does it have to be this way? We have so little time left—time which once I hurried away."

"Time, darling," he told her, "we can live a whole lifetime in what we have left, if, Judy, you will be my wife."

"Yes, John, it will make me the happiest woman in the world to be your wife."

A week later Dr. and Mrs. John Paul were the handsomest young couple on Elm Street in Glen Falls. Every evening John brought Judith roses, and after dinner they danced for hours to Strauss waltzes in their modest living room. Never again after their marriage had they mentioned Judith's heart condition. John enjoyed his work and felt that he was really being of service. Already the people of the town had begun talking of the new doctor, John Paul, and his good work.

One day three months after their marriage Judith had been quite dizzy for hours. When Paul came home, she told him of this. He took her pulse, heart-beat, and otherwise examined her. Then quite calmly he told her, "Darling, you are going to become a mother."

"John, oh, John, nothing could be more complete. A child for you. Oh, John, I'll have to see it through, I must. I'm so proud and happy."

"Judy, darling, I'm worried about you. Won't you see another doctor? I don't think it's safe," John said.

"No, John, you know what we said. Don't talk about it. Just be happy. Oh, darling, I love you," and she pulled him down and he put his head into her lap.

John did not sleep that night, he was afraid for Judith. She was not strong enough.

Time passed on and Judith grew happier day by day. Each day she took a walk, carefully ate the proper food, and did everything possible to protect her unborn child.

Finally the time came. Judith had been in the hospital for a week. It was a miracle to the doctors how she had held on. Her two years had been up two months ago. They wondered what had kept her alive. Her heart had practically stopped beating.

As this endless night began, John sat in the waiting room. Here he was just another expectant father anxiously awaiting the outcome. This time it was the other way around. Usually he was the doctor.

Around midnight the attending doctor came to John, "Dr. Paul, it's either the child or the mother. As you know the mother has practically no chance anyway, but there is a good chance for the child." John shook his head from side to side. The doctor thought he'd never seen a more miserable being as John struggled to get the words out——"The child."

After the doctor had left, John cried over and over, "Judy, my darling, my love"—and then there was silence. Ages seemed to roll on and he felt as if lost in a great desert. With other expectant fathers he waited in the hall for news of those who were to be.

Finally he heard someone say, "Dr. Paul." Instantly he rose and almost ran to the room where his wife was waiting for him. The nurse held the little brown baby with gleaming eyes like those of Judith.

"Judy, my darling, it is just like you," said the happy father.

"John, it is a girl." Then to the nurse she said, "Place my baby in my arms."

"Mother and daughter alike, both heavenly and beautiful. We'll name her after you, Judith," John said with great pride.

"No, John, not Judith." Then to the nurse, she said, "Take her now to her bed, my jewel, John, that I'm proud to give to you. Take my hand."

As he held her hand, automatically his fingers slid to her pulse. It was barely beating. He kissed her tenderly and his tears began to flow.

"My love," she faintly said, "you knew I had to go. I knew it too. My dear, I go unafraid and happy, because you brought joy into my life." Taking his hand with both of hers, she said, "John, call our baby Hope." Then she released his hand slowly and said, "I am happy, John, because there will always be hope."

"Judy, my darling, don't go!"

Then he heard the cry of their little daughter. At once he sighed, "All right, my little girl. Oh, I must live fully now, because, as my Love said, 'There will always be hope.'"

PART VIII

The Novel

Introduction   The Negro author has produced some interesting novels. One of the earliest pioneers in this field was William Wells Brown, who wrote *Clotele*. Charles W. Chesnutt shows power especially in *The House Behind the Cedars*. Jessie Fauset shows promise in *There Is Confusion* and in *The Chinaberry Tree*. Most Negro novelists deal with the uneducated Negro; on the other hand, Jessie Fauset and Nella Larsen deal with the intelligent Negro. Rudolph Fisher's *The Walls of Jericho* is another effective novel, which develops its plot around several piano movers in New York City. A short novel showing real genius is Paul Laurence Dunbar's *The Sport of the Gods*. There are many other novels by Negro authors; but most of the recent ones are pervaded with modern realism, which is frequently a combination of the vulgar and the profane.

An anthology cannot do justice to the novelist. However, some idea of the novelist's style can be discerned from an excerpt. Accordingly, the greater part of one of the latter chapters of Jessie Fauset's *The Chinaberry Tree* is here reproduced, to give some idea of the style of a representative Negro novelist. For the same reason this volume carries an excerpt from Arna Bontemps' *Drums at Dusk,* an historical novel, and Countee Cullen's *One Way to Heaven*.

The student at this point would do well to review the introduction on the short story; for much that is stated there comes within the province of the novelist. The novelist, however, with the extensive space allowed him, has much more freedom than the writer of the short story. He can use all the forms of discourse effectively in his novel. He has greater range in the development of plot, being able to introduce into his literary work any number of characters he desires and to spread the events over any extent of time. Besides, like Thackeray or George Eliot, he may comment extensively upon his characters and upon situations, making his philosophy of life an integral part of the novel.

One principle that the writer of fiction must regard is this: the incidents of the story must be presented with reference to the truth. The novelist may develop a story which presents impossible truth, as did Jules Verne in his novel, *Twenty Thousand Leagues Under the Sea.* He may aim to present actual truth, as Frank Yerby aspires to do in his historical novel, *The Foxes of Harrow.* Finally he may, like most novelists, strive for probable truth. Such is the aim of William Dean Howells in *The Rise of Silas Lapham,* Booth Tarkington in *The Turmoil,* Winston Churchill in *The Crisis,* and Sinclair Lewis in *Main Street.* This is the principle of verisimilitude. The events presented need not have occurred; but the reader is to be so impressed that he believes that the events are true to life; that is, that they are such as would very likely occur.

There are other techniques of the novelist; but these will not be discussed here. They will be left for the classroom teacher.

Finally, the novel, like the short story, may or may not have plot. *Banjo,* a novel by Claude McKay, has already been mentioned as one without plot. Similarly, De Foe's *Robinson Crusoe* has no plot, since the events of the story are related strictly in chronological order. Most novelists, however, do develop their stories with plot.

At this point, there must be mentioned again one of the most versatile of Negro writers, W. E. B. Du Bois, whose short story, "The Comet," and whose two novels, *The Quest of the Silver Fleece* and *Dark Princess,* place him among the best writers of American fiction.

Jessie Redmond Fauset

Jessie Redmond Fauset, the novelist, was born in Philadelphia. After attending the public schools of Philadelphia, she graduated from Cornell University. Later she attended the Sorbonne in Paris. After teaching for a number of years at the Dunbar High School of Washington, D. C. and in the public schools of New York City, she served as literary editor for the *Crisis*.

Among her publications are the following novels: *There Is Confusion, Plum Bun, The Gift of Laughter, The Chinaberry Tree,* and *Comedy, American Style.*

CHRISTMAS TIME [1]

The weather suddenly accepting its responsibility, Christmas arrived in due time as Christmas should. Red Brook on Christmas Eve bore out the scene on the conventional Christmas card. There must be something very basic and true, Malory Forten thought, plodding his way through the soft-falling, clinging snow, in a scene or a remark which was depicted or uttered again and again. Here for instance was the individual house, the moon visible over its peaked roof, its windows bright with light all over the dwelling, its children glimpsed through those same windows uncurtained and unshaded, busied about a Christmas tree. Over beyond loomed a thin church spire, and just above him in the sky there should be——there certainly was——the star.

[1] From *The Chinaberry Tree*, Copyright, 1931, by Jessie Fauset. Published by J. B. Lippincott Company, Philadelphia.

Somehow the accuracy, the truthfulness of the scene to type, both magnified and appeased the pain in his own young aching heart. Like many boys and men, Malory had a very definite sense of what a home should be . . . perhaps if in his home there had been the warmth, the jollity, and the light which one expects on Christmas Eve, he might have with sheer masculine perversity turned both his thoughts and footsteps elsewhere and sought a far different and less suitable means of spending the occasion. As it was, thwarted, baffled, embittered by the presence of the increased gloom which the holiday season seemed to bring to his cheerless household, he would have sacrificed almost every hope that he had for the future to have been able to see enacted within his walls the scenes which he was sure were being enacted in every normal household in Red Brook that night.

In spite of continued disappointments, he had thought that Reba in some way——he had long since ceased expecting anything of his mother or of Harriett——would have responded to the supremeness of the Christmas season. After all this was his first Christmas home, he was a boy, he was young. Great Scott, what did those folks of his have in their veins anyway! And what in God's name was the matter with them, he'd like to know! If Aunt Viny——good old sport if ever there was one——had only lived, he might have asked her. But Aunt Viny was dead now, lying straight and still under her first blanket of snow . . . could the dead feel the change in seasons he wondered, trying to think what the bare negation of life must mean. . . .

Only last Christmas Aunt Viny had given him the best party! True, she would ask only the grandchildren of her own pet cronies, whereas there were one or two new(!), very new, Philadelphians whom her very slightly more democratic nephew would gladly have welcomed. But after the guests arrived, Aunt Viny made it clear that they might do as they pleased; the old lady's only password to "society" being a valid claim to "old Philadelphian-ism." Having satisfied that, one might do what he wished. They had had a good time, "raising sand," (Aunt Viny's equivalent for the modern "whoopee,") dancing a discreet forerunner of the rumba, dispensing beribboned gifts. . . .

Late this afternoon Reba had come into his room and had placed on his bed a large flat package wrapped in a most un-Christmas-like covering of whitey-brown paper, the edges pinned together. How Malory's taste revolted at that!

"You might just as well have your presents now, Malory," she said faintly. "Harriett and I will be out serving a party to-night, so we'll be sleeping late, and mother never gets up on Christmas Day. She's gone to bed now . . . if you should go out you won't disturb her coming back will you? . . . If you want me to, I'll take your present in to her for you."

He'd give it to her himself when he saw her, he told her just as audibly. He was really suffering from the restraint which he felt he must put on the unreasoning anger welling within him. . . .

After she left he examined the bundle—two suits of underwear, two pairs of heavy worsted gloves—greeny-gray—with ugly, shapeless fingers, a whisk broom, a black neck-tie—a black neck-tie with small white rings in it! A tie old for a man of fifty! He left the articles reclining on their paper covering on the bed.

Melissa had given him a half-dozen fine handkerchiefs, the large size that made a fellow feel so opulent. They were monogrammed in simple, elegant lettering. With them had come a pair of heavy, short, tan gloves and a small pencil in silver and black marcasite. . . . He hadn't given her his present yet; it hadn't been completed until late this afternoon. . . . That was it, he'd go over to Melissa's this evening and hand the gift, a little monogrammed wrist watch in white gold——to whomever came to the door. No proud cousin could find fault with that! She'd probably take him for a messenger. If he could just set foot in Melissa's house to-night he would take it as an omen that next year she would be in his.

"She will, too," he vowed silently.

．　．　．　．

He started on his rounds early—there was candy for Kitty Brown, a copy of *Moby Dick* for Herbert Tucker whose family he liked. The Tuckers hailed him in, they made him sit down to supper. "We've got baked beans," Mrs. Tucker said hospitably, "it's so hard to decide what you're going to eat just before Christmas. You've got your mind so set on turkey and mince-meat. But boys always like baked beans."

It was great to be sitting in the warm cozy room, Malory thought, gratefully stowing away man-like portions of beans and corn-bread. They pressed him to stay. "We're not having company," Mrs. Tucker explained amiably, "we just like the family to be together on a night like this. Herbert usually goes out on New Year's Eve but he always stays home with his mother on Christmas Eve, don't you, Herbert?" She bustled out into the kitchen without waiting for an answer.

The boys grinned at each other in complete understanding.

"You know how it is," Herbert explained, whimsically resigned. He didn't really mind; his father and he had a perpetual conflict on at chess.

Malory stopped at Kitty's; met her sister Gertrude home for the holidays. A nice restful girl, he thought, with none of Kitty's aimless activity. He pushed on to Mrs. Ismay's, at whose house Mrs. Tucker had asked him to leave a small package. He liked Mrs. Ismay immediately, accepted her pleasant invitation to "drop in any evening, Doctor likes young men." He would go there sometime, he thought definitely, she seemed such a fine sort. . . . Melissa's cousin called there too, he remembered, maybe he'd meet her and make a good impression. . . . Wasn't it just his luck, though, to have absolutely no home and then to fall in love with a girl whose home he couldn't visit either?

"Well, there'll only be six months more of it," he muttered, and came to Melissa's house.

•   •   •   •

Assuredly this house ran true to type; its windows were blazing, its curtains up high. Malory stepped across the lawn in the soft snow up to, but not on, the front porch, and peered through the window. He saw a dark brown slender woman of about forty-five, he judged ——she had small, well-defined features. Then he saw Laurentine, smiling and excited, handing Christmas trinkets to Dr. Denleigh who, mounted on a step-ladder, was trimming a fine, tall Christmas Tree.

"Gosh, what a beautiful girl!" thought Malory. "What a 'wow' of a girl!" He shifted his position to see Laurentine better. Another man was standing there, middle-aged, in his overcoat, hat in hand, apparently ready to leave. Dr. Ismay, he saw later. Probably he had come over to bring a remembrance from his wife. Melissa wasn't there. He walked around to the side of the house and saw for the first time the Chinaberry Tree with its circular hexagonal seat under it. It was only a skeleton now, with here and there a leaf fluttering in the chilly night, but the moon sifting through its branches cast a pattern on the smooth snow about its base and made the tree more enchanting than ever.

Malory stopped to look at it, his quick mind visualizing it in its real glory. He said aloud what he'd said about Laurentine: "Gosh, what a beautiful tree! Why didn't Melissa ever tell me about this?" He started to knock on the side door but desisted, for fear one of the others might answer him and he did so want to see Melissa.

There was another room in back—that must be the kitchen— surely she must be in there, she wouldn't be up in her room alone on a night like this.

The kitchen windows were wide but shallow and placed high. Malory, looking about the yard in the clear moonlight, found a soap-box and stood on it to peer in the window. Yes, there she was in a white dress with a bright yellow smock; she was standing near an old-fashioned kitchen range, the oven-door was open and from it she had evidently drawn a pan of cookies.

He tapped softly on the door. Without a moment's hesitation, she opened it. "Malory! oh, Malory! Come in!"

He came in. He kissed her. His girl, Christmas Eve, the warm, safe room with its aura of living about it! "I suppose I should say, 'Together, at last.' "

She laughed with him. "Malory, this is the best present! How'd you dare come?"

"That reminds me, I've got your present—was that a hint—young lady?" He began to tap his various pockets, handed her a small package, "Don't open it 'til to-morrow morning——thus sparing my blushes. Melissa Paul, you wouldn't dare tell me you're making ginger cookies!"

"I certainly am; all hot and hot, and softy-like before they get cold, you know. Wait a minute." She vanished through the door, ran through the sewing-room, peeped into the room where the others were. She came back, her face glowing. "I told them to be very good and stay in there and later on I'd bring them something. Take off your overcoat and stay awhile." She helped him with it. "Oh Malory, Malory, to think you're actually in my house. . . . I think that's a good sign. . . . I've been so troubled, Malory . . . but now I believe everything will be all right."

He had on galoshes, but recklessly she bade him take those off too. He sat by the kitchen fire and she fed him hot gingerbread and cider and sandwiches which, already prepared, appeared fresh and dainty swathed in a thick white napkin. And all the time she was piling similar viands on a huge tray which she set in turn on a rolling tea table. Trundling this, she disappeared again, returned for plates and glasses, disappeared for a last moment and reappeared triumphant.

"There, that ought to hold them. They won't even think of me for the next hour." She dragged up a chair beside him, rested her head in one of her rare gestures of familiarity against his arm. "Malory, isn't it too grand? Have you opened your presents yet? Did you like them?"

"Like them? Look here!" He pulled one of the handkerchiefs from his pocket and flourished it. Another pocket in his vest revealed the smart new pencil.

"You shouldn't have used them so soon—greedy!"

"I couldn't help it, honey. Know what I've been thinking about, Melissa?"

"No, tell me!"

"This time, next year, we'll be together, you and I, in our own home. Say it and believe it." She said it and didn't believe it, though she wanted to.

He looked around at the kitchen, its bright orderliness, the rows and rows of shining, gaily colored plates, the clever furniture, the Dutch clock on the wall. Colonel Halloway had fitted out the place thoroughly, but that was long ago. Laurentine was responsible for bringing it thus up-to-date.

"You've never told me anything at all about your folks, you know, Melissa," he said looking around him with frank curiosity. "I had no idea you lived like this. I had no idea any colored folks in Red Brook lived like this. What's it your aunt's husband does?"

"He's dead," said Melissa uneasily. "Malory, I hate to hurry you, but I think you'd better go—see, I'm going to put these gingersnaps in your pocket." She wrapped them in a small fringed napkin. "Which I know I'll never see again," she teased him.

"You bet you won't. All right, honey. I'll be going, but I'm so glad I came, aren't you glad? Perhaps we can manage it again."

"Perhaps," she said breathlessly. "Here, I'll slip outside with you." She snatched a fleecy pink and white wool scarf from a hook, wrapped it around her rosy face in the old-fashioned style of the fascinator and stepped out into the path with him. "My boots are around on the side porch. I left them there this afternoon. I'll slip them on and walk a block with you."

But once near the side porch he remembered the Chinaberry Tree again. "Why didn't you ever tell me about it, Melissa? Here you've got your boots on, let's sit under it for a minute. Wait, I'll brush the snow off—and you can sit on the famous handkerchief. . . . Why, this place is too good to be true; isn't it really just the right place for a lover—and his lass?"

"Yes, it is," she agreed faintly. Why on earth must she remember, sitting here with Malory, her lover, the many, many times she had sat thus with Asshur?

"Listen, Malory, I'll have to be going in—I'll take cold and then anyway they might come out in the kitchen and miss me."

"Of course they will, better run along in. But let me tell you something, young lady. In the spring, come warm weather, we're going to sit out under this tree many's the night."

"How can we?"

"Easily enough. What time do your folks go to bed?"

"Oh, I don't know. Ten, half-past ten, eleven except when Laurentine's at Mrs. Ismay's or Dr. Denleigh's here."

"Well, we wouldn't expect to meet every night," he said reasonably. . . . "Say, your cousin is a stunning looking girl. Why didn't you ever tell me about her? 'Fraid I might look at her too hard?"

She laughed at that. "Silly! She's years older than you."

"Well, we'll slip out while the fair Laurentine and her mother are sleeping—I'll probably be here already—and we can talk and make plans. That's better than the Romany Road, Melissa, for you'll be already home then. I hate to see you starting off by yourself when you leave the Road."

She thought this over in silence. "Yes, yes, why I guess that would be better. I'm sorry darling—my teeth are chattering. Do go, Malory."

Once beyond the radius of the Chinaberry Tree, her uneasiness left her, her old adoration for him surged up. She put her arms about his neck in a sudden abandonment of love and regret at his going.

"Good-night, Malory. Merry Christmas, Malory."

"Merry Christmas, Melissa. Don't forget to come to Kitty's tomorrow."

"I'll come right after dinner."

"And we're having our own dinner, you remember, the next day at Pompton Lakes."

"Oh, yes, and I'm to bring the celery."

He walked off thinking it hadn't been such a bad Christmas Eve after all. "And when I know I don't have to have another one like it, I imagine this will be a very sweet and romantic memory," he told himself sensibly.

Melissa crept in the side door, rushed noiselessly up to her room, kicked off her wet boots and unwound her fascinator. Then bethinking herself of Malory's present reposing in the pocket of her smock, she took it out, pulled off its wrappings.

A wrist watch! In spite of herself she threw herself face downward across the bed and giggled almost hysterically. Asshur had sent her the selfsame gift, even to the design, from far off Alabama. It had arrived by special delivery just an hour before Malory came. Recovering presently, she arose and bearing the two watches under the electric light on her dressing table, she examined them carefully.

Yes, they were exact replicas——save that Asshur's watch had a tiny green jewel in the top of its minute winder, and Malory's had a blue one. And perhaps there was some slight difference in the monograms.

She took off her smock, smoothed her hair, applied powder and rouge and went back to the warm, spicy kitchen. . . . Mr. Stede came in with a present from Johnasteen. Aunt Sal emerging from the

living-room for a fresh supply of cookies found Melissa in the role
of Pentecost, staying the insatiable old man with platters of sandwiches and cookies, comforting him with flagons of cider.

Countee Cullen
(See page 67.)

ONE WAY TO HEAVEN [1]

Constancia Brandon, for whom Mattie worked, was the mirror in
which most of social Harlem delighted to gaze and see itself. She was
beautiful, possessed money enough to be willful, capricious, and rude
whenever she desired to deviate from her usual suave kindness; and
she was not totally deficient in brains. Tall and willowy, with a fine
ivory face whose emaciation spelled weakness and weariness, she
quickly dispelled such false first impressions when she began to talk,
with either her eyes or her tongue, in the use of both of which she
was uncommonly gifted. Her gray eyes had strange contractile powers,
narrowing into the minutest slits of disbelief and boredom, or widen-
ing into incredibly lovely globes of interest and amazement. They
were not the windows of her soul, but they were the barometers by
which one might gauge her interest in what he was saying.

Synthesis seemed to have had no part in her making. She had been
born in Boston, and baptized Constance in the Baptist Church; but at
sixteen she had informed her astounded parents and her equally
astounded and amused friends that thenceforth her name was to be
Constancia; that she found the religious ecstasies of the Baptist and
Methodist faiths too harrowing for her nerves; and that she would
attempt to scale the heavenly ramparts by way of the less rugged
paths of the Episcopalian persuasion. From the beginning her manner
was grand, and she gave one the impression that the great triumvirate,

composed of God, the Cabots, and the Lodges, had with her advent into the world let down the color bar and been reorganized, to include hereafter on an equal footing Constancia Brown. She had never experienced any racial disturbances or misgivings at attributing her equanimity on this score to one English grandfather, one grandfather black as soot, one grandmother the color of coffee and cream in their most felicitous combination, one creole grandmother, and two sane parents. She was interested in her genealogy only because she wanted to ascertain if there really was somewhere in the medley a gypsy woman or man whose slowly diminishing blood was responsible for her incessant and overwhelming love of jewelry. From the moment her ears had been pierced they had never been devoid of ornaments; sleeping or waking, she gave evidence of wise and charming investments in bracelets, rings, and pendants.

But her tongue was her chief attraction, ornament, and deterrent. Her linguistic powers, aided by an uncanny mnemonic ability, had brought her high honors at Radcliffe and the headlong devotion of George Brandon. Her schoolmates called her Lady Macbeth, not that she was tragic, but that she never spoke in a monosyllable where she could use a longer word; she never said "buy" when she might use "purchase," and purchased nothing to which she might "subscribe." The first night he met her at an Alpha Phi Alpha fraternity ball George Brandon had pleased her mightily by dubbing her Mrs. Shakespeare.

George Brandon, short, thick-set, light brown, and methodical, was an Oklahoma Brandon whose very finger tips were supposed to smell of oil and money. Constancia, whose lawyer father enjoyed a comfortable if not opulent living, had really lacked for no good thing, and so had been able to meet George Brandon with a disinterestedness and reserve that other young girls of colored Boston had not been able to simulate. She had been amused at his enervated, drawling speech and his dog-like devotion to her, but from that first meeting she had harbored kindly feelings for him because he had recognized her verbal literary ability by the sobriquet of Mrs. Shakespeare. It was inevitable, then, that after six months of frantic courting she should have accepted him when he pleaded that if she failed to do so he would be in no fit condition to be graduated from the Harvard Medical College.

"Not for your money, my dear," she had assured him, "nor for any inherent and invisible pulchritude in yourself, but in order to spare the world an accomplished physician, will I enter the enchanted realms of wedlock with you."

George had been happy to have her, even on the basis of so stilted and unromantic an acceptance. But the small-sized Oklahoma town to which he had taken her had not been able to reconcile itself to Mrs. Shakespeare. The small group of the Negro élite found her insufferable; they never knew what she was talking about. When she was hostess her guests generally left feeling that they had been insulted by her grandiose manners and complicated words; when she was guest her hostess never knew whether her comments on the party were commendable or derogatory. Matters fared no better at the monthly interracial meetings where the races met to exchange ideas and mutual good-will pledges, but not to touch hands. Constancia was elected secretary of the association, and thereafter the minutes were totally unintelligible save to herself, and when read made the bewildered workers for racial adjustment feel guilty of dark and immoral intentions. Mrs. Marshall, the wife of the white Baptist minister, and Mrs. Connelly, the wife of the leading white merchant, resented beyond concealment Constancia's chic vestments, blazing rings, and pendants; nor did they like the composed tone in which she would rise to say, "I unequivocally disagree with Mrs. Marshall," or, "I feel that Mrs. Connelly is in grievous error on this question."

In Oklahoma the Brandons could keep no servants; for Constancia had a strong democratic leaning which would not permit her to speak down to her menials. "I shall speak as I always do," she would say to the vainly expostulating George, "and they must learn to understand me. I do not want to embarrass them by making them self-conscious, by causing them to think that I do not believe that they have as much intelligence as I." And she continued to exhort her unintelligent help to "Come hither," to "Convey this communication to the doctor," or to "Dispatch this missive," until in utter self-defense they rebelled, and in true native fashion quit without giving notice.

Finally, at the repeated prayers of their respective ladies, the Reverend Mr. Marshall and Mr. Connelly, along with several colored members of the interracial committee, intimated to George that for the sake of racial amity it would be better if Constancia no longer kept the minutes of the meetings. And it was in order to placate Constancia for this loss of power and prestige that George brought her to Harlem.

In Harlem, Constancia had found her paradise. The oil-wells of Oklahoma were the open-sesame for which the portals of that extensive domain which goes by the name of Harlem society had swung wide to her. Wherever she went she conquered, and her weapons were various and well selected. Her interest in social activities won over the doctors' and lawyers' wives with whom, as Dr. Brandon's wife, she must naturally spend a part of her time; her democratic treatment of actors, writers, and singers made them her devoted slaves, while the very first week she was in New York her astounding vivacity and bewildering language completely floored Mrs. Vanderbilt-Jones of Brooklyn, who sent her an invitation to the Cosmos ball, and who even consented in all her rippling glory of black silk spangled with jet to attend Constancia's first Sunday night at home. For six days Harlem buzzed with the astonishing sight of Mrs. Vanderbilt-Jones in an animated and gracious conversation with Lottie Smith, singer of blues. Constancia had indeed been more than conqueror.

The Brandons purchased a fourteen-room house in what was called by less-moneyed, and perhaps slightly envious, Harlemites, Striver's Row. George, who, despite the unceasing emissions from the Oklahoma wells, came of industrious stock and willed to be a capable practicing physician, was relegated to the ground floor, while Constancia ruled supremely over the rest of the house.

She was endowed with taste of a diffusive sort, which communicated itself to the furnishings of her home as well as to her guests. What money could secure she bought, but indiscriminately. A survey of her home found ages and periods and faddistic moments juxtaposed in the most comradely and unhistoric manner, while the contributions of countries were wedded with the strictest disregard for geography.

Constancia never moved an eyelash to corral, but every author who came to her home either brought or sent an autographed copy of his books. Constancia dutifully and painstakingly read them all, after which she would give George an intricate résumé (which he promptly forgot) in order that, should he ever emerge into society, he might converse with intelligence and while talking to Bradley Norris not compliment him on the beauty of a poem which had been written by Lawrence Harper. No artist or singer was permitted to plead fatigue or temperament at Constancia's *soirées*. He might offend once, but Constancia would remark within ample hearing distance that temperament was the earmark of vulgarity and incapacity. If the erring virtuoso sinned a second time, she blue-penciled him, and remembered him with an elephant's relentlessness. For this reason her innumerable parties never lacked excitement and verve, and there was seldom a week in which the *New York Era* or the *Colonial News* did not carry a portrait of "Harlem's most charming hostess."

Lest it be thought that Constancia was built along strictly frivolous lines, let it be noted in all fairness and in her defense that she found time to belong to sixteen lodges which she never attended, but in which she was never unfinancial, and at whose yearly women's meetings she was always called upon to speak. She was a teacher in the Episcopalian Sunday School, because it convened in the morning and so left her free for her afternoon visits and her Sunday-evening at-homes. She was a member of the Board of the National Negro Uplift Society and a director of the Diminutive Harlem Theater Group; and she yearly donated fifty dollars for the best poem "by any poet," (never would she consent to stipulate "by any colored poet," although a colored poet had always won the award) published during the year in the *Clarion,* the Negro monthly magazine. Added to this, she belonged to two bridge clubs, one sorority, a circulating library, and she gave one hour a week in demonstrating household duties at the Harlem Home for Fallen Girls.

The freemasonry existing between the races in New York neither pleased nor disturbed her. She was equally gracious to an eccentric dancer from the Lafayette Variety Theater and to a slumming matron from Park Avenue, out with fear and trembling to discover just how the other color lived. When at one of her parties it was suggested to her in fiery language by a spirited young Negro, who could neither forget nor forgive, that a celebrated white writer present was out to exploit and ridicule her, she had replied:

"Ridicule me? If he contrives to depict me as I am, he shall have achieved his first artistic creation. If he does less, he shall have ridiculed himself. And besides, don't be so damnably self-conscious or you will be miserable all your life. Now vouchsafe me your attendance and let me introduce you to the ogre who has come to devour us all."

She had then taken the protesting youngster by the hand, piloted him through her groups of chattering guests, and brought him to a standstill before Walter Derwent.

"My dear Mr. Derwent, I want you to do me a kindness. Here is a young man who is laboring under the apprehension that your frequent visits to Harlem have an ulterior motive, that you look upon us as some strange concoction which you are out to analyze and betray. I wish you would either disabuse him of, or confirm him in, his fears."

And she had left them together, both equally frightened.

After leaving them, she had paused to shout into Mrs. Vanderbilt-Jones' deaf and sparkling ear:

"I have just coupled a diminutive god with a sprouting devil." She had passed on before Mrs. Vanderbilt-Jones could summon courage enough to demand an explanation of the riddle.

Mattie had been Constancia's maid for over six years, six days out of seven. Being maid meant making herself generally useful, and giving orders to Porter, *l'homme à tout faire,*[1] who was disinclined to see work which was not pointed out to him. Mattie adored Constancia, although she disapproved of her parties and thought her guests exceedingly strange and curiously mannered. Constancia spoke of Mattie as the perfect maid, a jewel of the first water. She had reached this conclusion when, coming home one afternoon, she had interrupted Mattie in the midst of her dusting, to inform her:

"Mattie, I have just been psychoanalyzed."

Mattie had said nothing for a moment, but had ceased dusting, and had then delved down into her apron pocket, whence she extracted a small pocket dictionary. After turning its pages and scanning the word

[1] A general utility man, a jack of all trades.

carefully, she had turned to the fascinated Constancia and, without a ripple stirring her smooth black face, had said:

"Yes, ma'am. I hope you liked it."

Constancia had flown to her, had kissed her, and called her a *rara avis*,[1] which had disturbed Mattie throughout the day because she could not find that in her dictionary.

Arna Bontemps

Calm or fiery as the occasion may require, but always virile in his writings, Arna Bontemps is chiefly an apostle of the classic style. His poetry shows restraint, though it carries an undercurrent of protest against the inconsistencies of our age. His novels are unusually moving, powerfully dynamic and swift, and realistic. Especially is this true of *Drums at Dusk,* from which an excerpt is taken for this volume. This chapter, the disturbed feast, the flight, and the return to Bréda of Celeste, are passages that reach the stage of epic grandeur.

Bontemps was born in 1902 in Alexandria, Louisiana. Because of the early death of his mother, his school attendance was irregular. Most of his training he received in the schools of California, and Pacific Union College.

Among his publications are the following: novels, *God Send Sunday* (1931), *Black Thunder* (1936), and *Drums at Dusk* (1939). In 1948 he published for young people *Story of the Negro.* In the same year he published a comprehensive anthology of poetry of the Negro of the Americas in collaboration with Langston Hughes. He has won several prizes for his poetry.

DRUMS AT DUSK [2]

Among those who heard the scuffling of the count and his female antagonist was the old, soft-voiced coachman of M. de Libertas. Toussaint, trusted beyond his fellows and respected for his judgment, had been assigned to the wine cellar during the festivities. When the trouble broke in the dining hall, he was pleased to remain at his post where

1 Rare bird.
2 From *Drums at Dusk,* by Arna Bontemps. Copyright, 1939, by The Macmillan Company, New York, and used with their permission.

he was presently joined by Mars, major-domo among the house servants.

"Baissou is theatrical," the coachman had remarked following Mars's description of the tumult at supper.

"He's not afraid, though."

"He makes himself conspicuous——foolishly conspicuous."

An hour had passed. The two old blacks, fastidiously clean and well-dressed, sat on stools in the flickering light of a candle. Half a dozen times they were visited by slaves who reported what was happening on the countryside and at various neighboring estates visible from the tree tops or from the roof of the stable. The insurrection of the blacks was indeed something more than a dream now, they declared. The slaves of Bréda, notoriously well-treated at the hands of M. de Libertas and his wife, had not yet joined, but a dozen or more of those who had been borrowed for this occasion had, like Baissou, scampered across the fields to join the batteries of drums, the rude cavalry detachments mounted on plow horses, oxen, mules, and donkeys, the horde of barefooted followers carrying torches and armed with machetes, pikes, and clubs.

"When do we join?" Mars asked, stifling a cough.

"I'll give the word. Not now," Toussaint told him decisively.

A few moments later they put their heads together and tried to comprehend the scuffle on the second floor. When it was over and one of the antagonists stumbled down the stairs and out the back door, Toussaint decided to leave the wine cellar and get busy.

"I won't be here when you come back," Mars told him on the ladder.

Toussaint paused.

"Feeling weak?"

Mars nodded.

"I want to lie down," he admitted.

"Well, get better. Tell Suzette where I am."

When he reached the hall above, the girl was still on the floor, her naked breasts exposed, her skirt twisted around her hips, her face long with exhaustion. She had the look of one who had been ravished; but when Toussaint squinted questioningly, she quickly corrected him. It wasn't what he thought.

"I fought back," she said. "The count struck me in the face; what's going to happen, *vieux* [1] Toussaint?"

"War is beginning," he told her. "The slaves are breaking free. They'll have to fight the army by morning."

"I'm already free," the girl suggested.

"Yes, you are—scuffling with the count. Go to your quarters now."

The hall was empty, save for these two; and when the girl left, Toussaint walked back and forth nervously. Through the window that led out on the balcony, he saw the burning fields, but there was now no one out there enjoying the spectacle. The rooms within seemed deserted, too. Still a few sounds could be heard. Several doors stood open. In each case the occupant had fled leaving the lamp burning. The gentlemen's coatroom had been left with a great number of neglected hats and riding garments.

M. Bayou de Libertas opened his door and came into the hall, stood silently, hands behind him on the knob, as tears filled his eyes and began running down his face. Seeing tears in the comical eyes of the overseer touched Toussaint immediately. He stopped pacing; his pitifully rounded shoulders, his hands, his wiry pigtail, his protruding teeth, together these made him an inexpressibly forlorn figure.

"Sad, Toussaint?" the overseer asked. "Or just tired?"

"Joy, like sorrow, has its tears," the coachman answered. "But I have no joy."

"You want to be free, don't you?"

"Is there a chance?"

"You know there is. Everything is with you."

"I haven't joined them——yet."

M. de Libertas looked at the shrewd old black with the utmost candor and sympathy.

"Why?" he asked simply, his eyes still tearful.

"Because of you and Madame."

"You mean——"

"Our people are not ungrateful, monsieur. Knowing how our

1 Old.

brothers have fared on other plantations has convinced us that you are not an ordinary master of slaves."

"That's flattery, Toussaint."

"At any rate, I shall not leave your side till you and Madame de Libertas are safe. The slaves are a lustful pack tonight."

"They're drunk——drunk with freedom. I suppose it's natural, after what they've been through."

"We can carry one trunk in the coach, monsieur. If you'll have Madame indicate what she'd like to save, I'll come back and make it ready after I've harnessed the horses."

"Toussaint, I hadn't thought of running away."

"It's your only chance, monsieur. There's been blood-letting to-night, and there may be more. I'm not sure I can stop them when they reach Bréda."

Fresh tears filled the blinking, round eyes of M. de Libertas.

"No, Toussaint, no! It's like quitting a ship. I'm a hired man on this place. There's no running away."

The door opened as M. de Libertas's voice rose. He was hysterical. His wife and Céleste, both pale as ghosts, came out and stood beside him.

"Don't shout," the older woman implored. "I can't stand to see you worked up."

"We'll have to stay and take our chances," he said more calmly. "It's our penalty for being blind while all this was brewing."

"But you have no right to risk danger for these ladies." Toussaint spoke with unusual firmness.

"We risk danger if we go or if we stay."

"Monsieur, we're wasting time. Tonight, if you please, I am the master of Bréda. You don't seem to realize that slavery ended this evening when the servants walked out of the dining room and returned to their quarters without permission."

The overseer was too shaken to answer.

"What are your orders, Toussaint?" Mme. de Libertas asked.

"Lay out the things you wish to save," he told her. "I'll be back presently to pack them in a trunk. Be ready to leave promptly. I hope to get the three of you to Le Cap."

He had turned before he finished his remarks. On the stairs he fairly bounded. Toussaint had an old face, but his body was made of hard, vibrant muscles. He had resources of strength that one discovered with surprise after long acquaintance.

A moment later he was on the path, hastening toward the stables. A pair of old carriage lamps gleamed on either side of the door leading into the harness room. Toussaint entered, his heels thumping solidly on the clean wooden floor. A lighted lantern swayed from a cross beam. Bare feet frisked excitedly on the roof overhead, like rats in an attic—black youngsters, perhaps, watching the fires from the distance.

When he had rolled a sturdy coach out into the yard by hand, he found bridles and quickly laid hands on the horses he preferred. Less than five minutes had passed when he swung himself to the coachman's place and, standing with feet braced apart, cracked a whip over the nervous, eager teams.

He was tying up at a sapling near the back door when he realized that he had delayed almost too long. The horde had reached Bréda. A flurry of drum beating broke out among the trees of the grove. Toussaint rushed to the door, paused long enough to feel his own quaking, dashed through the lower rooms and up the stairs. A moment later he was pounding on the door of Mme. de Libertas's room.

When the door was flung open, the old coachman was pleased to discover that the woman and the girl were already in their capes, the girl apparently wearing one that belonged to the larger woman. M. de Libertas, his sorrel hair in disorder, had plopped a hat heedlessly on his head. The room itself looked as if plunderers had already visited it. The trunk in which Mme. de Libertas kept the mementos of her bellehood had been uncovered and drawn into the middle of the room. A square affair, its top had been thrown back and its contents hurriedly sorted. On the floor at one side was a heap of outmoded clothes that had been discarded. In their place was to go a stack of wearable garments, spread at the moment on the bed and chairs. A quantity of silver was at the moment being stuffed into a plush bag already tight with small table-pieces and metal ornaments. The task had been given to the girl who, as she worked, trembled so noticeably that the old black took it out of her hands.

"Are we too late?" the overseer asked.

Toussaint did not answer. Instead he pointed to the bottles on a table.

"Drink something, monsieur."

"That's all he's been doing since you left," the stout wife replied, pushing the discarded things aside with her foot.

"They're coming through the grove," Toussaint said unsteadily. "You'd better go down now. The horses are tied near the back steps. I'll finish with these things. Monsieur, I suggest you lead the team around the house and get the coach out of sight. It's the safest way."

The three responded swiftly, carrying only as much as their arms could manage. With M. de Libertas it was his squirrel gun, two sets of duelling pieces, a small ornamental pistol with a carved handle. Céleste carried two fragrant dress boxes; and tucked under an orange satin coat Mme. de Libertas bore the heavy chestlike box that contained the gold they had on hand.

"Are we the last?" M. de Libertas asked, passing through the door.

Toussaint had already fallen on his knees before the open trunk and begun with swift efficiency to complete the job. He did not look up when he answered.

"Almost the last, I imagine, monsieur."

The overseer's wife was behind him now, however, and there was no chance of his turning. Toussaint heard their steps on the stairs a moment later. He heard the voices of Claire, Annette and perhaps a third woman in another part of the house. He felt, rather than heard, the soft thunder of drums, the impact of which fired his blood like a drug. But what, he wondered, gave him that tingling unsteadiness? Why did his teeth chatter? Was he afraid of Boukman or Baissou or the crowd they had been able to assemble?

Scarcely. There was no fear left in *vieux* Toussaint. Furthermore there was no time now for pointless questions of that sort. His task was clear. Madame and Monsieur had been kind and reliable friends to him and to many others in a time when the rule was cruelty and inhumanity toward slaves. When these were dispatched safely, along with their young friend, then—then he could hurl himself into the struggle. Toussaint lost none of his former care, but he completed his work with such deft speed that he was a trifle astonished himself as he realized that the jewel boxes, the corsets, the petticoats and pantalets, the morocco slippers, the bales of India silk turbans, the camphor and the sachet were all inside and that the trunk was full.

He was standing the box on end and securing it with straps and a rope when bedlam broke in the rooms downstairs. Glass shattered, chairs and tables toppled in a succession of wanton crashes. At the same moment heavy feet stormed the stairway.

Toussaint, calmer than he had been since the trouble first broke, recognized some of the savage voices and promptly decided to plead with the infuriated blacks in behalf of Bréda. On second thought, however, he swiftly changed his plan. There was no stopping them now. For a black who wished to see discretion and sober wisdom play a part in this thrust for liberty, the best line to follow—perhaps the only one—was to stay out of the picture until the bloody intoxication, the pent-up fury, had been spent. There was no need forgetting that a powerful French army was garrisoned in Cap Français, that this force contained veterans who had fought under the Marquis d'Estaing at the Siege of Savannah on the soil of continental America. Battalions would be in the field by morning, and this night of jungle heroics and wild abandon on the part of the slaves would be sure to have its sequel in fighting of another sort. The second and more important phase would not be firing great houses, turning on masters and pillaging. Permanent freedom would have to be won by tedious patience in a hard, prolonged campaign against armed forces. The chiefs of the blacks would be confronted with the near-impossible task of commanding this madness and transforming it into an organized force fit to cope with military arms and discipline. In that fighting old Toussaint was sure to have a part. A flash of benign confidence gleamed on the coachman's mask-like face. One could not be overconfident, knowing the odds and the chances of failure, but Toussaint knew that in his own heart he had already accepted the challenge. He was not a great one for the sort of havoc this night was producing; his mind was offended by messiness, confusion, and turmoil. He hadn't the power to draw a brawling sword. But he was ready and anxious to meet a military foe if by doing so he could strike a blow for the freedom of the blacks. In fact, the prospect thrilled him, and he was feeling drunk with it.

At the moment, however, with the wild element in control and the pack on the stair, his business was to drop the trunk with its treasures through the window and make way for the plunderers. He raised the box and, hurrying before the approaching steps, sent it hurtling through the pane and to the ground below. When he turned, he looked into the faces of slaves who knew him well.

"*Vieux* Toussaint!" one cried.

The old black straightened the kink in his back, made a dignified salute.

"*Vive la liberté!*" he replied, embarrassed.

"*Vive la liberté!*" The second voice was as hoarse and untamed as a lion's. It belonged to the gigantic, barrel-bellied Boukman.

Presently the room was filled with the slave pack. The fruits of plunder dangled from them grotesquely. One wore a yellow satin coat. Another had evidently fallen upon a jewelry box. A chain of vivid stones glittered about his neck. A handsome plumed hat adorned a savage head. There was a girl in the group, a lean bronze tomboy in an orange turban, an abbreviated skirt and gleaming boots.

"You should be home," Toussaint told her, not unkindly. "The apron should work for the pantaloons."

"Tomorrow," she said. "Everyone is out tonight. I couldn't stay."

The crowd drifted out of the room and into the hall.

"The time is slipping," Boukman growled impatiently. "Dig in. We've got to move along."

"Bréda deserves a better fate than the other estates," Toussaint suggested.

"You're soft, *vieux* Toussaint. You've been petted. See, your back is smooth. Look at these scars. I say spare none."

The burly giant gave the others his back, tore off his shirt and showed them the record of his servitude. Even Toussaint winced at the sight. Boukman had been more badly used than any beast. He snorted with ribald laughter as the others became pop-eyed with amazement.

"There is no answer to that," Toussaint remarked sadly.

The crowd quickly divided, breaking into the empty rooms like hungry jackals. Here and there a door had to be forced. This was followed each time by a resounding crash. Machetes and pikes, pirate sabers and rude spears, brandished overhead, smote one against the other in awkward confusion. A vast ravishment of curtains and hangings, of canopies and beds, of dressing tables and mirrors began. In the midst of it Claire and Annette suddenly appeared in the hall, their eyes bright with rum.

"Wait," Claire said, running after one of the wildest insurgents and slapping him on his shoulder. "Give me a machete," she cried through the din.

The slave, so surprised he seemed frightened, raised his spear before her.

"What's this?"

"I've been waiting twenty years for something like this. Give me a weapon. I can fight, too. You can't leave me out."

"Nor me," Annette insisted, "I'll help."

The slaves shook them off but refrained momentarily from running them through with their blades.

"They aren't very playful," Toussaint told the women.

He turned and slipped swiftly down the stairs. From the bottom, he saw the enchanted Claire persuading Annette to slide down the banister.

A moment later, dragging the trunk across a flower bed, he reached the coach where M. de Libertas had secluded it in a clump of tall shrubbery and low trees.

"There is no peace, Toussaint," Mme. de Libertas whimpered, drowsy with long excitement. "No peace anywhere. Turmoil, turmoil, turmoil—one fight after another."

"Each hour wounds," the coachman replied. "The last kills."

"We sent a word for Mme. Jacques Juvet, this child's grandmother," the overseer's wife reminded. "Have you heard whether or not it was delivered?"

"A stableboy carried it," Toussaint assured her. Reluctantly he added, "It was too late."

"No. Oh, no. You don't mean——"

"The excitement, perhaps. Her heart."

He touched the horses and the coach moved heavily on the soft earth. Inside the carriage sobs broke. Toussaint was unable to distinguish between the voices.

PART IX

The Drama

Introduction   The word "drama" comes from the Greek verb "dramein," which means to act. Accordingly Aristotle in his *Poetics,* in setting forth laws governing the Greek drama, stated that the essential of a drama is action, which is the very life of a play. The most successful plays have been those that abound not in provocative thought but from beginning to end teem with action. The form of the drama is dialogue, not mere conversation but dramatic dialogue; it is conversation which can be helped by action. Consider, for instance, just a few lines of a soliloquy from Shakespeare's *Macbeth:*

MACBETH. Go bid thy mistress, when my drink is ready,
    She strike upon the bell. Get thee to bed. (*Exit Servant*)
    Is this a dagger which I see before me,
    The handle toward my hand? Come, let me clutch thee.
    I have thee not, and yet I see thee still.
    Art thou not, fatal vision, sensible
    To feeling as to sight? or art thou but
    A dagger of the mind, a false creation,
    Proceeding from the heat-oppressed brain?
    I see thee yet, in form as palpable
    As this which now I draw.

This passage offers many opportunities for gestures and body movements. This is possible because of the images the language arouses in the mind of the reader or the hearer.

Drama also requires a conflict. It may be a conflict of physical, intellectual, or emotional forces or it may be a combination of two or of all of these. A fight, a duel, and a collision are examples of a conflict of physical forces. A quarrel or an argument or a debate or a court trial would be an example of an intellectual conflict. The quarrel and argument might be more emotional than intellectual. The debate and the court trial are supposed to be more intellectual than emotional. If there is a struggle between two or more individuals, there is a conflict. All these situations are dramatic; the greater the amount of action involved and the greater the contrast of the emotions involved in the conflict, the more dramatic will be the situation. Polar ideas creating excellent dramatic situations are love and hate, loss and gain, joy and sorrow, poverty and wealth, fear and courage. There are other strong contrasts.

The unusual is also an inspirer of the dramatic. The ordinary event may not arouse the deep emotions, but the unusual happening will. There is an element of allurement about the strange.

Showiness is also helpful in inspiring the dramatic. Beautiful scenery and showy costumes will stir the emotions and, if carefully selected to blend with an incident, will greatly aid the drama. Because the drama may use music, dancing, speech, poetry, painting, sculpture, and architecture, it has been called the greatest of the fine arts.

There is much of the dramatic in everyday life: an automobile accident, a fire which has brought a response from the fire department of a community, an athletic contest, a funeral, or a wedding. The funeral and the wedding, because of the large numbers of people involved, generally partake of the nature of a pageant. A pageant is a type of drama in which there are many characters, in which the interest is more in the action, the scenery, and the costumes than in the conversation. There is not a rapid change in the pageant from speaker to speaker; one character may be the only speaker in the scene. Such is not true of the regular drama; for in the regular drama, if it is to be effective, there must be frequent change from speaker to speaker.

The vehicle of the drama may be prose or poetry. Shakespeare in his dramas used both prose and poetry. He used prose to show the rank of the lowly people or the peasants, and to convey humor. The drunken porter in *Macbeth* speaks in prose; the clowns or peasants in *Hamlet*, that is, the gravediggers, are humorous characters and speak in prose. The noblemen and kings in Shakespeare's plays speak in poetry, generally unrhymed verse. When they speak in rhymed poetry, Shakespeare is giving emphasis to a particular part within a play or to the end of a scene. Since rhymed poetry, if used regularly, would have given artificiality to his characters, Shakespeare had the supernatural characters speak regularly in rhymed stanzas. He uses stanzas chiefly to intensify an emotion. The stanzas of *A Midsummer Night's Dream* give lightness to that play and intensify the emotion of joy; the stanzas in *Hamlet,* a tragedy, as sung by Ophelia, intensify the emotion of sadness.

The dramas of Arthur Wing Pinero and Henry Arthur Jones, as well as those of George Bernard Shaw, are in prose. The dramas of Henrik Ibsen, though apparently in prose, are written in poetic language. So far the American Negro dramatists have adhered to prose.

On the plantation during slavery days, many Negroes, with their gifts of mirth and song, won great applause from masters and overseers. These were so impressed with their ability as entertainers that some white men blackened their faces and began professionally to imitate the antics of the Negro. Thus there came into existence the minstrel show, with such great minstrels as Lew Dockstader, the Primrose Minstrels, and then Negro troupes.

Later there came musical comedies with a team of two black-faced comedians, or one black-faced comedian who supplied the fun of the show. The other principal actor appeared in the most stylish attire; but his black-faced friend wore clothes that were flashy or bizarre. Such a team was that of Egbert Williams and George Walker in *In Dahomey* and *Bandana Land;* or Bob Cole and J. Rosamond Johnson in *The Shoofly Regiment* and *Red Moon;* or Miller and Lyles, in *Shuffle Along,* assisted by Noble Sissle and Eubie Blake.

The first classic play by an American Negro author, *The Escape,* or *A Leap for Freedom,* was written by William Wells Brown.

The performance of the Negro actor certainly indicates that he has a sense of dramatic appreciation. Ira Aldridge's rendition of Shakespearean roles in Glasgow, Liverpool, London, Paris, Berlin, and Moscow brought generous acclaim from Edward Bulwer-Lytton. Charles

Gilpin as the Emperor Jones, Paul Robeson as the Emperor Jones, the Hairy Ape, and Othello, and Frederick O'Neal as the brother of Anna Lucasta—all bespeak the ability of the Negro as an actor and his appreciation for the dramatic.

This appreciation has expressed itself in Little Theater movements in various cities. Frederick O'Neal organized the Ira Aldridge Players in Saint Louis and the American Negro Theater in New York. Out of the American Negro Theater of New York came "Anna Lucasta," a Broadway success and one of the most popular plays ever to appear on Broadway. In Saint Louis some years ago, Ruth Gaines Shelton, who wrote for the *Crisis* the prize comedy, *The Church Fight,* made a specialty of giving full-length plays of her own composition for the benefit of churches. One of her most popular plays was *Lord Earlington's Broken Vow.* Observing that the church offers an excellent opportunity for religious drama, the National Baptist Sunday School and Training Congress is offering a course in "The Use of the Drama in Religious Education."

In Washington, D. C., the great spirit encouraging the creation of a Negro Theater Movement with original plays was Willis Richardson. His plays well interpret Negro life, whether of the past or the present. He is one of the most popular of Negro playwrights. The other individual nationally known for his efforts to promote a Negro Theater Movement is Randolph Edmonds, professor of the drama at Dillard University, New Orleans. He organized the Negro Intercollegiate Drama Association and the Southern Association of Drama and Speech Arts.

A playwright needs actors to interpret his plays, a producer to stage them and an audience to witness them. The Negro playwright has not accomplished much in the drama because of this interlocking relationship. Ira Aldridge, Paul Robeson, Charles Gilpin, Frederick O'Neal, Muriel Smith, Ethel Waters, Eva Matthews, Lena Horne, Hilda Simms, and many others—all prove that the Negro playwright can get competent actors. His difficulty has been to find a producer. Most spoken dramas of the professional stage make their debut on Broadway. To take a play there is very expensive. Besides, a play will not remain there long, so far as the Negro is concerned, if it has an all-Negro cast, unless the play is full of comedy, comedy of the primitive Negro, as in *Porgy, Cabin in the Sky,* and *The Green Pastures.* Since the primitive Negro is more dramatic than the sophisticated Negro, more frank and more natural, plays about this type of Negro, who constitutes a stereotype, are more readily received by a Broadway audience than would be a play of the life of the Negro who is intellectual. The sophisticated Negro wants plays of sophisticated Negro life; Broadway wants the other type. As a result, if the Negro writes a play of sophisticated Negro life, he must expect to have a Negro audience. Those demanding this type of Negro play are not sufficiently numerous to make it profitable for a Negro to produce the kind of play they desire.

A classic example of this is the effort of Garland Anderson of San Francisco. His play, *Appearances,* took well there. It was recommended for Broadway.[1] By his own financing, it did reach Broadway. However, though it was an excellent play, its run was short.

Langston Hughes' *The Mulatto,* it is true, was a Broadway success and toured many of the large cities; but it was a play of primitive life, a play of race relations on a farm where poor white people and poor Negroes of the Deep South lived side by side in accordance with the folkways of the Deep South. In such plays the Negro is disadvantaged and oppressed. Such a picture is presented as appears in *Tobacco Road.* There are, there have been, intelligent Negro heroes, like Frederick Douglass, Josiah Henson, William Wells Brown, Richard Allen; but a dramatist cannot yet expect to have a Broadway success with a play presenting such a hero. The American public is year by year becoming more liberal; but justice in the drama, so far as the Negro is concerned, is still a long way off. However, that day will eventually come. When it does, then will appear the great Negro drama and the great Negro dramatist. Willis Richardson and Randolph Edmonds are ready now. America some day will give them a chance.

---

[1] Garland Anderson, *From Newsboy and Bell Hop to Playwright,* p. 7.

Willis Richardson

Willis Richardson, dramatist and essayist, was born at Wilmington, North Carolina. He was educated in the public schools of Wilmington and Washington. His interest in literature led him to pursue a correspondence course in Poetry and the Drama.

Among his publications are the following: Essays, "The Hope of a Negro Drama," *Essays on the Drama;* plays, *Four Plays in the Brownie Book, Mortgaged, The Deacon's Awakening, The Broken Banjo* (which won the Amy Spingarn Prize in the contest conducted by the *Crisis* in 1925. The same prize was awarded this author in 1926 for his three-act play, *Bootblack Lover.*) He edited *Plays and Pageants from the Life of The Negro* and *Negro History in Thirteen Plays.*

THE HOUSE OF SHAM [1]

Characters

JOHN COOPER, *a real estate dealer*	JOYCE ADAMS, *Enid's cousin*
	DR. BILL HOLLAND
MRS. COOPER	HAL FORD
ENID, *their daughter*	DORSEY

The house of Cooper is that of a well-to-do colored family, and the room we see is what might be called a reception room. At the right is a door which leads outside, and above and below this respectively stand a desk and a chair. Directly in front of us at the upper end of the room is a bay window from which the street can be seen by those

[1] Permission for the performance of this play must be obtained from the author, Willis Richardson, 2023 13th St. N.W., Washington, D. C.

in the room. On the left side of the room is a mantel below which is a
fireplace. In front of the mantel stand two comfortable chairs, and
other comfortable seats are about the room. At the present moment
Mrs. Cooper, Enid, Joyce, and Bill Holland are visible. Bill and Enid
are about to go motoring. A door at the left leads to other parts of the
house.

BILL. (*As they are about to go.*) Don't you want to take a spin
around the block with us?

MRS. COOPER. (*Who is the only one sitting.*) No, thanks, Doctor, I
haven't long come in. I'm very tired.

BILL. (*To Joyce.*) How about you, Joyce?

JOYCE. No, I guess not. I thank you just the same.

ENID. (*Who is not overanxious for a third party.*) Expecting any one,
Joyce?

JOYCE. (*Adjusting Enid's collar.*) Not exactly.

ENID. But if any one comes you mean to be here, don't you?

JOYCE. Yes, but I don't exactly expect any one.

BILL. Is that why you won't go with us, because you don't exactly
expect any one?

JOYCE. No, that's not it.

BILL. What is it, then? Honestly, now?

ENID. Let her alone, Bill; can't you see she's got a secret?

JOYCE. (*Smiling.*) You know I'm too young to have secrets, Enid.

BILL. (*Throwing up his hands in mock despair.*) That settles it; come
on, Enid.

ENID. (*Putting her arm around Joyce.*) The younger they are the
more secrets they have these days, dear; now tell us who it is, what
it is, when and why and how.

JOYCE. You don't want to know much, do you?

MRS. COOPER. Let Joyce alone and go on for your ride. How long do
you mean to be gone?

BILL. We won't be gone many minutes. We hope to pick Mr. Cooper
up on our way back.

ENID. (*Lingering.*) I've just got to learn what this child is all a-flutter
about.

JOYCE. But I'm not all a-flutter.

MRS. COOPER. Don't tell her a thing, Joyce.

ENID. Do you know what it is, Mama?

MRS. COOPER. I have an idea.

ENID. (*Going to her mother.*) Whisper it to me.

MRS. COOPER. No, I won't.

ENID. Well, I'll get the idea when I come back. (*She and Bill go out.*)

MRS. COOPER. I think I know your secret, Joyce.

JOYCE. (*Turning to her quickly.*) Which secret?

MRS. COOPER. How many have you?

JOYCE. I didn't say I had any.

MRS. COOPER. Oh, but you have; and it's about you and Hal.

JOYCE. (*Feigning innocence.*) Hal?

MRS. COOPER. Now don't try to fool an old woman. Every woman knows when another one is in love.

JOYCE. (*Confused.*) But—Hal—you know Hal—

MRS. COOPER. (*Rising.*) Yes, I know. I understand perfectly. Come here to the window a minute. I want to show you something. (*She and Joyce go up to the window.*) Don't Enid and the doctor make a fine-looking couple?

JOYCE. Yes, they do. And here comes Hal down the street. He'll just miss them.

MRS. COOPER. To miss them is just what he wants to do, I'll bet.

JOYCE. He sees them, though. See how he's watching the car.

MRS. COOPER. (*Pointing.*) I wonder who that man is?

JOYCE. The one walking up and down?

MRS. COOPER. Yes; and holding his hand in his pocket. He's been walking up and down there for the last hour.

JOYCE. I suppose he's waiting for some one.

MRS. COOPER. But he always looks up at this house.

JOYCE. If he wanted to see any one in here he'd come in, wouldn't he?

MRS. COOPER. I don't know. There's so many rascals about nowadays a person can hardly tell what to think.

JOYCE. Ask Hal about him.

MRS. COOPER. That's what I mean to do as soon as he comes in.

JOYCE. (*Turning from the window.*) I'll go in and read my magazine while you talk to him.

MRS. COOPER. Don't you want to talk to him?

JOYCE. (*Blushing.*) Yes, but—yes, I'll see him later.

MRS. COOPER. Oh, you want to see him alone. I'll send him to you. (*The bell rings and Mrs. Cooper goes to the door while Joyce goes out left.*)

HAL. (*Entering.*) Good evening.

MRS. COOPER. (*Closing the door.*) Well, Hal, how're you this evening?

HAL. Fair. (*He looks about and sees that no one else is present.*) All alone?

MRS. COOPER. (*Indicating the other room.*) Joyce is in there reading. (*Looking at him closely.*) You look worried. Is there anything wrong?

HAL. I acknowledge I am a little worried, and I'm glad you're alone. I want to talk to you——ask your advice about something.

MRS. COOPER. Why so serious?

HAL. It's a serious matter.

MRS. COOPER. (*Sitting.*) Well, take a cigarette and tell me the sad news.

HAL. (*Taking a cigarette from his pocket and lighting it.*) It's not serious that way. It's about Enid and me.

MRS. COOPER. (*Enlightened.*) Oh, I see.

HAL. You know we've been——I've been taking up a great amount of her time, and now I think it's only right for me to——

MRS. COOPER. (*Kindly.*) There isn't any use going any further, Hal; I understand what you would say. You think it's your duty to propose to Enid and you want my consent. Well, you know I'm your friend, but I'm not going to give my consent to that because I know you're in love with Joyce, and I know Dr. Holland is in love with Enid. Now, aren't you in love with Joyce?

HAL. You're frank with me, so I'll be frank with you. There isn't any doubt that I think a great deal of her.

MRS. COOPER. I knew it. It's hard to fool a woman about being in love; and especially an old woman like me.

HAL. I wouldn't try to fool you.

MRS. COOPER. I hope not. Now to be more frank with you. I like you very much, Hal; better than I do Dr. Bill, but I could hardly give my consent to a marriage between you and Enid even if things were different from what they are.

HAL. (*Puzzled.*) You mean even if we were in love with each other?

MRS. COOPER. That's just it.

HAL. Why?

MRS. COOPER. One simple reason: Because you don't make money enough. And what Enid will need most of all will be money. You couldn't begin to take care of her, but Dr. Bill can. You see, he's a doctor and has prospects of making plenty of money. I hope you understand me, Hal.

HAL. (*Relieved.*) Yes, I understand you, and I'm glad things haven't gone any further than they have.

MRS. COOPER. Well, that's settled and I hope we'll be just as good friends as we ever were.

HAL. We will, you bet we will.

MRS. COOPER. (*Rising.*) I'm glad you take it that way. You've always been a darling. Now I think I'll go and take a little rest and let you and Joyce talk to each other until Enid and Bill come back.

HAL. Is Mr. Cooper in?

MRS. COOPER. No, he hasn't come in yet——by the way, did you notice a man walking up and down in front of the house?

HAL. I saw Dorsey outside as I came in.

MRS. COOPER. (*Puzzled.*) Dorsey? Who is Dorsey?

HAL. He's a man who claims Mr. Cooper owes him five hundred dollars.

MRS. COOPER. Look out here and see if you're talking about the same man I am. (*They go to the window.*) That man there with his hand in his pocket—is he the one?

HAL. Yes, that's Dorsey.

MRS. COOPER. It's a business deal, is it?

HAL. Yes, he had us buy a house for him.

MRS. COOPER. Then he ought to settle it at the office and not come hanging around here. He makes me nervous the way he carries his hand in his pocket.

HAL. Don't worry about him, it'll be settled all right.

MRS. COOPER. I hope so. I don't like to have people like that around. He seems to have a gun or something in his pocket.

HAL. He seems to be in a tight place too.

MRS. COOPER. A tight place?

HAL. Yes; he's out of a job and his wife's been sick for some time.

MRS. COOPER. I suppose he holds us responsible for that too.

HAL. I don't know; but if it were left to me, I'd settle with him and let him go.

MRS. COOPER. Then John really owes him?

HAL. That's what he claims. Of course, it's a matter of business and there are two sides to it.

MRS. COOPER. (*Going towards the left door.*) I'll talk to John about it as soon as he comes in. That man gives me the shivers. Now I'll send Joyce in and take a few minutes' rest. (*She goes out through the hall. Hal paces the floor a few moments until Joyce appears.*)

HAL. (*Taking her hands.*) Oh, there you are. I had begun to think I wouldn't have the pleasure of seeing you.

JOYCE. I was coming in as soon as you finished telling Aunt Edna how much you wanted to marry Enid.

HAL. You know better than that. I wanted to tell her how much more I care for you than I ever did for Enid, but she seemed to know it before I could tell her and paired us off—you and me, Enid and Bill.

JOYCE. What will Enid think after all the time you two spent together before I came here and before Bill started coming around so regularly?

HAL. Enid will just love it. What girl wouldn't be glad to get a promising young physician these days?

JOYCE. I suppose you could find one or two who wouldn't.

HAL. For instance?

JOYCE. I, for one, wouldn't be overjoyed.

HAL. (*Putting his arm around her.*) I'm glad of that, because I've just been told that I'm not good enough for Enid; but I'm just the one for you.

JOYCE. Did Aunt Edna say that?

HAL. Words to that effect. What do you say?

JOYCE. (*Smiling.*) Well, you're not a promising young physician, you know.

HAL. I'm glad I'm not, if you think that way about it. (*He draws her close, and just as they are about to kiss there is a loud ring of the bell. Hal is disappointed.*) I could kick the one who did that! (*Joyce goes to the door and opens it, then starts back, for Dorsey is standing there with his hand in his pocket as usual.*)

DORSEY. Good evenin'.

HAL. (*Who has moved forward.*) Oh, it's you, is it, Dorsey?

DORSEY. Yes, young feller, it's me. Where's your boss?

HAL. He's not in yet.

DORSEY. (*Turning to Joyce.*) When will your Pa be in?

HAL. That's not his daughter.

DORSEY. Oh, excuse me for tryin' to make you kin to a rat like John Cooper.

JOYCE. (*Resentfully.*) But I am kin to him. He's my uncle.

DORSEY. (*To Hal.*) Is his wife in?

HAL. Yes, but I don't believe she wants to be disturbed.

DORSEY. Well, Ah've got to see somebody. Ah've waited long enough and this thing's got to be settled this evenin'. (*To Joyce.*) Tell your aunt somebody's here to see her husband, and she'd better come in cause it's mighty important.

JOYCE. Yes, I'll tell her. (*She goes out.*)

DORSEY. (*To Hal.*) You know Ah've been done dirty. You know it as well as you know you're standin' there.

HAL. But why didn't you say something about it before? It's been two years.

DORSEY. Two years ago Ah was workin' and makin' good money; and besides, Ah didn't find it out till two weeks ago.

HAL. You know you couldn't do much if you went to court about it —after waiting all this time.

DORSEY. Maybe Ah couldn't; Ah know Ah couldn't. Ah wouldn't

have the money to fight him in court. But Ah'm goin' to get ma money. Ah'll either get ma money or get him.

HAL. I wouldn't make threats, Dorsey. That won't do you any good, and it may do you a great deal of harm.

DORSEY. If you was in ma fix you'd make threats and carry 'em out too.

MRS. COOPER. (*To Hal.*) Some one to see me, you said, Hal?

HAL. Some one to see the chief, but since he's not in——

DORSEY. Ah'm the man wants to see him. Dorsey's ma name and he owes me money. Five hundred dollars in round numbers, and Ah need it—need it like a man never needed money before.

MRS. COOPER. (*Coldly.*) I don't see in what way that concerns me.

DORSEY. It will concern you if Ah don't get ma money; because Ah'll either get ma money or get him.

HAL. I told you this was no place to make threats, Dorsey.

MRS. COOPER. It seems to be a matter of business; and my husband always looks after his own business affairs.

DORSEY. When will he be in?

MRS. COOPER. (*Shortly.*) I don't know.

HAL. (*To Dorsey.*) I sympathize with you, Dorsey; but you shouldn't have agreed to buy the house if you thought the price was too much for you.

DORSEY. Ah wanted the house when Ah bought it, and Ah didn't know Ah was bein' robbed till ma wife took the notion that the owner didn't get as much as we paid for the place. Then she wrote to the owner and found out that we paid five hundred dollars more than the owner got from you people. Ah'd take it for ma share if Ah didn't need the money and need it bad.

HAL. I guess all of us need money.

DORSEY. But Ah need it in the worse way. Ah've got a sick wife and four hungry children. Maybe none of you all know what that means, but it means hell for a man that's got any feelin's for his family.

MRS. COOPER. I'll tell my husband you were here and he'll make an engagement to see you at his office.

DORSEY. No, Ah won't see him at his office. Ah'm goin' to see him right here if he comes home tonight.

MRS. COOPER. But he may be late.

DORSEY. Late or not late, Ah'll see him. Ah've got to see him.

MRS. COOPER. I hope you don't mean to stay here till he comes.

DORSEY. No, Ah won't stay in here in your way. Ah'm goin' home to see how ma wife is, then Ah'm comin' back here ready to park maself out there the rest of the night.

HAL. (*As he opens the door for Dorsey.*) I hope you'll cool down a little before you come back, Dorsey. You know the kind of threats you're making don't get a man anywhere.

DORSEY. Ah'm in a mood to keep them threats too. You know Ah've been done dirty. (*To Mrs. Cooper.*) This young feller can tell you Ah've been robbed. He's got a spark of honesty in him and he knows Ah've been cheated.

HAL. (*Holding the door open.*) Good night, Dorsey.

DORSEY. Ah won't say good night. Ah'll be back this way before long. (*He goes out and Hal closes the door behind him.*)

MRS. COOPER. (*With a sigh of relief.*) That man makes me so nervous I don't know what to do. Even the sight of him—the way he carries his hand in his pocket—it looks as if he is about to drop a bomb or something.

HAL. I don't believe he's really harmful. He's excited, and I suppose he is in need.

MRS. COOPER. But listen, Hal; is what he says true? He says you know he's been cheated. Has he?

HAL. There's two sides to every question, you know.

MRS. COOPER. I know that, but when he made that statement you didn't deny it, you didn't say it wasn't true.

HAL. That's because he looks at it one way and the chief looks at it another.

MRS. COOPER. How do you look at it? What's your side of the question?

HAL. Well, he came to the office for us to buy a house for him and he paid what we charged.

MRS. COOPER. But he said you charged much more than the owner asked.

HAL. The chief holds that he wasn't obliged to pay it. He could've gone to some other office.

MRS. COOPER. Of course, you business people have your own peculiar way of looking at things, but was it all entirely honest?

HAL. (*Unconvincingly.*) I suppose so.

MRS. COOPER. It seems that you ought to know. They say you know more about real estate than any man in town under forty. Was it honest in your opinion?

HAL. (*Still evasively.*) There are many ways of looking at it, and a good number of real estate men do the same thing when they get a chance. Whether it's honest or not depends on the way you look at it.

MRS. COOPER. Would you have done it if you had been at the head of the firm?

HAL. Now that's something I'm not sure of.

MRS. COOPER. If you're not sure about it I know you wouldn't have done it. Now I'm sure there's something wrong about it. You're simply trying to uphold John in some trick of his.

HAL. I've stated the case exactly as it is.

MRS. COOPER. Still you wouldn't have done what was done. I'm going to talk to John about it. I don't want that man coming around here with his hand in his pocket ready to shoot or cut somebody.

HAL. I tried to get the thing settled more than a week ago when Dorsey first started coming to the office, but I couldn't work it.

MRS. COOPER. John wouldn't listen to you?

HAL. No.

MRS. COOPER. I'll see if he'll listen to me. That man's coming here has surely spoiled my evening.

HAL. I wouldn't let it affect me like that.

MRS. COOPER. Don't then, go in and talk to Joyce some more.

HAL. Where is she?

MRS. COOPER. She stayed back in the library. She thought the man had business to talk about.

HAL. I'll go in then, if you don't mind.

MRS. COOPER. Yes, do. I'll wait here until John comes. (*As Hal starts out.*) Just a minute, Hal. (*Hal stops.*) How much did that man say he had been cheated out of?

HAL. Five hundred dollars.

MRS. COOPER. Suppose John flatly refuses to pay him. He's like that, you know.

HAL. I don't know what may happen then.

MRS. COOPER. I have a plan I mean to work if John won't pay him.

HAL. What is it?

MRS. COOPER. I'll get him to sign an open check for the grocery and laundry bills, then if he refuses to pay this man I'll make the check for five hundred dollars and pay him myself.

HAL. (*Doubtfully.*) That may work, I don't know.

MRS. COOPER. It will work. I'll make it work.

HAL. A check for three hundred and fifty dollars just came back to him from the bank yesterday marked "no funds," and he said he'd have to be more careful.

MRS. COOPER. He told me about that. He fixed it up the same evening. So it's all right now.

HAL. I'm glad it is.

MRS. COOPER. All right, run along. (*Hal goes out and she goes to the writing table by the door, and opening the drawer takes out a check book and looks at it. Having done this she puts it back and starts towards the window just as the door is thrown open suddenly and Enid rushes in.*)

MRS. COOPER. (*Frightened.*) What in the world is the matter with you? You shouldn't rush in here like that! You frightened me! I'm as nervous as I can be anyhow!

ENID. (*Elated.*) I've got the best of news!

MRS. COOPER. What about?

ENID. Bill proposed!

MRS. COOPER. (*Forgetting her fright.*) He did? And of course you accepted?

ENID. That's understood. Can you blame me for rushing in like that?

MRS. COOPER. That does make a difference. It's delightful! Where is he?

ENID. We picked Papa up on our way home and Bill is outside showing him some kind of new brake on the car. (*Mrs. Cooper goes quickly to the window and looks out.*)

MRS. COOPER. I'm glad that man's not out there.

ENID. What man?

MRS. COOPER. The man who threatened to kill your father. That's what I'm so nervous about.

ENID. (*Breathlessly.*) Somebody threatened to kill Papa!

MRS. COOPER. Less than an hour ago.

ENID. What on earth for?

MRS. COOPER. He claims your father owes him money.

ENID. Oh, that can be easily settled. I thought it was something worth worrying about.

MRS. COOPER. But he's going around carrying some kind of weapon in his pocket. Just to look at him with his hand in his pocket all the time would give you the shivers.

ENID. Where did you see him?

MRS. COOPER. I saw him outside and in here too.

ENID. In here. What was he doing in here?

MRS. COOPER. He came in.

ENID. And were you alone?

MRS. COOPER. No, Hal and Joyce were here. They're in the library now. And by the way, Hal started to ask about proposing to you, but I cut him off and told him how everything stood. You're a lucky girl.

ENID. Lucky in what way?

MRS. COOPER. Here you are with two men wanting to propose to you in one night, while thousands of girls can't get one man to propose to them in a whole lifetime.

ENID. I don't call that so lucky. It's the way I charm them. Did Hal seem very much put out?

MRS. COOPER. No. To tell the truth, he seemed rather pleased when I mentioned Joyce in connection with him.

ENID. (*Disappointed.*) Well, let him be pleased, I'm pleased too. I'm tickled to death.

MRS. COOPER. Did you tell your father about Bill's proposing?

ENID. No, I'll leave that for you to do. You know how much he wanted me to marry Hal.

MRS. COOPER. I'll tell him; don't you worry. As if Hal could ever make enough money to take care of you. (*At this time Cooper, a prosperous looking colored man of eight-and-forty, enters from the right.*)

COOPER. Well, here I am.

MRS. COOPER. (*As if displeased.*) It's about time you were coming home.

COOPER. What's the matter?

MRS. COOPER. Everything has tried to happen this evening.

ENID. (*To her father.*) Is Bill coming in?

COOPER. (*Turning to the door.*) Here he is now.

BILL. (*Entering.*) That was quite a spin, wasn't it?

ENID. Yes, the car runs fine, Bill. Don't you think so, Papa?

COOPER. Yes; a car at that price ought to run fine.

MRS. COOPER. (*Taking Bill's hand.*) And, doctor, before we go any further, let me congratulate you and Enid. I hope you'll make her a good husband and I hope she'll make you a good wife.

BILL. Then I have your consent?

MRS. COOPER. Most certainly.

BILL. (*Looking from her to Cooper.*) And Mr. Cooper's?

COOPER. (*Puzzled.*) This is the first I've heard of it.

ENID. (*Quickly taking Bill's hand.*) Come on, let's break the news to Hal and Joyce. Mama will fix Papa all right. (*She leads him out left.*)

COOPER. (*Sternly.*) What's this about Enid and Bill Holland? Do you mean to tell me—

MRS. COOPER. Yes, that's just it. Dr. Holland proposed to Enid and she accepted him.

COOPER. But I thought it was understood that Enid and Hal—

MRS. COOPER. Will you please tell me how on earth you think Hal could ever take care of Enid on the money he makes?

COOPER. I didn't make half what he makes when I married you, and I took care of you all right.

MRS. COOPER. That's different. Everything has changed since that time. And besides, Enid was reared in a different way from what I was. Everything was lavished on her, and after she marries she'll expect it.

COOPER. Do you think Bill can give it to her?

MRS. COOPER. More so than Hal, and that you know.

COOPER. But Hal is a fine fellow.

MRS. COOPER. I don't deny that, but what woman can eat and wear good clothes and enjoy herself on the mere fact that her husband is a fine fellow?

COOPER. (*Impatiently.*) Yes, that's all you think of. Eating, wearing good clothes, and enjoying yourself.

MRS. COOPER. You'll have to be reasonable, John; even if that weren't all there's still a greater reason why Enid and Hal could never make it as man and wife.

COOPER. What's that?

MRS. COOPER. Hal and Joyce are in love with each other.

COOPER. (*Surprised.*) Hal and Joyce!

MRS. COOPER. Yes.

COOPER. How do you know?

MRS. COOPER. A woman can see those things. She doesn't have to be told.

COOPER. (*Surrendering.*) If what you say is true Joyce will certainly get a good husband.

MRS. COOPER. What about Enid? Is there anything wrong with Bill?

COOPER. I don't say there's anything wrong with him, but compared to Hal I can't see him.

MRS. COOPER. He may surprise you.

COOPER. I hope he does. Now tell me what are all the things that have happened since I've been gone.

MRS. COOPER. Before we talk about that you'd better sign me an open check for the grocery and laundry bills.

COOPER. Don't you know how much they are?

MRS. COOPER. Not yet. How should I?

COOPER. All right, I'll sign it. (*He goes to the desk by the door and signs an open check which he gives her.*)

MRS. COOPER. (*Putting the check into the drawer.*) I'll fill it in.

COOPER. Now what?

MRS. COOPER. Do you know a man named Dorsey?

COOPER. (*Starting.*) Dorsey! Yes. What do you know about him?

MRS. COOPER. He's been here.

COOPER. What for?

MRS. COOPER. He says you owe him money.

COOPER. He doesn't know what he's talking about.

MRS. COOPER. (*Earnestly.*) But he's desperate, John: I'll swear to goodness he's desperate.

COOPER. Let him be desperate. What else did he have to say?

MRS. COOPER. He said he meant to kill you if he didn't get his money. And I'm sure he's carrying a weapon of some kind. He always holds his hand in his pocket. (*Pointing to the chair.*) Even when he was sitting there he always held his hand in his pocket.

COOPER. (*Surprised.*) He's been inside here sitting down?

MRS. COOPER. Less than an hour ago. And he says he means to come back.

COOPER. Coming back and carrying a gun, is he?

MRS. COOPER. He's carrying some kind of weapon. It may be a gun and it may be a knife. I don't know.

COOPER. (*Opening the desk drawer.*) All right, I'll be prepared for him.

MRS. COOPER. What're you going to do?

COOPER. I want to see if this gun is in good shape. (*Reaching into one of the lower drawers of the desk he brings out a revolver.*)

MRS. COOPER. If you owe the man why in heaven's name don't you pay him and save trouble?

COOPER. (*Unloading the revolver and snapping it.*) I don't think I owe him anything.

MRS. COOPER. You don't think so! You ought to know whether you owe him or not.

COOPER. (*Snapping the empty revolver several times.*) I say I don't owe him and he says I do; but I'm standing pat. If he wasn't satisfield with the price I charged he shouldn't've paid it.

MRS. COOPER. Even at that wouldn't it be better to pay him and let him go than to have bloodshed?

COOPER. (*Reloading the revolver.*) There won't be any bloodshed.

MRS. COOPER. He says his wife's sick, his children are hungry, and he's out of a job.

COOPER. Am I supposed to worry my head about that? That's his funeral.

MRS. COOPER. But, John, can't you see that he has good reasons to be desperate?

COOPER. I can't see that he has any cause to try to bulldoze me; and even if he has, I'm not afraid of him or anybody else. (*He puts the revolver into the top drawer of the desk.*)

MRS. COOPER. (*Surprised.*) Are you going to leave it there?

COOPER. Why not?

MRS. COOPER. He has his weapon in his pocket. He could shoot or cut you before you could get to the table.

COOPER. I'll have to come to the table before I come to the door to let him in, or before I make a check for him.

MRS. COOPER. If it were left to me I wouldn't risk being hurt on account of a little money.

COOPER. I know you don't want to see me play the coward and throw up my hands as soon as he comes in here.

MRS. COOPER. But I do want you to do the right thing, John; you know that.

COOPER. That's what I mean to do.

MRS. COOPER. This thing has me so excited I can hardly appreciate the fact that Enid is engaged to Dr. Holland. I believe a cup of tea would quiet my nerves. Won't you take one too?

COOPER. I don't mind. (*As he and his wife start towards the hall they meet Hal entering.*)

HAL. (*To Cooper.*) Did Mrs. Cooper tell you about Dorsey?

MRS. COOPER. Yes, I told him, Hal.

COOPER. (*To Hal.*) I can't do anything for him. You know how I stand on that question.

HAL. He seems to be in a tight place.

COOPER. I can't help it. I didn't put him there.

HAL. I was going to say that if you could possibly do anything for him—

COOPER. (*Smiling.*) You're too tender-hearted, Hal. I suppose that's why everybody likes you; but I can't do a thing for Dorsey, and I don't believe I would if I could.

HAL. I'm sorry.

MRS. COOPER. Won't you have a cup of tea with us, Hal?

HAL. No, thanks, I— (*Just then Joyce enters from the hall.*)

MRS. COOPER. (*Looking from Hal to Joyce.*) Oh, I see; a rendezvous. I wouldn't spoil it for worlds. (*She and Cooper go out and Hal and Joyce come into the room.*)

HAL. (*Finishing a previous conversation.*) I want you to rest your mind about one thing.

JOYCE. What's the one thing?

HAL. About Enid and me.

JOYCE. Oh, I know all that's settled now since she and the doctor are engaged.

HAL. You talk as if that doesn't make any difference to you.

JOYCE. Oh, yes, it does make a difference.

HAL. (*Putting his arm around her.*) How much?

JOYCE. A great difference. (*Just as Hal leans forward to kiss Joyce, Enid enters followed by Bill.*)

ENID. We're looking for the young lovers. (*Seeing them.*) Oh, here they are. (*Hal and Joyce step apart.*) We don't mean to intrude, but how are things progressing with you young lovers?

BILL. I can hardly keep my head, Hal. I didn't know being engaged affected a fellow like that. (*Just then there is a loud ring of the bell. The thing is so sudden that it startles them.*)

ENID. I wonder who's trying to break the bell.

BILL. He must've kicked it or something. (*Joyce, who is nearest the door, opens it.*)

DORSEY. (*Outside.*) Your uncle home yet?

JOYCE. Yes, he's here. Won't you come in? (*Dorsey enters. His hand is still in his pocket.*)

JOYCE. Take a seat and I'll call him. (*Dorsey sits in front of the desk. Joyce goes out through the hall and Enid follows her.*)

HAL. I see you're back, Dorsey.

DORSEY. Yes, Ah'm back. Ah told you Ah was comin' back.

HAL. I hope you've sobered up a little.

DORSEY. Ah wasn't drunk. How can Ah afford to get drunk with all the children Ah've got and a sick wife to boot?

BILL. That's the very time some men think they ought to get drunk. If you want to drown your troubles I'll fix you up.

DORSEY. No, nothin' doin' on that. Ah ain't got time to get drunk right now. Ah got bigger fish to fry.

HAL. I wasn't talking about being drunk anyhow. I wanted to know if you felt less like murdering somebody.

DORSEY. Ah wouldn't hurt a hair on no man's head; but Ah won't stand and be kicked around. Ah'm goin' to sit tight till Ah get paid off.

BILL. I didn't know I was butting in on a business matter. (*Cooper enters, followed by Mrs. Cooper, Enid, and Joyce.*)

COOPER. Well, Dorsey, what can I do for you?

DORSEY. (*Rising angrily.*) You know what you can do for me! There's only one thing Ah want out o' you and you know what that is! Pay me! (*He holds out his hand.*)

COOPER. But I'm not convinced that I owe you anything.

DORSEY. Ah'm convinced, if you ain't! (*Pointing to Hal.*) And there's a young feller that's convinced too, but he won't say so because he works for you! He's the only honest man in your whole crowd and he knows you owe me money!

COOPER. You don't have to bring any one else into the argument. The whole thing is between you and me, and I say I don't owe you anything! (*Turning to the others.*) Will you excuse us a few minutes while we talk this over?

MRS. COOPER. Do you think I'm going to leave you here alone when that man may have a revolver or something in his pocket?

DORSEY. You said it right, lady; Ah have got a gun in ma pocket. Ah don't mean to take no chances.

COOPER. Will the rest of you go out for a few minutes? (*Joyce, Enid, Hal and Bill go reluctantly out.*)

COOPER. (*After they have gone.*) Now, Dorsey, it seems to me that you ought to understand my position. (*Trying to get him away from the desk.*) Have a seat over here and we'll talk it over.

DORSEY. Ah only understand one thing, and that's that Ah want ma money! Ah'm willin' to sit right here and talk it over!

COOPER. You paid what I charged for the house. You should've thought before you bought it if you didn't like the price.

DORSEY. You can talk from now till doomsday if you want to; but Ah'm goin' to have ma money!

COOPER. You won't get it from me, not a cent!

DORSEY. (*Drawing the revolver from his pocket.*) Then Ah'll get you! Ah'll give you two minutes to make up your mind!

MRS. COOPER. (*Starting out.*) I'll call the police.

COOPER. (*Detaining her.*) No, don't call the police! He's not going to shoot!

DORSEY. (*Raising the revolver.*) You'll see that Ah'll shoot.

MRS. COOPER. (*Calling out in a frightened voice.*) Hal! Bill! (*Hal rushes in followed by Bill, Enid, and Joyce.*)

HAL. (*Starting towards Dorsey.*) For God's sake, Dorsey; what're you doing? Put that gun down!

DORSEY. (*His face set.*) Don't come over here, young feller. Ah like you pretty good, but if you come another step Ah'll pull the trigger!

JOYCE. (*Catching Hal's arm.*) Don't, Hal! Don't!

MRS. COOPER (*Almost screaming.*) Why don't you pay the man, John?

COOPER. (*Bravely.*) I won't pay what I don't owe!

ENID. But, Papa, he'll shoot you! I can see it in his eyes!

DORSEY. In another minute Ah'll shoot him if he won't come across!

COOPER. Let me come to the desk and get my check book.

DORSEY. Nothin' doin'. Ah don't want you comin' too close to me. Stay over there and Ah'll throw it to you. (*He opens the drawer and sees the revolver which he takes out and unloads.*) Ah reckon you wanted this gun more than you did the check book. Ah don't see no check book nohow. It's a fake and your time's up! (*Dorsey is aiming when Mrs. Cooper leaps in front of her husband.*)

MRS. COOPER. Wait a minute! Wait a minute! I'll pay you! I'll make a check! (*She goes to the desk.*)

COOPER. Don't do that, Edna! You'll ruin me! I'll swear to God you will! (*He starts for Mrs. Cooper, who is at the desk.*)

DORSEY. (*Checking him.*) Stand back there! You'd better let her save your cheap life if she's willing to!

HAL. Don't you know you'll hang if you shoot that man, Dorsey?

DORSEY. Ah don't care! Ah'll know he's gone in front of me!

MRS. COOPER. (*After making the check.*) Here's the check for your money.

DORSEY. (*Taking it.*) Is it any good?

COOPER. No, it's no good! I'll swear it's not worth the paper it's written on!

DORSEY. (*Putting it into his pocket.*) Ah'll take a chance on that. (*As he backs to the door.*) This might look like a holdup to you all, but Ah did what Ah thought was right. Ah didn't take what wasn't mine. (*To Cooper.*) You can tell the police if you want to; but if you do Ah'll tell 'em a lot of things on you that won't do you no good. Good night and bad luck to you! (*He goes out, slamming the door behind him.*)

COOPER. (*Turning to his wife.*) You've ruined me! Ruined me! Ruined us all!

MRS. COOPER. Ruined you how? Do you think I'd stand here and let that man shoot you down?

COOPER. That would've been better! I haven't got that money in the bank and I've been warned that they won't cash another check for me! When they turn that one down Dorsey'll set up a howl and the whole town will know what I've been doing! Creditors will be on my neck from everywhere!

ENID. *Creditors!*

MRS. COOPER. What do you mean?

COOPER. I mean we don't own a thing! This very house we live in doesn't belong to us! I've been living by my wits! Shamming!

MRS. COOPER. But, John!

COOPER. Yes, it's true! Every word of it!

ENID. How in the world can it be true, Papa?

COOPER. (*Turning to her.*) How in the world do you think I ever got money enough to keep you living in your style? Fine clothes, new cars, parties, trips to Europe, and everything to try to imitate millionaires! I stole and did everything else crooked, and now I'm done for! We're all done for! (*He goes out through the hall broken in spirit.*)

MRS. COOPER. (*Turning to Hal.*) Hal, is this true? You know——

HAL. (*Nodding.*) Yes, things have been going very badly with his business for months.

ENID. And you never said anything?

HAL. He ordered me not to.

MRS. COOPER. What in the world shall we do? He says even this house will go along with everything else.

JOYCE. (*Innocently.*) Perhaps we can all go to work and pay the mortgage off the house so we can still live here.

MRS. COOPER. Go to work! Work where?

JOYCE. We ought to be able to find work.

ENID. Don't talk foolish, Joyce; think of something reasonable.

JOYCE. What's more reasonable than going to work when you have to?

ENID. Oh, a lot of things. (*Turning to her mother.*) After Bill and I marry I'm sure we can take you and Papa in until you can get on your feet.

MRS. COOPER. (*Relieved.*) That is an idea! But what of Joyce?

HAL. (*Quickly.*) Oh, Joyce will be cared for. She promised to marry me right away.

MRS. COOPER. (*Going out left.*) I must tell John. I don't know what he may do.

JOYCE. (*Who has been staring at Hal.*) But, Hal, you haven't ever asked me to marry you!

HAL. Won't you?

JOYCE. (*Smiling.*) I suppose there isn't anything else for me to do now since you have everything planned out.

ENID. (*To Bill.*) That will be all right what I told Mama, won't it, Bill?

BILL. (*Who is sitting silently by smoking and staring into space.*) Well, to tell the truth about it, Enid, I'm not quite ready to marry and start a house of my own. I had thought I'd be able to live here with your people until my practice picked up a little.

ENID. I understood that your practice was already good.

BILL. (*Not meeting her eyes.*) No, not anything like it.

ENID. But, Bill, the way you spend money, the new car you just bought and everything!

BILL. A fellow has to put up a front, you know. A young doctor has to look prosperous even if he's not.

ENID. So we won't be able to marry soon?

JOYCE. (*Turning to her.*) Enid! What a question!

BILL. I'm afraid the way things are now we won't be able to marry for a long time.

ENID. The way things are! You mean about Papa?

BILL. Yes.

ENID. Oh, I see; you thought my father was a rich man.

BILL. (*Carelessly.*) You can't blame me for that, can you? Everybody thought so.

ENID. And everybody was mistaken. I hope you will excuse me, Dr. Holland; I must look after my father. (*Bill rises. Enid goes into the hall and gets his hat.*) (*As she hands him his hat.*) I'm glad you found out before we married that my father wasn't a rich man.

BILL. (*Taking his hat.*) I don't see that it's necessary to take this tone about it, Enid. (*Without replying she holds the door open for him.*)

ENID. Good night, Dr. Holland.

BILL. (*Looking towards Hal and Joyce.*) Good night.

HAL. Good night, Bill.

JOYCE. Good night. (*He goes and Enid closes the door behind him.*)

HAL. (*With sympathy.*) Everything will come out all right, Enid.

ENID. (*Almost sobbing.*) I hope it will, Hal; but I'm sick of all this pretense and sham! Sick to death of it! (*She goes out through the hall.*)

HAL. (*Tenderly to Joyce.*) Are you sick of all this sham, too, dear?

JOYCE. I've always been, but most of all I'm glad you don't belong to this house of sham. (*As he takes her in his arms the curtain falls.*)

(Curtain)

Elizabeth Maddox Huntley

Elizabeth Maddox Huntley, dramatist, musician, and teacher of religious dramatics, was born at Eatonton, Georgia. She was educated in the public schools of Eatonton, Washington High School of Atlanta, and Morris Brown College, doing her graduate work at Atlanta University. She teaches a course in The Use of Dramatics in Religious Education. One of her anthems is "Allelujah, the Prince of Peace Shall Reign."

LEGION, THE DEMONIAC [1]

Cast of Characters

JULE, JOANNA, *Workers in the Field*
MICHAEL, EMMITT, *Friends of Rachael*

RACHAEL, *Mother of Legion*
LEGION, *A Man Possessed of Devils*
JOEL, *Brother of Legion*

Introduction

Jule and Joanna, peasant women, are gleaning in the field. They hear a weird howling from the forest-side. Rachael and Joel are seen approaching. Rachael is carrying a small package in her hand and there are signs of grief on her face.

(*Curtains open. Jule and Joanna are gleaning in the field. Soft music, "Bringing in the Sheaves," as they glean silently for one or two moments. Legion, who is back-stage, begins howling in many different tones of voice. Jule pauses and stares at Joanna in amazement.*)

JULE. (*Excitedly.*) What is that?

JOANNA. I don't know. It sounds like some kind of wild animal.

JULE. If it is anything that will harm us, where shall we go for safety?

1 Reprinted with the permission of the author.

JOANNA. Verily, there is no place to hide unless we climb the syca-
more tree or hide in one of those rock tombs. (*Howling continues.
The women continue to work, but at irregular intervals, staring at
each other now and then as if to determine whose voice it is.*)

Enter RACHAEL *weeping, carrying bread; Joel follows, riding
a stick for a horse.*

(JULE *and* JOANNA *speak almost simultaneously to* RACHAEL.) Do
you hear that howling? (RACHAEL *stares at the floor and then bursts
into tears.* JULE *and* JOANNA *look at each other and then at* RACHAEL
in amazement.)

JULE. What troubles theé, my friend?

JOANNA. (*Rushing to her.*) May we do something for thee?

RACHAEL. Nay . . . Nay. (JOEL *looks on in wonder.*) (*Howling continues.*)

JOANNA. Why weepest thou?

RACHAEL. Didst thou not know that the voice which thou hearest over
in the forest is that of my son? (*Weeping.*) My own son!

JULE. Your son?

RACHAEL. Yes. (*Between sobs.*) He is possessed of many devils and
he will not stay at home. He lives in caves and tombs.

JOEL. Yea, and we have tied him with chains but he breaks the chains.
Sometimes he is quiet, but not for long. Most of the time he is in a
rage. This is the way he does——(JOEL *then demonstrates in voice
and bodily movements the actions of* LEGION, *his older brother, while
the women watch him with pathetic interest.*)

JULE. (*To* RACHAEL.) What is that in thine hand?

JOEL. (*Interrupts.*) That's bread. She is going to put it——

RACHAEL. (*Interrupts.*) Let me answer, Joel! Hear thou me. See, the
child will not eat at home and I have brought this crust of bread to
lay on a stone so that in his wandering for food he will perchance
find it and eat. (*Howling;* RACHAEL *weeps.*)

JOANNA. There is a man in town whose name is Jesus. He has much
power, so I hear, the power to raise the dead. (RACHAEL *looks with
interest;* JOANNA *continues.*) Did you ever take your son to see
that man?

RACHAEL. Nay (*sniffing*), I have heard of him, but he has never passed my way so that I might see him.

JOANNA. Thou shouldst invite him into thine home. If thou invite him he will come. And he will heal thy son. I know he can do it, because I have seen people whom he healed. He healed the Centurion's servant.

JULE. Yea, and he raised the widow's son from the dead.

JOEL. (*Quickly and with much interest.*) Thinketh thou that he can heal my brother?

JULE. I *know* he can.

JOEL. Let's find him, Mother, verily, he must be a great man.

RACHAEL. (*Tearfully and prayerfully.*)

My God, grant that I might find this man Jesus, that my child might be MADE WHOLE. (*Howling continues.*) How can I stand it —how can I, O God! (*At this point* JOANNA *and* JULE *begin wiping their eyes also.*) (*Soft music while* RACHAEL *continues.*) O, Jehovah, give Peace to my heart and courage to my soul (*howling is heard*). I lay this bread here so that he may find it and eat. (*Exit* RACHAEL *and* JOEL.)

(JULE *and* JOANNA *resume their work; howling gets louder.*)

JOANNA. How sad it must be for a mother to carry such a burden.

JULE. Yea, that mournful groaning of her son *must* make her weep, because it haunts me, too.

(*Enter* LEGION, *dressed in the manner of a tramp, crawling on his knees and making weird noises, his eyes staring before him.*)

JOANNA. (*Having just discovered* LEGION.) *Look! Look!* (*Both women stare in silence as* LEGION *approaches them. Suddenly,* LEGION *leaps at them. They fight at him and scream for help. Enter* MICHAEL *and* EMMITT *hurriedly, carrying chains with which to tie* LEGION. *While* LEGION *fights at them they tie his hands and feet.* LEGION *should be making weird noises all the while the scuffle is under way. The chains should have one cotton string link so as to be easily broken. After* LEGION *has been tied and becomes calm,* MICHAEL *speaks.*)

MICHAEL. What is thy name? (LEGION *groans loud and long.* MICHAEL *repeats.*) What is thy name? (LEGION *jumps at him as he answers.*)

Randolph Edmonds

LEGION. My name is Legion (RACHAEL *and* JOEL *rush in and* RACHAEL *attempts to calm* LEGION*, while* JOEL *looks on in awe.*)

MICHAEL. Why doth thou call thyself Legion?

LEGION. DEVILS—DEVILS—DEVILS—I KILL YOU ALL— (LEGION *leaps to his feet bursting the chains from his hands and feet. All other characters flee except* RACHAEL. *She tries to calm him. When she sees she cannot, she bursts into tears while* LEGION *howls and squirms. Suddenly he looks with interest toward an exit. Then screams in a* loud voice.) I see Jesus, Jesus. Thou Son of David, what have I to do with thee? (*Exits running.*) (RACHAEL, *amazed, follows slowly, even stopping at times. Before she has had time to get off stage,* LEGION *reappears in white robe, singing an appropriate hymn.* RACHAEL *shouts with waving arms in gratitude to the Master. All other characters reappear and join in the hymn.*)

(Curtain)

Randolph Edmonds

Randolph Edmonds, the dramatist, was born in Lawrenceville, Virginia. He went to the St. Paul Normal and Industrial School of Lawrenceville. He obtained the degree of Bachelor of Arts from Oberlin College, and the degree of Master of Arts from Columbia University. He also studied the Drama at Yale University. As a result of a Rosenwald Fellowship he studied drama organizations in Ireland and Great Britain, especially the production methods of the Abbey Theater in Dublin. Among his publications are *Shades and Shadows, Six Plays for a Negro Theater,* and *The Land of Cotton and Other Plays.*

"OLD MAN PETE" [1]

Cast

"PETE" COLLIER, *an old man*
MANDY COLLIER, *his wife*
SAM COLLIER, *their oldest son*
MARIA LEWIS, *their daughter*
WILMUR LEWIS, *her husband*

JOHN COLLIER, *their youngest son*
VIVIAN COLLIER, *his wife*
A POLICEMAN, GUESTS, ETC.

Scene 1. John's Apartment in Harlem
Scene 2. A section in Central Park

Scene 1. *The living-room of a cozy little flat in Harlem. It is a place furnished and arranged in good taste. There are two doors; the one to the left leads from outside, and the one to the right leads to the kitchen and other rooms in the house. There are two large windows near the back.*

The furniture, while not the most expensive kind, shows that the inhabitants are living well. There is a small baby grand piano on the left, a settee stretching along the wall under the two windows, and a bookcase filled with volumes on the right. Lamps and chairs are placed conveniently about. Everywhere there are feminine, artistic touches which give a genuine atmosphere of comfort to the modern Harlem apartment.

(At the opening of the curtain MARIA LEWIS *and her husband,* WILMUR, *are seated. They are well dressed in the latest conservative styles. When* JOHN *comes in he is dressed in a work suit which needs pressing, and has an overcoat on his arm.* MARIA *and her husband are around forty and* JOHN *is about thirty-five. It is about eight o'clock on a winter evening.)*

JOHN. (*Tossing a newspaper to* WILMUR, *and getting his overcoat.*)
I'll be back in a minute. I've got to beat it down to the laundry and get my shirt before that Chinaman at the corner closes up his shop. By that time Sam ought to be here. Vivian will be in later.

[1] From *Six Plays for a Negro Theater*, by Randolph Edmonds. Copyright, 1934, by Walter H. Baker Company, Boston.

MARIA. All right, John. But put on your overcoat. It is freezing weather outside.

(*John goes out.*)

WILMUR. (*Lighting a cigarette and blowing out a cloud of smoke.*) What is this family conclave about tonight?

MARIA. I'm sure I don't know. John said he wanted to see all of the members of the family together here tonight.

WILMUR. (*Rising and moving about as if slightly agitated.*) Well, it wouldn't take a prophet to foretell what the meeting is called for.

MARIA. What do you mean?

WILMUR. You know exactly what I mean. You know as well as you know your name that John called us here tonight to decide what is to be done about your mother and your Old Man. He wants to get rid of them.

MARIA. (*Evasively.*) He didn't say what he wanted.

WILMUR. You all ought to have left the old people down in Virginia where they were born. I always thought it was a dumb idea bringing them up here. You ought to have known they wouldn't fit in. No, all of you had to be so generous.

MARIA. It isn't a crime to want to do something nice for your mother and father, Wilmur.

WILMUR. I know it isn't; but why bring them to New York? With all due respect to them, they will never adapt themselves to Harlem. Where are they now?

MARIA. John said something about their going out to an early service in the church.

WILMUR. Yeah, I know. They've gone around to that sanctified dump on 133rd Street again. I wish they would go around there and stay.

MARIA. (*Resenting his remarks.*) That's unkind of you, Wilmur, to talk about my father and mother like that.

WILMUR. Well, if you must know the truth, I am tired of being made the laughing-stock of Harlem. Everywhere I go somebody asks me, "Where is your pa?" "Where is your ma?" "Did they get happy at the meeting last night?" and a whole lot of other silly things until it's just gotten on my nerves, that's all. I don't see which one of you ever thought of bringing them up here in the first place.

MARIA. Oh, Wilmur, that can't really be you talking like that.

WILMUR. (*Vehemently.*) Oh, yes, it is too! I'm filled up, I tell you. I've got enough. I try to have a decent home where my friends can come and enjoy themselves; but I can't do it as long as your mother and father act like they do. I——

MARIA. Don't talk like that, Wilmur.

WILMUR. I wouldn't mind it so much if they acted like human beings. Sam gave the old man two suits. Why can't he put them on? Why do they have to wear those antique rags of the south? One day Slim came around to see me before he left the city. Your father sat around and entertained him in his undershirt about farming and driving railroad spikes. When Charles and Betty came one day, he entertained them with his plantation dialect. (*Exasperated.*) I'm filled up, I tell you.

MARIA. What can I do about it, Wilmur? I have told them about it time and time again. I can't hurt their feelings.

WILMUR. You've got to do something. When they discuss the matter tonight, you let them stay here with John or send them back to Sam. I don't care what you do as long as you don't take them back in our house.

MARIA. Somebody has got to take care of them.

WILMUR. (*Putting on his coat, and speaking with an air of finality.*) I am going on home to let you three discuss the matter without any embarrassment. You can take your choice, however; if they come to our house, I will leave. That's all. (*Starts to leave.* MARIA *tries to stop him.*)

MARIA. Oh, Wilmur! Wilmur!

(WILMUR *pays no attention to her, but rushes on out of the door. She looks after him for a second, then bursts into tears. She dries her tears quickly, however, and powders her face as she hears the key in the lock.* JOHN *and* SAM *come in.* SAM *is about forty-five and is dressed in a conservative business suit. They take off their over-coats. They rub their hands and ears from the cold.*)

JOHN. I met Sam just as I was entering the building on my way back.

SAM. I thought he would walk right over me, too.

JOHN. (*Looking around.*) Where is Wilmur?

MARIA. He was expecting someone to call tonight on business, so he went on home. Didn't you meet him in the hall? He just stepped out.

SAM. No, we didn't. We came up on the elevator. Maybe he went down the stairs.

JOHN. I'll put this laundry in the bedroom. I'll be right back. (*He exits.*)

SAM. Do you know what John wants?

MARIA. I don't know; but I think it's about Father and Mother.

SAM. I guess you are right.

MARIA. What are we going to do?

(*Before he can answer* JOHN *comes back into the room.*)

JOHN. I had to have a clean shirt. The gang is going to drop by here tonight and have a cocktail or two before going on a cabaret party.

MARIA. It's too cold for me to think of cabarets. Where are you going?

JOHN. It is cold, but the gang will go anyway. We'll start out at the Bamboo Inn. I don't know where we will end up.

SAM. You'd better take it easy. Too many cabarets will wreck you, you know.

JOHN. Don't worry. We don't go out often enough for that. (*Abruptly changing the subject.*) I asked you to come over tonight because I wanted to see which of you will take Father and Mother. You know they have been here two weeks now.

SAM. I figured that was about what you wanted when I got your message. Maybe Maria will take them. I've got to go out of town next week on business.

MARIA. Maybe you could keep them for another week, John. They could go to Sam's when he comes home.

SAM. I'd like to have a little time to get straight when I get back. Why can't you take them, Maria?

MARIA. (*Confused.*) Well, Wilmur will be so busy next week, perhaps the next two or three weeks working overtime. I'd like to be without anybody until he can be home more.

JOHN. Come on now. You are not playing fair. I'm busy, too. I've got to go out of town next week for a few days myself, and Vivian and

I would like to be alone for a while, too. You remember they have been here two weeks.

MARIA. You know we kept them about two weeks and a half.

JOHN. (*Annoyed.*) Neither of you seems to want them. Well, it's a cinch that Vivian and I can't keep them all the time.

SAM. I'm thinking we ought to have left them at home in Virginia.

MARIA. I think so, too.

JOHN. (*Impatiently.*) But we're not dealing with suppositions and oughts. We're dealing with a problem right here and now. Maria was the first to suggest bringing them up here; and now she is the main one wanting to get out of keeping them.

MARIA. Now don't put it all on me. You and Sam were just as anxious as I was.

JOHN. But that isn't solving the problem. What are we going to do with them? I know Vivian and I can't take care of them all the time.

MARIA. You take them again, Sam. Then maybe I'll take them again; and then it will be John's turn once more. I just can't take them now.

SAM. (*Meditating.*) Maybe we ought to get a little two-room apartment for them. Each of us would have to chip in to pay the expenses.

MARIA. I'll have to see what Wilmur says about that.

SAM. Maybe we'll be able to get them into a home in a few months.

JOHN. We've got to do something.

SAM. I tell you what, John, you keep them another week. By that time we can settle what to do.

JOHN. I suppose I can persuade Vivian to keep them. She had counted on one of you taking them to-morrow.

MARIA. That is the best thing to do, John. We can then work out what we ought to do. We certainly can't give them the impression of not wanting them. I think it would break their hearts.

SAM. (*Putting on his overcoat.*) Are you going on home now, Maria?

MARIA. (*Putting on her coat.*) I guess I might as well.

SAM. Come on, then.

(*Maria puts on her coat, and they prepare to leave.*)

JOHN. Remember now, we keep them for another week. After that somebody else will have to look after them. We positively can't keep them any longer.

(*There is the rattle of a key in the lock.* VIVIAN *comes in. She is a typical flapper. Her hair is cut in the latest bob, and she has a lot of rouge and paint on her face.*)

VIVIAN. My, but it's cold outside! I thought I would freeze before I got here.

JOHN. It is cold outside.

VIVIAN. How are you, Maria? And you, Sam?

SAM. How are you, Vivian?

(VIVIAN *and* MARIA *kiss each other.*)

VIVIAN. You aren't going so soon? You needn't hurry.

SAM. I can't stay. I've got to get right on back home. Maybe Maria will stay.

MARIA. No. I've got my things on, so I might as well run along. We'll be over sometime this week.

VIVIAN. All right, then, if you must go. But come around any old time. You must bring your wife to see us soon, Sam.

SAM. I will, Vivian.

(*They say good-bye and go out.*)

VIVIAN. Well, what's the verdict?

JOHN. They asked me to keep them another week. Neither one could take them just now.

VIVIAN. And what after the week?

JOHN. Sam said something about making some arrangements for a small apartment or seeing about getting them in a home.

VIVIAN. And we are to keep them until all these arrangements are made. You are a fine one to let them pull that stuff over on you.

JOHN. Somebody's got to look out for them until all arrangements are made.

VIVIAN. But why should it be us? I wouldn't mind it, but they are such nuisances. I hope I'm not like that when I get old.

JOHN. Remember, dear, they are my father and mother.

VIVIAN. You know they are nuisances as well as I do, only you don't want to say so. You know I always say just what I think, John. It is too late for me to change now. Sam and Maria dumped them on us because they found out that it is true they're nuisances.

JOHN. Well, let's not discuss it.

VIVIAN. Very well; but I just want you to know that I'm tired having them in the way, too. They've been here for two weeks now and Sam and Maria should take them.

JOHN. Don't talk like that, Vivian.

VIVIAN. . Talking like that won't settle matters, and you know it.

JOHN. I can't ask them to leave.

VIVIAN. Well, that's your red wagon. I just want you to know that I am tired, that's all.

JOHN. They won't bother us tonight anyway.

VIVIAN. I do hope they show at least that much common sense.

JOHN. You're unsympathetic, Vivian.

VIVIAN. Call it what you will, my patience is at an end.

JOHN. We can tough it out another week. So let's forget it. I've got everything for the cocktails.

VIVIAN. (*Looking at her wrist watch.*) Let's go in and get dressed and have everything ready. The gang will be by here in a few minutes. You know the bunch plans to stop at several houses before winding up at the cabaret.

JOHN. (*Following her into the room to the right.*) I know. Billy told me all about the plans.

(*As they go out, a key rattles in the lock.* PETE *and* MANDY *come into the room unbuttoning their winter coats. They take them off and throw them on chairs.* PETE *is old and grey headed, and walks with a stick. He is wiry and tough, however. He is dressed in a pair of close-fitting grey breeches and a wide swinging black coat. His whiskers are long and unshapely.* MANDY *is elderly, with grey hair, and is dressed in a long sweeping calico dress. When she takes off her coat and old-fashioned hat, she leaves a red shawl around her shoulders.*)

PETE. Hit's cold out dere, Mandy. De air is raw. Winter is sho heah.

MANDY. And dey tells me dat snow stays on de ground de yeah 'round, too.

PETE. We don't hab tuh wurry 'bout no winter up heah. Yuh don't hab tuh chop wood fuh dese houses. Dey is heated wid steam.

MANDY. Ah'll miss hit, dough, setting by de chimley and lookin' at de open fire.

PETE. (*Seating himself.*) Let's set down a few minutes in heah befo' goin' tuh our room. 'Tain't nobody using hit.

MANDY. Yeah, we mought ez well set awhile. (*Seating herself.*) Didn't yuh lak dat sermon tu-night, Pete?

PETE. I sho did. Dat's de best sermon we is heard since we been heah.

MANDY. Hit's de best, all right. I couldn't keep from shouting tuh save ma life, and a sermon sho has tuh be good tuh make Mandy Collier shout.

PETE. We's been tuh many dese fine buildings since we been heah; but hit all go tuh prove dat fine buildings don't make fine churches 'less de sperit is dere.

MANDY. Dat's de gospel truf. Ah didn't heah a single "Amen" in all dem fine churches.

PETE. Well, Mandy, we's been heah 'bout six weeks now. How does yuh lak New York?

MANDY. Ah can't say Ah's crazy 'bout hit, Peter. Does yuh lak hit up heah?

PETE. Sho Ah does. Whut make yuh don't lak hit, Mandy?

MANDY. Well, everybody is in sich a hurry. Ef yuh don't git outen dere way, dey will walk right over yuh. Den everything is so crowded heah. People is cooped up lak chickens. De room we sleep in ain't beig as a closet. Den yuh hab tuh climb so many steps 'cause de elevator is broke mos' de time. Ah ain't used tuh climbin' a thousand pair steps tuh sleep in a hen coop.

PETE. Yuh'll git used tuh hit by and by. Why, Ah's almos' a born New Yawker by now.

MANDY. (*Sighing.*) Ah'd ruther live in Fuginia any day.

PETE. Come on, Mandy, git over dem blues.

MANDY. Ah hates tuh set 'round all day and do nothing. Ah ain't used tuh hit. At home Ah always had somethin' tuh do. Ef hit wa'nt cleaning, Ah was feedin' de pigs, milkin', churnin' er somethin'. Heah Ah ain't gut nuthin' tuh do.

PETE. Ah don't min' settin' 'round. Ah's wurked hard all ma life. Ah needs a res' now.

MANDY. Yuh mean yuh is lazy.

PETE. Wal, we's gut our chilluns anyway. Ah'll always keep dis letter dat Sam writ us when we was home.

MANDY. Read hit ag'in, Pete. Let me heah how hit sounds once mo'.

PETE. (*Getting out his glasses and reading.*) "Dear Mother and Father: John, Maria, and myself thought the farm was too much for you to attend to in your old age; so we would like for you to sell the farm and come up and live with us in New York. Sell out as soon as possible and send us a telegram when you start. You took care of us in childhood and the three of us certainly ought to be able to take care of you in your old age. We are anxiously awaiting your coming. Your affectionate son, Sam." Dat boy really show his eddication, don't he, Mandy? Dat's whut Ah calls a real eddicated letter. Folks thought we was fools when we sent our chilluns tuh school. In fact, old Doot Williams told me so hisse'f. But yuh ought tuh seen de 'spression on his face when Ah showed him dis letter from Sam.

MANDY. Maggie Yates told me de same thing when Ah told huh 'bout dat letter. She said, "Yuh won't never git 'long in dat big city. Yuh is too old-fashioned. Yo' chilluns will git 'shamed o' yuh."

PETE. Ah guess old Maggie is still waggin' huh mouf. As ef we could ever git too old-fashioned fuh our chilluns! Dat is a good one.

MANDY. Sometimes Ah thinks Maggie Yates is right.

PETE. Yuh ain't gittin' cold feet, is yuh, Mandy?

MANDY. No, Pete. Hit ain't dat; but yuh never can tell.

PETE. Yuh certainly is gut a lot o' faith, Mandy. Won't Ah hab a good time tellin' de chilluns how yuh doubted 'em.

MANDY. Ah don't mean tuh doubt dem, Pete. Ah s'pose hit's jes' being in a strange place.

PETE. Dat's hit, Mandy. We's gut a chance tuh see somethin' in dis strange place. Why up heah we's gut trains under de groun' and trains in de air. Plenty dese buildings up heah is eight times ez high ez de Fust National Building at home. Jes' think of hit, eight times ez high! And yuh remember de building wid de rollin' steps

whar yuh git right on and dey carry yuh right up tuh de top. Dere
is always sometin' tuh see dat's new heah.

MANDY. Yeah, Ah jes' hopes hit las', dough.

PETE. Cose hit's gwine tuh las'. How come yuh think hit ain't? (*The
bell rings.* JOHN *comes into the room and pushes the buzzer. He
has changed his clothes.*)

JOHN. How are you, Mother? How are you, Father?

PETE. We's up and 'bout, Son. We jes' come in frum de church. De
air is raw outside.

JOHN. It is cold. The papers say tonight will be the coldest we have
had in twenty years.

MANDY. Ah'm glad we don't hab tuh git up early.

JOHN. (*Diplomatically.*) We are having some company for a little
while. They won't be here long. If you and Mother will stay in your
room, we won't bother you at all.

PETE. Sho, sho. We'll go right in. We don't want tuh be in yo' way.

MANDY. Come on, Pete. (*They get their coats and go out.* VIVIAN
*comes in in a beautiful gown in the latest fashion. She seems far
more the flapper type since she has dressed up.*)

VIVIAN. Everything ready?

JOHN. Yes, I think so.

(*Pete comes in with his shirt tails out and in his socks. He searches
around the room, then bellows.*)

PETE. Mandy! Whar did yuh say ma chawin' 'backer is at?

VIVIAN. (*Very much annoyed.*) What are you looking for? Here,
get into your room before those people get up here. The idea of
your coming out here like that!

PETE. 'Scuse me, daughter. 'Scuse me.

(*He hurriedly disappears. There is a ring on the bell.* JOHN *opens
the door. Several couples come in. They greet* VIVIAN *warmly. She
kisses one or two women.* JOHN *shakes hands with the men.*)

A GIRL. Give me a shot of something, Vivian. I am freezing to death.

A MAN. It is ten below zero now, and the papers said it is going to get
colder.

A GIRL. It is beginning to snow outside.

A MAN. Ah, can't you think of something else to talk about except the weather?

ANOTHER MAN. Here is something else to think about anyway. Let's drink. (*He indicates the tray of glasses that* JOHN *has brought in.*)

JOHN. Here you are, folks. This is just a starter-off for the night. (*He passes the glasses. All take one and drink.*)

VIVIAN. Here is a table. Would some of you like to play a game of contract before we go?

A GIRL. I will, kid. Come on, somebody.

(*Two couples sit at the table and begin playing.*)

VIVIAN. Have a cigarette? (*She passes the cigarettes and the men and women take them and begin smoking.*)

ONE MAN. Say, John, how is your pa?

(*A snicker goes around the crowd.*)

JOHN. He's all right, thank you. I fail to see the joke, however.

VIVIAN. Never mind. It wasn't meant for you to see, dear.

ONE GIRL. Play a piece, Jack.

(JACK *goes to the piano and begins to play a low mournful blues.*)

A GIRL. (*To one of the men.*) Come dance with me, papa. I can't stand it no longer.

(*Several couples dance for a short time. Then* JACK *stops playing for a second.*)

A GIRL. Give me another drink, somebody.

ANOTHER GIRL. I hope I don't get drunk tonight. I got high as a kite the last time we had a cabaret party.

(*After the piano player gulps down a drink that is given him, he starts another fast number.*)

A GIRL. How about a dance, Vivian?

(*She gets out in the center of the floor and does the dance. The others clap their hands and shout various things at her. She stops amid a burst of applause.*)

ONE GIRL. Well, it's time for the party to be breaking up, if we want to go by Alice's.

ANOTHER GIRL. Yes, let's get going. By the time we stay there awhile, the cabaret will be in full swing when we get there.

VIVIAN. You don't have to hurry.

JOHN. No. Stay as long as you like.

A GIRL. I guess we'd better go on.

ANOTHER GIRL. I'll have another shot before I go.

A MAN. Let's all have another shot.

(*The glasses are filled once more. Everybody drinks.* JOHN *and* VIVIAN *help them with their coats. All are about to leave.*)

VIVIAN. John and I will join you at Alice's in a few minutes—just as soon as we get the room a little straight.

A GIRL. We'll look for you, kid.

(*They all go out.*)

JOHN. That's a dizzy bunch.

VIVIAN. Yes, but they're heaps of fun, though. Come on, let's hurry and get things straightened up so we can join them. (VIVIAN *lights a cigarette. They commence to get the chairs straight.* PETE *comes in with his night cap on and his breeches. He also has on a red flannel undershirt with his suspenders hanging behind him.*)

PETE. 'Scuse me.

VIVIAN. (*Irritated.*) What do you want?

PETE. Daughter, Ah mus' hab a chaw o' 'backer befo' Ah can sleep.

VIVIAN. (*Half to herself.*) You and your old tobacco make me sick.

JOHN. Vivian!

VIVIAN. (*So irritated she doesn't care what she says.*) Yes, they make me sick.

(*Before anybody can say anything further* MANDY *comes in dressed in an old-fashioned nightgown covered by an old robe.*)

MANDY. Yuh is de fugittenist man in de wurl, Pete. Ah knows Ah saw dat 'backer 'round heah somewhar. (*She looks around and finds it on the bookcase.*) Heah 'tis right on de bookcase in front yo' eyes.

PETE. Thank yuh, Mandy. Ah don't know whut Ah'd 'a' done without a chaw.

(*He takes a chew.*)

MANDY. (*To* VIVIAN.) Yuh shouldn't smoke cigarettes, honey. Hit don't look nice. Good gals don't smoke.

VIVIAN. (*Bursting out.*) What have you got to do with it? What do you mean by meddling in my business?

JOHN. Vivian! Vivian, please, dear.

MANDY. Ah didn't mean no harm, honey. Ah didn't mean no harm.

VIVIAN. (*Sarcastically.*) No. You never mean any harm. You are always doing something dumb that you don't mean. I know what you want. You just want to start your usual sermon about wild parties and drinking whiskey. I know what you're going to say, and I don't want to hear it!

PETE. (*Getting angry.*) John, is yuh gwine stand dere and let dat gal talk tuh yo' mammy lak dat?

JOHN. What can I do, Father?

VIVIAN. Why don't you do something about it, you grey-headed old fool?

JOHN. Come on, Vivian. Let's go to Alice's.

PETE. Yeah. Take huh away befo' Ah lose ma temper. She's too brazen. A gal lak dat ought tuh be horsewhupped. She ain't got no manners.

VIVIAN. (*Very angry.*) You ought to learn some manners yourself. You act like somebody half civilized. The idea of your talking about whipping somebody! (*Crying.*) You get out of my house, both of you! Get out!

JOHN. (*Catching her by the hand.*) Come on, Vivian!

PETE. We'll git out, all right. We'll go tuh Maria's in de mawning.

MANDY. Calm yo'se'f, Pete.

VIVIAN. (*Jerking her hand out of* JOHN's.) Turn me loose. (*To* PETE.) It ain't no use of your going to Maria's, nor Sam's neither. They were here this evening, and neither one would take you. You'd better go back to the sticks where you came from.

MANDY. (*Getting a little angry herself.*) Yuh is a liar, gal. Sam and Maria never done nothin' lak dat.

VIVIAN. Well, go on to them, then. Go anywhere, just so you get out of my house.

JOHN. Don't, Vivian. It's not necessary to have a quarrel.

VIVIAN. It ain't no use for you to try to smooth things over. You think just as I do, but you're not man enough to say so.

PETE. Dat gal is spiled. A good fannin' would straighten huh out.

VIVIAN. (*Very angrily to* JOHN.) You standing there talking and looking, and letting them say anything to me. You're no man, that's what. If you don't make them go, I'll go myself. I'll never put my foot in this house as long as they're here.

JOHN. Vivian! Vivian!

(VIVIAN *darts into the other room and gets her coat and goes out with a grim determination. She slams the door after her.*)

PETE. A gal dat ain't gut no manners is better off gone.

JOHN. I don't thank you a bit for coming here and causing trouble between my wife and me.

PETE. (*Surprised.*) What! You uphold dat gal in huh sassiness?

JOHN. She is my wife.

PETE. Wife or no wife, she ain't gut no business talkin' tuh folks lak dat. She is a hussy, dat's whut.

JOHN. Father, don't say another thing about my wife. I'm going out to get her now, and I don't expect you to give her any more trouble. (JOHN *gets his coat and goes. As he shuts the door,* PETE *shakes his fist at the door, and shouts.*)

PETE. Follow yo' wanton strumpet! Fugit de ones dat bawned yuh! Turn yo' back on de ones dat nursed yuh! Git out o' ma sight, plague take yo' ungrateful hide, git out o' ma sight!

MANDY. (*Trying to console him.*) Don't git wurked up so, Pete. Calm yo'se'f.

PETE. (*Meditating for a moment.*) Mandy, dat gal is right. We is no longer wanted. We's gwine.

MANDY. Gwine whar, Pete?

PETE. Back tuh Fuginia.

MANDY. But we ain't gut de money, Pete.

PETE. Ah, yes we is. Ah always kept de fare back home. Ah didn't trust to no chances, aldough Ah never thought we would come tuh dis.

MANDY. (*Wiping her eyes.*) But hit's too cold outside. Listen tuh dat wind.

PETE. Don't le's argue, Mandy. Ah said we is gwine, and we is gwine tuh do hit. Ah wouldn't stay in dis house another instant—no siree, not another instant. Let's git dressed and leave dis place behind us.

MANDY. But we can't go back home and tell de folks dat our chilluns don't want us. Ah can heah Maggie Yates' mouf now. Dat's too hard fuh us to do, Pete. (*She starts to cry.*)

PETE. Life is hard, Mandy, hard as pig iron! Don't cry, Mandy, we's done no mo' dan others. We jes' bawned chilluns tuh turn on us lak spiders. Whut do we care whut Maggie Yates say, or anybody else say 'long ez we's gut each other. Fuh nearly fifty yeahs now yuh is leaned on de strong arm ob Old Man Pete Collier. He is de one who is gwine tuh stick till de end. Come on, let's pack up, Mandy. We'll leave dese ungrateful chilluns in de hands ob a just God. (*He takes her by the hand and leads her into the next room.*)

(Curtain)

Scene 2. *A section of Central Park. The trees and ground are draped with snow. The wind is blowing, and the snow is falling. A park bench is stretched along the walk. Pete and Mandy are bundled up with heavy coats. Pete has an old rusty suitcase in his hand, and Mandy has a red shawl tied around her head.*

MANDY. (*Showing great weariness.*) Ah wonder how much futher de station is frum heah.

PETE. Hit ain't fu. De man said ef we went right thru heah, we wouldn't be fur away from a car dat would take us right dere.

MANDY. Ah's tired, Pete. Le's res' heah a bit.

PETE. Jes' a minute, den. Hit's too cold tuh stop long.

MANDY. Look at de snow fall and listen at de wind.

PETE. Don't mind de elements. Do lak me. (*Shaking his fist in the air.*) Wind, blow yo' darndest gale. Heavens, pile yo' snow in drifts ez high ez de tallest building; an' we'll wade thru dem somehow tuh git away from dem ungrateful chilluns.

MANDY. Don't take on so, Pete. Ah's been thinkin' since we left de house. Maybe hit ain't de chilluns' fault; maybe hit is us who is tuh blame. Maybe we is jes' done got old and outgrowed our chilluns. Le's go back tuh de house.

PETE. Ah'd ruther go to hell and burn in torment fire a thousand yeahs befo' Ah'd go back tuh dat ungrateful house.

MANDY. Don't say dat, Pete.

PETE. Chilluns ain't got no business outgrowing dere parents, or dere parents outgrowing dem. De way we slaved tuh send dem all tuh school—no siree, yoh can't let dem off dat easy.

MANDY. Ah s'pects yuh is right. (*Silence for a second.*) Ain't yuh feelin' cold, Pete?

PETE. Nah. Never felt hotter in ma life.

MANDY. Ah ain't so cold. Ah's jes' tired. We's walked a long ways.

PETE. Le's push on, Mandy. De night is raw out heah. Hit'll be better in de fine railroad station.

MANDY. Ah can't, Pete. Ah's gut tuh res'. (*She props her head up with her hands.*)

PETE. Wal, res' a bit, Mandy. Ah'll walk 'round tuh keep warm. Yoh was right—back dere in de house. 'Tain't gwine tuh be easy tuh live down de 'sults ob de people at home; but somehow we's gut to do hit. We's faced things tugether fuh many a yeah, dough, and always come out de big end ob de hawn. (*Shakes her.*) Wake up, Mandy, dis is a cold night. Hit's too cold tuh stay out heah long. Wake up!

MANDY. Don't bother me, Pete. Let me sleep jes' a little longer. Ah feels so nice and warm.

PETE. All right, jes' a little longer den. (*Walking around and hitting himself to keep warm.*) Ah's sho hit's de bes' tuh go back home and live our las' yeahs among fr'en's dan in dis Gawd fusaken city whar nobody cares whether yuh lives er dies. (*Stops and shakes her.*) Wake up, Mandy. Le's go. 'Tis cold out heah. Wake up, Mandy! She is fast asleep all right. (*He pulls off his coat and puts it around her.*) Ah can keep warm walkin' bout. (*After awhile.*) Wake up, Mandy. Dis is a raw night, and we mus' move on. (*Drops beside her on the bench and puts his arm around her.*) Ah don't blame yuh much. Ah is tired mase'f. Ah is sort o' sleepy, too. (*He rests his head on her shoulder for awhile. Then he sleepily shakes her.*) Wake up, Mandy! Wake up, Mandy! (*Silence.*) Wake up, Mandy! Ah heah de cows low'ring; but hit's dark and cold out heah. Only de snow makes hit light. (*Brokenly.*) De sky is dark, Mandy; but down in Fuginia de sun is shining. Le's git in de sun. (*A brief silence, then he feebly continues.*) Wake up, Mandy! Ah heah de horses neighing and de pigs is squealing. Dey is hongry, Mandy. Le's go feed de pigs. (*Silence for a while. Day breaks. A* POLICE-MAN *enters.*)

POLICEMAN. (*Hitting on the seat with his club.*) Move on folks! It is twenty below zero. It is the coldest wave that ever struck New York, and here you are sitting in the park. You'll freeze here. (*Hitting the seat again.*) Move on, I tell you. (*Pushes them.*) Gosh, them fools are frozen stiff. (*He looks sorrowfully at them.*)

(Curtain)

A BRIEF

Bibliography

For Supplementary Readings
or Further Study [1]

FOLK LITERATURE

HURSTON, ZORA NEALE: *Jonah's Gourd Vine*, 1934; *Mules and Men*, 1935; *Tell My Horse*, 1937; all published by Lippincott Company, Philadelphia.

JOHNS, ALTONA TRENT: *Play Songs of the Deep South*. Associated Publishers, Washington, D.C., 1944.

JOHNSON, JAMES WELDON: *God's Trombones*. Viking Press, 1941.

JOHNSON, JAMES WELDON, AND JOHNSON, J. ROSAMOND: *The Book of American Negro Spirituals*, Viking, New York, 1925.

TALLEY, THOMAS W.: *Negro Folk-Rhymes*. The Macmillan Company, New York, 1922.

WOODSON, CARTER GODWIN: *African Myths*. Associated, 1928.

WORK, JOHN WESLEY: *American Negro Songs*. Howell, Soskin, and Company, New York, 1940.

POETRY

BELL, JAMES MADISON: *The Poetical Works of James Madison Bell*. Wynkoop, Hallenbeck, Crawford Company, Lansing, Mich., 1901.

BRAITHWAITE, WILLIAM STANLEY: *Lyrics of Life and Love*. Herbert B. Turner and Company, Boston, 1904.

BROOKS, GWENDOLYN: *Annie Allen*. Harper, 1949.

BROWN, STERLING: *Southern Road*. Harcourt, Brace, and Company, New York, 1932.

COTTER, JOSEPH S., JR.: *A White Song and a Black Song*. Bradley and Gilbert Company, Louisville, Ky., 1909.

CULLEN, COUNTEE: *Color*, 1925; *The Ballad of the Brown Girl*, 1927; *Copper Sun*, 1927; *Caroling Dusk* (Ed.), 1927; *The Black Christ*, 1929; all Harper and Brothers, New York.

DUNBAR, PAUL LAURENCE: *Complete Poems*. Dodd, Mead, and Company, New York, 1927.

HILL, LESLEY PINCKNEY: *The Wings of Oppression*. The Stratford Company, Boston, 1921.

---

[1] The compiler has deliberately included in this bibliography a number of books which are out of print. Many or most of them may be found in the major public libraries.

327

HUGHES, LANGSTON: *The Weary Blues,* 1926; *Fine Clothes to the Jew,* 1927; *The Dream Keeper,* 1932; all Alfred A. Knopf, New York.

JOHNSON, GEORGIA DOUGLAS: *The Heart of a Woman and Other Poems,* The Cornhill Company, Boston, 1918; *Bronze,* B. J. Brimmer Company, Boston, 1922; *An Autumn Love Cycle,* Harold Vinal, New York, 1928.

JOHNSON, JAMES WELDON: *Fifty Years and Other Poems.* Cornhill, 1917; *The Book of American Negro Poetry,* (Ed.), Harcourt, 1922; *Saint Peter Relates an Incident of the Resurrection Day,* 1930; *God's Trombones,* 1941; both Viking.

The Scribes, *Sing, Laugh, Weep.* The Press Publishing Co., St. Louis, Mo., 1944.

WHEATLEY, PHILLIS: *Poems on Various Subjects.* London, 1773. Revised Edition by R. R. Wright, Philadelphia.

BIOGRAPHY AND AUTOBIOGRAPHY

ALLEN, RICHARD: *Life and Times.* African Methodist Episcopal Book Concern, Philadelphia, 1833.

BRAITHWAITE, WILLIAM STANLEY: "House under Arcturus," in *Phylon.* Atlanta University Press, 1941.

BRAWLEY, BENJAMIN GRIFFITH: *Doctor Dillard of the Jeanes Fund.* F. H. Revell Company, New York, 1930; *Negro Builders and Heroes.* University of North Carolina Press, Chapel Hill, North Carolina, 1924; *Your Negro Neighbor.* Macmillan, 1918.

BROWN, HALLIE QUINN: *Homespun Heroines.* Wilberforce University Press, Xenia, Ohio, 1926.

BULLOCK, RALPH W.: *In Spite of Handicaps.* Association Press, New York, 1927.

CROMWELL, JOHN WESLEY: *The Negro in American History.* American Negro Academy, Washington, D. C., 1914.

DANIEL, SADIE: *Women Builders.* Associated, 1931.

DOUGLASS, FREDERICK: *Life and Times of Frederick Douglass.* Park Publishing Company, Hartford, Conn., 1881.

DU BOIS, WILLIAM EDWARD BURGHARDT: *John Brown.* The Jacobs Publishing Company, Philadelphia, 1909; *Dusk of Dawn.* Harcourt, 1943.

FAUSET, ARTHUR HUFF: *Sojourner Truth, God's Faithful Pilgrim.* University of North Carolina Press, 1938.

HANDY, WILLIAM CHRISTOPHER: *Negro Authors and Composers of the United States.* Handy Brothers Music Company, Inc., New York, 1938; *Father of the Blues.* Macmillan, 1941.

HAYNES, ELIZABETH ROSS: *Unsung Heroes.* Du Bois and Dill, New York, 1921.

HUGHES, LANGSTON: *The Big Sea.* Knopf, 1940.

JOHNSON, JAMES WELDON: *Along This Way.* Viking, 1937.

LANGSTON, JOHN MERCER: *From the Virginia Plantation to the National Capitol.* Author, Hartford, Conn., 1894.

MCKAY, CLAUDE: *A Long Way From Home.* Harcourt, 1937.

MOTON, ROBERT RUSSA: *Finding a Way Out.* Doubleday, Page & Company, New York, 1920.

PAYNE, DANIEL A.: *Recollections of Seventy Years.* African Methodist Episcopal, 1888.

PICKENS, WILLIAM: *The Heir of Slaves,* An Autobiography. Pilgrim Press, Boston, 1911; *Bursting Bonds* (Revised Autobiography). Jordan and More Press, Boston, 1923.

WASHINGTON, BOOKER T.: *Frederick Douglass.* Jacobs, 1907; *Up from Slavery.* Doubleday, 1901.

WESLEY, CHARLES HARRIS: *Richard Allen, Apostle of Freedom.* Associated, 1935.

ESSAYS

ANDERSON, GARLAND: *From Newsboy and Bell Hop to Playwright.* Author, San Francisco, 1926.

BOND, FREDERICK WELDON: *The Negro and the Drama.* Associated, 1940.

BRAWLEY, BENJAMIN GRIFFITH: *The Negro in Literature and Art in the United States.* Duffield Company, New York, 1918.

BROWN, STERLING: *Negro Poetry and the Drama.* The Bronze Booklet Series, No. 7, Washington, D. C., 1937; *The Negro in American Fiction.* Howard University, Washington, D. C., 1938.

DONALDSON, ULYSSES S.: *The Humanity of Jesus.* Douglass University Press, St. Louis, Mo., 1937.

DU BOIS, W. E. B.: *The Gift of Black Folk.* Stratford, 1924; *The Souls of Black Folk.* A. C. McClurg, Chicago, 1903.

ELLIS, GEORGE WASHINGTON: *Negro Culture in West Africa.* Neale Publishing Company, New York, 1914.

FRAZIER, EDWARD FRANKLIN: *The Negro Family in the United States.* University of Chicago Press, Chicago, 1939.

HARRIS, ABRAM LINCOLN: *The Negro as Capitalist.* American Academy of Political and Social Science, Philadelphia, 1936.

HENDERSON, EDWIN BANCROFT: *The Negro in Sports.* Associated, 1939.

JOHNSON, CHARLES SPURGEON: *The Shadow of the Plantation.* University of Chicago Press, 1934; *Growing up in the Black Belt.* American Council on Education, Washington, D. C., 1941.

LEWIS, JULIAN HERMAN: *The Biology of the Negro.* University of Chicago Press, 1942.

LOCKE, ALAIN: *The Negro and His Music.* Bronze Booklet Series, No. 2, 1936; *Negro Art.* Associates in Negro Folk Education, Howard University, 1936.

LOGAN, RAYFORD WHITTINGHAM: *What the Negro Wants.* University of North Carolina Press, 1944.
LOGAN, SPENCER: *A Negro's Faith in America.* Macmillan, 1946.
MCKAY, CLAUDE: *Harlem, Negro Metropolis.* Harcourt, 1940.
MILLER, KELLY: *Race Adjustment.* Macmillan, 1909; *The Everlasting Stain.* Associated, 1924.
MOTON, ROBERT RUSSA: *What the Negro Thinks.* Doubleday, 1929.
PICKENS, WILLIAM: *The New Negro.* Neale Publishing Company, New York, 1916.
POWELL, ADAM CLAYTON, JR.: *Marching Blacks.* The Dial Press, New York, 1945.
STYLES, FITZHUGH LEE: *Negroes and the Law.* Christopher Publishing Company, Boston, 1937.
VAUGHN, GEORGE L.: *The Negro Origin of Free Masonry; The Sumerian Civilization; Antar, Arabian Negro Poet and General; The Negro's Armageddon;* all St. Louis Argus Publishing Company, 1926.
WOODSON, CARTER GODWIN: *The Negro Professional Man and His Community.* Association for the Study of Negro Life and History, Washington, D. C., 1934.

ADDRESSES

DUNBAR-NELSON, ALICE: *Masterpieces of Negro Eloquence.* Bookery Publishing Company, New York, 1914.
JOHNS, VERNON S.: "Transfigured Moments" in *The Best Sermons of 1926.* Joseph Forte Newton, Editor; Harcourt, 1927.
WESLEY, CHARLES HARRIS: *The Look Forward; The Pursuit of Things;* both Wilberforce University Press, Wilberforce, Ohio, 1946.
WOODSON, CARTER GODWIN: *Negro Orators and Their Orations.* Associated, 1925.

SHORT STORIES

CHESNUTT, CHARLES WADDELL: *The Conjure Woman and Other Stories,* 1899; *The Wife of His Youth and Other Stories,* 1899. Both Houghton, Mifflin Company, Boston.
COTTER, JOSEPH E.: *Negro Tales.* Cosmopolitan Press, New York, 1912.
DUNBAR, PAUL LAURENCE: *Folks from Dixie,* 1898; *The Strength of Gideon and Other Stories,* 1900; *In the Old Plantation Days,* 1904; all Dodd, Mead.
HUGHES, LANGSTON: *The Ways of White Folks.* Knopf, 1935.
MATHEUS, JOHN F.: "Swamp Moccasin." *The Crisis,* New York, December, 1926.
COLEMAN, ANITA SCOTT: "Two old Women A-Shopping Go!" (A Fantasy). *The Crisis,* May, 1933.
WYNBUSH, OCTAVIA B.: "The Black Streak." *The Crisis,* October, 1945.

NOVELS

ATTAWAY, WILLIAM: *Let Me Breathe Thunder*. Doubleday, 1939.

BONTEMPS, ARNA: *Black Thunder*. Macmillan, 1936.

CHESNUTT, CHARLES WADDELL: *The House Behind the Cedars*, 1900; *The Marrow of Tradition*, 1901; *The Colonel's Dream;* 1905; all Doubleday.

CULLEN, COUNTEE: *One Way to Heaven*. Harper, 1932.

DU BOIS, W. E. B.: *The Quest of the Silver Fleece*. McClurg, 1911; *Dark Princess*. Harcourt, 1928.

DUNBAR, PAUL LAURENCE: *Uncalled*, 1898; *The Love of Landry*, 1900; *The Fanatics*, 1901; *The Sport of the Gods*, 1902; all Dodd, Mead.

FAUSET, JESSIE REDMOND: *There Is Confusion*. Boni and Liveright, New York, 1924; *The Chinaberry Tree*. Lippincott, 1932.

FISHER, RUDOLPH: *The Walls of Jericho*. Knopf, 1928.

HUGHES, LANGSTON: *Not Without Laughter*. Knopf, 1930.

JOHNSON, JAMES WELDON: *Autobiography of an Ex-colored Man*. Sherman, French, and Company, New York, 1912.

LARSEN, NELLA: *Quicksand*, 1928; *Passing*, 1929; both Knopf.

HURSTON, ZORA NEALE: *Jonah's Gourd Vine*, 1934; *Their Eyes Are Watching God*, 1937; both Lippincott.

McKAY, CLAUDE: *Home to Harlem*, 1928; *Banjo*, 1929; both Harcourt.

PETRY, ANN: *The Street*. Houghton, 1946.

THURMAN, WALLACE: *The Blacker the Berry*. Macaulay Publishing Company, New York, 1931.

WHITE, WALTER: *The Fire in the Flint*, 1924; *Flight*, 1926; both Knopf.

YERBY, FRANK: *The Foxes of Harrow*. Dial, 1946.

DRAMA

ANDERSON, GARLAND: *Appearances*. Frolic Theater, New York, 1925.

COTTER, JOSEPH S., JR.: *Caleb, The Degenerate*. Gilbert and Company, Louisville, Ky., 1903.

EDMONDS, RANDOLPH: *The Land of Cotton and Other Plays*. Associated, 1942; *Six Plays for a Negro Theater*. Walter H. Baker Company, Boston, 1934.

RICHARDSON, WILLIS: *Plays and Pageants from the Life of the Negro*. Associated, 1930.

RICHARDSON, WILLIS, AND MILLER, MAY: *Negro History in Thirteen Plays*. Associated, 1935.

HISTORY

BRAWLEY, BENJAMIN GRIFFITH: *A Short History of the American Negro*, Fourth Ed., 1939; *A Social History of the American Negro*, 1921; both Macmillan.

COBB, W. MONTAGUE: *The First Negro Medical Society*, 1884-1939. Associated, 1939.

CROMWELL, JOHN WESLEY: *The Early Negro Convention Movement*, 1904; *The Negro in American History*, 1914; both American Negro Academy.

DREER, HERMAN: *History of the Omega Psi Phi Fraternity*. The Fraternity, Washington, D. C., 1940.

DU BOIS, W. E. B.: *The Gift of Black Folk*. Stratford, 1924; *Black Reconstruction*. Harcourt, 1935; *Black Folk, Then and Now*. Henry Holt and Company, New York, 1939.

EPPSE, MERL RAYMOND: *The Negro, Too, in American History*. National Educational Publishing Company, New York, 1938.

GREENE, LORENZO JOHNSTON: *The Negro in Colonial New England*. Columbia University Press, New York, 1942.

HARE, MAUDE CUNEY: *Negro Musicians and Their Music*. Associated, 1936.

PAYNE, DANIEL A.: *The History of the African Methodist Episcopal Church*. A. M. E., 1891.

STEVENS, GEORGE E.: *The History of Central Baptist Church*, 1847-1927. Central Baptist Church, St. Louis, Mo.

TAYLOR, ALRUTHEUS A.: *The Negro in South Carolina During the Reconstruction*. Associated, 1924.

WASHINGTON, BOOKER T.: *The Story of the Negro*. Two Volumes. Doubleday, 1883.

WESLEY, CHARLES HARRIS: *The Collapse of the Confederacy*. Associated, 1937.

WOODSON, CARTER G.: *History of the Negro Church*, 1921; *The African Background Outlined*, 1936; *The Negro in Our History*, Eighth Edition, 1945; all Associated.

MAGAZINES

The Crisis, National Association for the Advancement of Colored People, 70 Fifth Avenue, New York 11.

Ebony, Chicago.

The Negro Digest, Chicago.

The Journal of Negro Education, Howard University Press, Washington, D. C.

The Journal of Negro History, The Negro History Bulletin, Associated Publishers, Washington.

Opportunity, Journal of Negro Life, National Urban League, 1133 Broadway, New York 10.

The Negro, 4405 Enright, St. Louis, Mo.

The Phylon, Atlanta University Press, Atlanta, Ga.

Index

of Authors and Titles